SELECTED POEMS

ALGERNON CHARLES SWINBURNE (1837–1909) was an associate of the Pre-Raphaelite Brotherhood and one of the most prolific and versatile poets of the nineteenth century. Educated at Eton and Balliol College, Oxford, Swinburne left the latter without taking a degree and devoted himself to an increasingly scandalous life and a controversial literary career. His socially privileged background gave him the means and confidence to challenge Victorian middle-class values, while his remarkable gifts as a poet, novelist, linguist, and essayist ensured him a prominent place in the cultural life of the time. Rejected by his cousin, Mary Disney Leith, Swinburne never married. His later years were spent at the Pines, Putney, under the watchful eye of his friend and fellow *littérateur* Theodore Watts-Dunton. His muse never deserted him, nor did his interest in liberationist politics, ancient Greece, Charles Baudelaire and Victor Hugo, and English renaissance drama.

L.M. FINDLAY was educated at Aberdeen and Oxford universities and is now Professor of English and Director of the Humanities Research Unit at the University of Saskatchewan, Canada. As well as nineteenth-century studies, his interests include the history of the humanities and government policy pertaining to universities. In 2001 he co-edited for Purich Press *Pursuing Academic Freedom: 'Free and Fearless'?* He is currently preparing for Broadview Press a new edition and translation of *The Communist Manifesto.*

Fyfield*Books* present poetry and prose by great as well as some-times overlooked writers from British and Continental literatures. Clean texts at affordable prices, Fyfield*Books* make available authors whose works endure within our literary tradition.

The series takes its name from the Fyfield elm mentioned in Matthew Arnold's 'The Scholar Gypsy' and in his 'Thyrsis'. The elm stood close to the building in which the Fyfield series was first conceived in 1971.

> *Roam on! The light we sought is shining still.*
> *Dost thou ask proof? Our tree yet crowns the hill,*
> *Our Scholar travels yet the loved hill-side*

from 'Thyrsis'

ALGERNON CHARLES SWINBURNE

Selected Poems

Edited with an introduction by
L.M. FINDLAY

Fyfield*Books*

CARCANET

First published in Great Britain
in 1982 by
Carcanet Press Limited

This impression 2002

Introduction, selection and editorial matter
Copyright L.M. Findlay 1982, 1987, 2002

The right of L.M. Findlay
to be identified as the editor of this
work has been asserted by him in accordance with
the Copyright, Designs and Patents Act of 1988

ISBN 0 85635 728 6

The publisher acknowledges financial
assistance from the Arts Council of England

Printed and bound by SRP Limited, England

CONTENTS

SELECTED POEMS

INTRODUCTION

ALGERNON CHARLES SWINBURNE (1837-1909) lived long and wrote copiously—poetry, novels, letters, criticism. This very Victorian combination may arouse in us a mixture of envy and disbelief. Faced with the forbidding bulk of the Bonchurch Swinburne and the works and correspondence published since then, one must determine a basis for selection. How effectively selective was the poet himself in his choice of topics and in what he allowed to be published during his lifetime? How rigorously selective should the reader, editor and critic be, if justice is to be done to Swinburne's poetic range and development?

There are other difficulties too. Swinburne seems a bizarre amalgam of aristocratic breeding and revolutionary fervour. The interplay in him (as in Byron and Shelley) of privilege and libertarianism may bemuse the modern reader too eager to reduce poets and poetry to one or another modish orthodoxy. Swinburne attended Eton and Oxford, and maintained throughout his life a sense of family honour and tradition and a disdain for bad taste at least as intense as his republican ardour and Baudelairean *nostalgie pour la boue*. Alas, his more scandalous personal proclivities have attracted a disproportionate amount of critical attention. But was Swinburne homosexual, bisexual or asexual; was he alcoholic or sadomasochistic; a case of arrested development or avant-garde enterprise? And does any of this matter to those who wish to understand and assess his poetry aright? Correlation of the life and work is natural but hazardous. One may concede that Swinburne's flagellation poems are absurd and tedious, that his baby-poems are sentimental gush: and that in both cases his imagination is the creature of unhealthy compulsion. But in much of his work style is not empty mannerism, nor is theme the mechanical consequence of pathetic seizure. There is undoubtedly a pattern of submission and revolt in Swinburne's life, but it is wrong to see nothing but this in his poems; to explain away his talent for praise and blame, his exploration of love as both violence and tenderness, his marked reliance on antithesis, paradox, synaesthesia, his fondness for technically exacting verse forms, as functions of sadomasochism. Psychology, amateur or otherwise, cannot fully account for aesthetic success or failure. The real challenge facing those who would read Swinburne's poems in the light of his life is to determine the extent and nature of autobiographical elements in his best work: not only in an acknowledged *cri-de-coeur* like 'The Triumph of Time' or a self-styled spiritual autobiography like 'Thalassius', but in poems as diverse and distant in time from each other as the 'Hymn to Proserpine', *Erectheus* and 'Tristram of Lyonesse'. The transformations of experience into art are no less subtle in Swinburne than in any other great poet.

Swinburne's classical learning may also prove an obstacle in an age that has witnessed the dramatic decline of reading Greek and Latin literature in the original. To complicate matters further, Swinburne's neo-paganism draws on an intimate knowledge of the Bible and The Book of Common Prayer, a mastery of their measures and imagery that gives his poetry ironic resonances often at first inaudible to modern ears. Nor is this the full extent of his bookishness. His lifelong study of classical and contemporary literature in five languages, coupled with an unrivalled memory, drives his annotator to despair, and many ordinary readers to less 'literary' authors. But erudition by itself is no basis for depreciating any artist, just as it need not *a priori* count in his favour. The question is whether his learning lives in his art. Is it shaped and transmuted, or merely the accumulated lumber of a typical Victorian response to *horror vacui*? Perhaps at a time when many thinkers urge us to see all experience as a text—as the great and good book of traditional hermeneutics, or a secular scripture for an agnostic age, or as writing that is always phenomenologically primary yet always under erasure—we ought to take Swinburne's bookishness more seriously. Elizabeth Barrett Browning was subtler than is often recognised when she affirmed in *Aurora Leigh*, a poem that Swinburne admired, 'The world of books is still the world.'

Despite his reputation as one of the best-read poets and critics in the language, Swinburne incurred the scorn of friends as well as enemies for what they took to be an inherent inability to produce thoughtful poetry. It is a charge that haunts him still, although some fine recent appreciations of his poetic intelligence have turned the tide of uncritical censure. Perhaps the most influential formulation of this particular prejudice against Swinburne is Tennyson's: 'He is a reed through which all things blow into music.' All who encounter this assessment seem to interpret it as an indictment—and Tennyson probably meant it to be one, his admiration for the 'strength and splendour' and the 'fine metrical invention' of *Atalanta* notwithstanding. However, this continuity of interpretation is curious, especially when related to the received critical and creative wisdom of our time that insists all experience is potentially proper subject-matter for poetry. If Auden needs no forgiveness for assimilating industrial as well as academic Oxford, why does Swinburne need to be defended against the charge that his muse accommodates 'all things'?

Tennyson's words tend to be read with as little care as Swinburne's poetry. Critics who quote Tennyson respectfully feel that he has exposed with unrivalled wit and accuracy the central flaw in Swinburne's artistic makeup. His pagan prolificness (so the assumption goes) is nicely captured in the image of the personified calamus, more properly the poet's instrument not itself the poet. However, Tennyson's witticism reveals his own entrenched resistance to Swinburne's vision of poetic intelligence, not that Swinburne is mindlessly mellifluous. As early as 1830 in Οἱ ῥέοντες [all thoughts, all creeds] Tennyson gave notice of his abiding aversion to Heracliteans, ancient and modern, and their claim that '*all things* flow like a stream' (my italics). He sees a similar lack of discrimination in them and Swinburne. Yet the celebration of process, whether philosophic or poetic, need not be unthinking or intellectually empty. When critics follow Tennyson in finding intellectual barrenness and incoherence in Swinburne's poetry, they are too often recklessly subjective and prescriptive. If Swinburne is a reed, he is so not so much in Tennyson's sense as in Pascal's: 'L'homme n'est qu'un roseau, le plus faible de la nature; mais c'est un roseau pensant.'

An important clue to the nature of Swinburne's thinking is to be found in his undergraduate essay 'Of Analogy':

> It may be said that analogy, rightly used, lies at the root of all reason, of all progress, invention, discovery. . . . Of true analogy we may take two kinds as heads of the division: Poetic and Scientific Analogy. To the first we may suppose that Metaphor & such like forms are separately the perception of likeness & aptitude, of relation and community, which give to poetry the powers of comprehension & exposition through which he [the poet] becomes interpreter and prophet of things unapparent to ordinary men & this we may perhaps define as the special aim of poetry, to which the subordinate analogies of metaphor and rhythm serve as attendants; & rhyme itself thus assumes meaning & reason if we accept it as a musical balance & relation of sound corresponding to the analogy of sense expressed thro' it.

Poetic comprehension is too serious a matter to be unthinkingly assimilative. Swinburne's dependence on various kinds of analogy and parallelism, semantic and prosodic, is motivated by an unshakable belief in the accessibility of truth through such means. This is why he never ventured into *vers libre*, and why Samuel Daniel's *Defence of Rhyme* had an honoured place in his library. When Swinburne sings creation, analogy is ubiquitous and precise: 'Sunbeams and starbeams, and all coloured things,/ All forms and all similitudes began;/And death, the shadow cast by life's wide wings,/And God, the shade cast by the soul of man' ('Genesis' 16-20). His formalism is not so much illogical as post-logical, as he affirms early in an undergraduate essay on the 'Use of Logic': logic 'has no such exact message to deliver as art, mathematics, music, etc.—it makes the way clear for the entrance of something more than itself.' In his best poems logic is usually a framework for 'something more', and not itself the 'internal centre' that Meredith missed in Swinburne's prose burlesque, 'La Fille du Policeman', and that many critics have persisted in missing in most of the canon ever since.

For his contemporaries, there had to be some way of diminishing the challenge of Swinburne's neo-paganism in *Atalanta*, his unorthodox pursuit of *le frisson juste* in the first series of *Poems and Ballads*, the ringing republicanism of *Songs Before Sunrise*. Such diminishment took the form of denying coherence to Swinburne's analogical thought, and deploring the apparently effortless amplitude of his style. Depreciation on these grounds was made more inevitable by the association, by Swinburne as well as his detractors, of his analogies and synaesthetic effects with Baudelaire's *Correspondances*, with the attuned sensorium of Théophile Gautier, and the mordant historical parallels of Hugo's *Châtiments*. To conjure harmony from outrageous diversity in an age of waning faith was sufficiently galling. But the employment of virtuoso skills and considerable learning in the interests of polytheism was too much for Victorian *gravitas*. Faced with the erudite ironies of Swinburne's poetry, most of his contemporaries resorted to the language and strategy of Desiré Nisard a generation earlier in excoriating French romanticism as *l'art pour l'art*, and branding its leading figures as decadent. Once such labels were applied to Swinburne, it was difficult for his poems to secure a fair hearing, the verse of his later years being most sorely affected by prejudice.

In the twentieth century the grounds for disbelieving Swinburne's poetry have changed somewhat. Collapse of the context in which his work can best be savoured has already been mentioned. The growing popularity of the Metaphysical Poets among poets and critics also damaged his case: he showed little talent for compactness, while his irony, his management of the language of paradox, seemed either invisible or hysterical. The New Criticism cut its teeth on short poems, while the Victorians in general displayed an inconvenient facility, and Swinburne was one of the worst offenders. After the prosodic roughness of Donne, Swinburne might well seem to practise rhythmic regularity for its own sake. Even if, as Archibald Macleish argued, poetry had more to do with being than with meaning, Swinburne's apparent evasion of meaning was not what was meant at all. He seemed at odds with Symbolism, Imagism, Modernism; his imagery generalized and repetitious, unclear and imprecise.

Perhaps the poems collected here will help correct some of the mistaken impressions about Swinburne still current. I have included a good many of the pieces usually (and deservedly) anthologized, a number of excerpts (mainly from the verse dramas) suggestive of the flavour of the longer works, and a relatively heavy representation from *A Century of Roundels* where Swinburne's formalism is seen to good advantage. He was still capable of fine work in old age, a capacity rare enough among lyric poets. As an elegist he is intelligent and moving, whether his subject is recently dead—as in the case of Baudelaire, Gautier, or his own father—or a vital memory from an earlier age—as with his beloved Elizabethan and Jacobean dramatists. His Northumberland background contributes to the tact and vigour of his literary ballads, as may be seen in 'A Reiver's Neck-Verse' and 'The Witch-Mother'. His parodies are unerring, the anatomy of his own poetic faults in 'Nephelidia' reminding us effectively that Swinburne's irony was not directed exclusively at others. The translations from Villon are compelling evidence of his linguistic gifts, while the frequent reworking of passages from classical authors in his own poems is always purposeful: an appropriate tribute to or enlistment of Sappho or Aeschylus or Catullus; or an astutely filtered commentary on his own historical context.

The poems must of course stand or fall ultimately on their own merits. However, for those who relish fine writing, there is no lack of it in this selection—from accurate, sensitive description in 'The Sundew', to masterly evocation in 'In The Bay' where we move

> Past Hades, past Elysium, past the long
> Slow smooth strong lapse of Lethe—past the toil
> Wherein all souls are taken as a spoil,
> The Stygian web of waters.

There are innumerable local and technical felicities: as in the yawning enjambement between stanzas 12 and 13 of 'By The North Sea', reinforcing the sense of desire descending through darkness; the appropriate incremental force in 'The Eve of Revolution' of 'I set the trumpet to my lips and blow'; the synaesthetic reinforcement of entrancement in 'Laus Veneris'. In such poems as 'Hertha' and 'Thalassius' there is mythopoeia aplenty.

For the aficionado of epiphany, Swinburne has much to offer, as in 'On The Downs':

> Out of pale cliff and sunburnt heath,
> Out of the low sea curled beneath
>   In the land's bending arm embayed,
> Out of all lives that thought hears breathe
>   Life within life inlaid,
>   Was answer made.

> A multitudinous monotone
> Of dust and flower and seed and stone,
>   In the deep sea-rock's mid-sea sloth,
>   In the live water's trembling zone,
>   In all men love and loathe,
>   One God at growth.

Swinburne is undoubtedly monotonous, but in his best work he is multitudinously so, eliciting harmony from conflict in a way that typifies so much of the poetry that we value.

The rehabilitation of Swinburne is inevitably an uncertain enterprise, despite the impetus provided by Cecil Y. Lang, John S. Mayfield and Jerome McGann. To claim too much for Swinburne's poems may do more harm than good. There is no need to be blindly partisan, especially now that the worst excesses of New Criticism seem to be behind us. The recent revival of interest in typology—most notably in George Landow's study of Holman Hunt—augurs well for Swinburne. The virtues of such poems as 'Hymn to Proserpine', 'The Last Oracle' and 'Tiresias' may be more fully appreciated than ever before. An understanding of the anticipation and continuities informing the imagery and structure of a number of Swinburne's finer poems may in turn encourage acceptance of his role in effecting the transition from Victorianism to Modernism.

A NOTE ON THE TEXT

Except where otherwise indicated in the Notes, this selection is based on
The Poems of Algernon Charles Swinburne, 6 volumes (London, 1904);
The Tragedies of Algernon Charles Swinburne, 5 volumes (London,
1905); and *Posthumous Poems of Algernon Charles Swinburne*, ed.
E. Gosse and T. J. Wise (London, 1917). The Bonchurch edition of the
Complete Works, 20 volumes (London, 1925-7) is less reliable than the
collected editions of Poems and Tragedies published by Chatto and
Windus while Swinburne was still alive.

from ROSAMOND

ROSAMOND

Fear is a cushion for the feet of love,
Painted with colours for his ease-taking;
Sweet red, and white with wasted blood, and blue
Most flower-like, and the summer-spousèd green
And sea-betrothed soft purple and burnt black.
All coloured forms of fear, omen and change,
Sick prophecy and rumours lame at heel,
Anticipations and astrologies,
Perilous inscription and recorded note,
All these are covered in the skirt of love
And when he shakes it these are tumbled forth,
Beaten and blown i' the dusty face of the air.

from ATALANTA IN CALYDON

FIRST CHORUS

When the hounds of spring are on winter's traces,
    The mother of months in meadow or plain
Fills the shadows and windy places
    With lisp of leaves and ripple of rain;
And the brown bright nightingale amorous
Is half assuaged for Itylus,
For the Thracian ships and the foreign faces,
    The tongueless vigil, and all the pain.

Come with bows bent and with emptying of quivers,
    Maiden most perfect, lady of light,
With a noise of winds and many rivers,
    With a clamour of waters, and with might;
Bind on thy sandals, O thou most fleet,
Over the splendour and speed of thy feet;
For the faint east quickens, the wan west shivers,
    Round the feet of the day and the feet of the night.

Where shall we find her, how shall we sing to her,
　　Fold our hands round her knees, and cling?
O that man's heart were as fire and could spring to her,
　　Fire, or the strength of the streams that spring!　　　　20
For the stars and the winds are unto her
As raiment, as songs of the harp-player;
For the risen stars and the fallen cling to her,
　　And the southwest-wind and the west-wind sing.

For winter's rains and ruins are over,
　　And all the season of snows and sins;
The days dividing lover and lover,
　　The light that loses, the night that wins;
And time remembered is grief forgotten,
And frosts are slain and flowers begotten,　　　　　　　30
And in green underwood and cover
　　Blossom by blossom the spring begins.

The full streams feed on flower of rushes,
　　Ripe grasses trammel a travelling foot,
The faint fresh flame of the young year flushes
　　From leaf to flower and flower to fruit;
And fruit and leaf are as gold and fire,
And the oat is heard above the lyre,
And the hoofèd heel of a satyr crushes
　　The chestnut-husk at the chestnut-root.　　　　　　40

And Pan by noon and Bacchus by night,
　　Fleeter of foot than the fleet-foot kid,
Follows with dancing and fills with delight
　　The Mænad and the Bassarid;
And soft as lips that laugh and hide
The laughing leaves of the trees divide,
And screen from seeing and leave in sight
　　The god pursuing, the maiden hid.

The ivy falls with the Bacchanal's hair
　　Over her eyebrows hiding her eyes;　　　　　　　　50
The wild vine slipping down leaves bare
　　Her bright breast shortening into sighs;

The wild vine slips with the weight of its leaves,
But the berried ivy catches and cleaves
To the limbs that glitter, the feet that scare
    The wolf that follows, the fawn that flies.

CHORUS

Before the beginning of years
    There came to the making of man
Time, with a gift of tears;
    Grief, with a glass that ran;   60
Pleasure, with pain for leaven;
    Summer, with flowers that fell;
Remembrance fallen from heaven,
    And madness risen from hell;
Strength without hands to smite;
    Love that endures for a breath:
Night, the shadow of light,
    And life, the shadow of death.

And the high gods took in hand
    Fire, and the falling of tears,   70
And a measure of sliding sand
    From under the feet of the years;
And froth and drift of the sea;
    And dust of the labouring earth;
And bodies of things to be
    In the houses of death and of birth;
And wrought with weeping and laughter,
    And fashioned with loathing and love,
With life before and after
    And death beneath and above,   80
For a day and a night and a morrow,
    That his strength might endure for a span
With travail and heavy sorrow,
    The holy spirit of man.

From the winds of the north and the south
    They gathered as unto strife;

They breathed upon his mouth,
   They filled his body with life;
Eyesight and speech they wrought
   For the veils of the soul therein,   90
A time for labour and thought,
   A time to serve and to sin;
They gave him light in his ways,
   And love, and a space for delight,
And beauty and length of days,
   And night, and sleep in the night.
His speech is a burning fire;
   With his lips he travaileth;
In his heart is a blind desire,
   In his eyes foreknowledge of death;   100
He weaves, and is clothed with derision;
   Sows, and he shall not reap;
His life is a watch or a vision
   Between a sleep and a sleep.

MELEAGER

And I too as thou sayest have seen great things;
Seen otherwhere, but chiefly when the sail
First caught between stretched ropes the roaring west,
And all our oars smote eastward, and the wind
First flung round faces of seafaring men
White splendid snow-flakes of the sundering foam,   110
And the first furrow in virginal green sea
Followed the plunging ploughshare of hewn pine,
And closed, as when deep sleep subdues man's breath
Lips close and heart subsides; and closing, shone
Sunlike with many a Nereid's hair, and moved
Round many a trembling mouth of doubtful gods,
Risen out of sunless and sonorous gulfs
Through waning water and into shallow light,
That watched us; and when flying the dove was snared
As with men's hands, but we shot after and sped   120
Clear through the irremeable Symplegades;
And chiefliest when the hoar beach and herbless cliff

Stood out ahead from Colchis, and we heard
Clefts hoarse with wind, and saw through narrowing reefs
The lightning of the intolerable wave
Flash, and the white wet flame of breakers burn
Far under a kindling south-wind, as a lamp
Burns and bends all its blowing flame one way;
Wild heights untravelled of the wind, and vales
Cloven seaward by their violent streams, and white   130
With bitter flowers and bright salt scurf of brine;
Heard sweep their sharp swift gales, and bowing birdwise
Shriek with birds' voices, and with furious feet
Tread loose the long skirts of a storm; and saw
The whole white Euxine clash together and fall
Full-mouthed, and thunderous from a thousand throats:
Yet we drew thither and won the fleece and won
Medea, deadlier than the sea; but there
Seeing many a wonder and fearful things to men
I saw not one thing like this one seen here,   140
Most fair and fearful, feminine, a god,
Faultless; whom I that love not, being unlike,
Fear, and give honour, and choose from all the gods.

CHORUS

Who hath given man speech? or who hath set therein
A thorn for peril and a snare for sin?
For in the word his life is and his breath,
    And in the word his death,
That madness and the infatuate heart may breed
    From the word's womb the deed
And life bring one thing forth ere all pass by,   150
Even one thing which is ours yet cannot die—
Death. Hast thou seen him ever anywhere,
Time's twin-born brother, imperishable as he
Is perishable and plaintive, clothed with care
    And mutable as sand,
But death is strong and full of blood and fair
And perdurable and like a lord of land?

Nay, time thou seest not, death thou wilt not see
Till life's right hand be loosened from thine hand
 And thy life-days from thee.   160
For the gods very subtly fashion
 Madness with sadness upon earth:
Not knowing in any wise compassion,
 Nor holding pity of any worth;
And many things they have given and taken,
 And wrought and ruined many things;
The firm land have they loosed and shaken,
 And sealed the sea with all her springs;
They have wearied time with heavy burdens
 And vexed the lips of life with breath: 170
Set men to labour and given them guerdons,
 Death, and great darkness after death:
Put moans into the bridal measure
 And on the bridal wools a stain;
And circled pain about with pleasure,
 And girdled pleasure about with pain;
And strewed one marriage-bed with tears and fire
For extreme loathing and supreme desire.

What shall be done with all these tears of ours?
 Shall they make watersprings in the fair heaven   180
To bathe the brows of morning? or like flowers
Be shed and shine before the starriest hours,
 Or made the raiment of the weeping Seven?
Or rather, O our masters, shall they be
Food for the famine of the grievous sea,
 A great well-head of lamentation
Satiating the sad gods? or fall and flow
Among the years and seasons to and fro,
 And wash their feet with tribulation
And fill them full with grieving ere they go?   190
 Alas, our lords, and yet alas again,
Seeing all your iron heaven is gilt as gold
 But all we smite thereat in vain;
Smite the gates barred with groanings manifold,
 But all the floors are paven with our pain.
Yea, and with weariness of lips and eyes,

With breaking of the bosom, and with sighs,
    We labour, and are clad and fed with grief
And filled with days we would not fain behold
And nights we would not hear of; we wax old,   200
    All we wax old and wither like a leaf.
We are outcast, strayed between bright sun and moon;
    Our light and darkness are as leaves of flowers,
Black flowers and white, that perish; and the noon
    As midnight, and the night as daylight hours.
    A little fruit a little while is ours,
        And the worm finds it soon.

But up in heaven the high gods one by one
    Lay hands upon the draught that quickeneth,
Fulfilled with all tears shed and all things done,   210
    And stir with soft imperishable breath
    The bubbling bitterness of life and death,
And hold it to our lips and laugh; but they
Preserve their lips from tasting night or day,
    Lest they too change and sleep, the fates that spun,
The lips that made us and the hands that slay;
    Lest all these change, and heaven bow down to none,
Change and be subject to the secular sway
    And terrene revolution of the sun.
Therefore they thrust it from them, putting time away.   220

I would the wine of time, made sharp and sweet
    With multitudinous days and nights and tears
    And many mixing savours of strange years,
Were no more trodden of them under feet,
    Cast out and spilt about their holy places:
That life were given them as a fruit to eat
And death to drink as water; that the light
Might ebb, drawn backward from their eyes, and night
    Hide for one hour the imperishable faces.
That they might rise up sad in heaven, and know   230
Sorrow and sleep, one paler than young snow,
    One cold as blight of dew and ruinous rain;
Rise up and rest and suffer a little, and be
Awhile as all things born with us and we,
    And grieve as men, and like slain men be slain.

For now we know not of them; but one saith
   The gods are gracious, praising God; and one,
When hast thou seen? or hast thou felt his breath
   Touch, nor consume thine eyelids as the sun,
Nor fill thee to the lips with fiery death?   240
   None hath beheld him, none
Seen above other gods and shapes of things,
Swift without feet and flying without wings,
Intolerable, not clad with death or life,
   Insatiable, not known of night or day,
The lord of love and loathing and of strife
   Who gives a star and takes a sun away;
Who shapes the soul, and makes her a barren wife
   To the earthly body and grievous growth of clay;
Who turns the large limbs to a little flame   250
   And binds the great sea with a little sand;
Who makes desire, and slays desire with shame;
   Who shakes the heaven as ashes in his hand;
Who, seeing the light and shadow for the same,
   Bids day waste night as fire devours a brand,
Smites without sword, and scourges without rod;
   The supreme evil, God.

CHORUS

The house is broken, is broken; it shall not stand.

ALTHÆA

Woe, woe for him that breaketh; and a rod
Smote it of old, and now the axe is here.   260

CHORUS

   Not as with sundering of the earth
      Nor as with cleaving of the sea
   Nor fierce foreshadowings of a birth
      Nor flying dreams of death to be
   Nor loosening of the large world's girth
   And quickening of the body of night,

And sound of thunder in men's ears
And fire of lightning in men's sight,
   Fate, mother of desires and fears,
    Bore unto men the law of tears;   270
But sudden, an unfathered flame,
   And broken out of night, she shone,
She, without body, without name,
   In days forgotten and foregone;
And heaven rang round her as she came
Like smitten cymbals, and lay bare;
   Clouds and great stars, thunders and snows,
The blue sad fields and folds of air,
   The life that breathes, the life that grows,
   All wind, all fire, that burns or blows,   280
Even all these knew her: for she is great;
   The daughter of doom, the mother of death,
The sister of sorrow; a lifelong weight
   That no man's finger lighteneth,
Nor any god can lighten fate;
A landmark seen across the way
   Where one race treads as the other trod;
An evil sceptre, an evil stay,
   Wrought for a staff, wrought for a rod,
   The bitter jealousy of God.   290

For death is deep as the sea,
   And fate as the waves thereof.
Shall the waves take pity on thee
   Or the southwind offer thee love?
Wilt thou take the night for thy day
Or the darkness for light on thy way,
   Till thou say in thine heart Enough?
Behold, thou art over fair, thou art over wise;
The sweetness of spring in thine hair, and the light in thine eyes.
The light of the spring in thine eyes, and the sound in thine ears;   300
Yet thine heart shall wax heavy with sighs and thine eyelids with tears.
Wilt thou cover thine hair with gold, and with silver thy feet?
Hast thou taken the purple to fold thee, and made thy mouth sweet?
Behold, when thy face is made bare, he that loved thee shall hate;
Thy face shall be no more fair at the fall of thy fate.

For thy life shall fall as a leaf and be shed as the rain;
And the veil of thine head shall be grief; and the crown shall be pain.

from CHASTELARD

CHASTELARD

        Most sweet queen,
They say men dying remember, with sharp joy
And rapid reluctation of desire,
Some old thing, some swift breath of wind, some word,
Some sword-stroke or dead lute-strain, some lost sight,
Some sea-blossom stripped to the sun and burned
At naked ebb—some river-flower that breathes
Against the stream like a swooned swimmer's mouth—
Some tear or laugh ere lip and eye were man's—
Sweet stings that struck the blood in riding—nay,   10
Some garment or sky-colour or spice-smell,
And die with heart and face shut fast on it,
And know not why, and weep not; it may be
Men shall hold love fast always in such wise
In new fair lives where all are new things else,
And know not why, and weep not.

MARY

When this last year the fight at Corrichie
Reddened the rushes with stained fen-water,
I rode with my good men and took delight,
Feeling the sweet clear wind upon my eyes   20
And rainy soft smells blown upon my face
In riding: then the great fight jarred and joined,
And the sound stung me right through heart and all;
For I was here, see, gazing off the hills,
In the wet air; our housings were all wet,
And not a plume stood stiffly past the ear
But flapped between the bridle and the neck;
And under us we saw the battle go
Like running water; I could see by fits

Some helm the rain fell shining off, some flag   30
Snap from the staff, shorn through or broken short
In the man's falling: yea, one seemed to catch
The very grasp of tumbled men at men,
Teeth clenched in throats, hands riveted in hair,
Tearing the life out with no help of swords.
And all the clamour seemed to shine, the light
Seemed to shout as a man doth; twice I laughed—
I tell you, twice my heart swelled out with thirst
To be into the battle; see, fair lord,
I swear it seemed I might have made a knight,   40
And yet the simple bracing of a belt
Makes me cry out; this is too pitiful,
This dusty half of us made up with fears.—

from POEMS AND BALLADS, FIRST SERIES

A BALLAD OF LIFE

I found in dreams a place of wind and flowers,
    Full of sweet trees and colour of glad grass,
    In midst whereof there was
A lady clothed like summer with sweet hours.
Her beauty, fervent as a fiery moon,
    Made my blood burn and swoon
        Like a flame rained upon.
Sorrow had filled her shaken eyelids' blue,
And her mouth's sad red heavy rose all through
        Seemed sad with glad things gone.   10

She held a little cithern by the strings,
    Shaped heartwise, strung with subtle-coloured hair
    Of some dead lute-player
That in dead years had done delicious things.
The seven strings were named accordingly;
    The first string charity,
        The second tenderness,
The rest were pleasure, sorrow, sleep, and sin,
And loving-kindness, that is pity's kin
        And is most pitiless.   20

There were three men with her, each garmented
 With gold and shod with gold upon the feet;
  And with plucked ears of wheat
The first man's hair was wound upon his head:
His face was red, and his mouth curled and sad;
  All his gold garment had
   Pale stains of dust and rust.
A riven hood was pulled across his eyes;
The token of him being upon this wise
   Made for a sign of Lust.   30

The next was Shame, with hollow heavy face
 Coloured like green wood when flame kindles it.
  He hath such feeble feet
They may not well endure in any place.
His face was full of grey old miseries,
  And all his blood's increase
   Was even increase of pain.
The last was Fear, that is akin to Death;
He is Shame's friend, and always as Shame saith
   Fear answers him again.   40

My soul said in me; This is marvellous,
 Seeing the air's face is not so delicate
  Nor the sun's grace so great,
If sin and she be kin or amorous.
And seeing where maidens served her on their knees,
  I bade one crave of these
   To know the cause thereof.
Then Fear said: I am Pity that was dead.
And Shame said: I am Sorrow comforted.
   And Lust said: I am Love.   50

Thereat her hands began a lute-playing
 And her sweet mouth a song in a strange tongue;
  And all the while she sung
There was no sound but long tears following
Long tears upon men's faces, waxen white
  With extreme sad delight.
   But those three following men

Became as men raised up among the dead;
Great glad mouths open and fair cheeks made red
    With child's blood come again.   60

Then I said: Now assuredly I see
    My lady is perfect, and transfigureth
    All sin and sorrow and death,
Making them fair as her own eyelids be,
Or lips wherein my whole soul's life abides;
    Or as her sweet white sides
      And bosom carved to kiss.
Now therefore, if her pity further me,
Doubtless for her sake all my days shall be
    As righteous as she is.   70

Forth, ballad, and take roses in both arms,
    Even till the top rose touch thee in the throat
Where the least thornprick harms;
    And girdled in thy golden singing-coat,
Come thou before my lady and say this;
    Borgia, thy gold hair's colour burns in me,
      Thy mouth makes beat my blood in feverish rhymes;
    Therefore so many as these roses be,
      Kiss me so many times.
Then it may be, seeing how sweet she is,   80
    That she will stoop herself none otherwise
      Than a blown vine-branch doth,
    And kiss thee with soft laughter on thine eyes,
      Ballad, and on thy mouth.

LAUS VENERIS

Asleep or waking is it? for her neck,
Kissed over close, wears yet a purple speck
    Wherein the pained blood falters and goes out;
Soft, and stung softly—fairer for a fleck.

But though my lips shut sucking on the place,
There is no vein at work upon her face;

Her eyelids are so peaceable, no doubt
Deep sleep has warmed her blood through all its ways.

Lo, this is she that was the world's delight;
The old grey years were parcels of her might;   10
    The strewings of the ways wherein she trod
Were the twain seasons of the day and night.

Lo, she was thus when her clear limbs enticed
All lips that now grow sad with kissing Christ,
    Stained with blood fallen from the feet of God,
The feet and hands whereat our souls were priced.

Alas, Lord, surely thou art great and fair.
But lo her wonderfully woven hair!
    And thou didst heal us with thy piteous kiss;
But see now, Lord; her mouth is lovelier.   20

She is right fair; what hath she done to thee?
Nay, fair Lord Christ, lift up thine eyes and see;
    Had now thy mother such a lip—like this?
Thou knowest how sweet a thing it is to me.

Inside the Horsel here the air is hot;
Right little peace one hath for it, God wot;
    The scented dusty daylight burns the air,
And my heart chokes me till I hear it not.

Behold, my Venus, my soul's body, lies
With my love laid upon her garment-wise,   30
    Feeling my love in all her limbs and hair
And shed between her eyelids through her eyes.

She holds my heart in her sweet open hands
Hanging asleep; hard by her head there stands,
    Crowned with gilt thorns and clothed with flesh like fire,
Love, wan as foam blown up the salt burnt sands—

Hot as the brackish waifs of yellow spume
That shift and steam—loose clots of arid fume

From the sea's panting mouth of dry desire;
There stands he, like one labouring at a loom.   40

The warp holds fast across; and every thread
That makes the woof up has dry specks of red;
    Always the shuttle cleaves clean through, and he
Weaves with the hair of many a ruined head.

Love is not glad nor sorry, as I deem;
Labouring he dreams, and labours in the dream,
    Till when the spool is finished, lo I see
His web, reeled off, curls and goes out like steam.

Night falls like fire; the heavy lights run low,
And as they drop, my blood and body so   50
    Shake as the flame shakes, full of days and hours
That sleep not neither weep they as they go.

Ah yet would God this flesh of mine might be
Where air might wash and long leaves cover me,
    Where tides of grass break into foam of flowers,
Or where the wind's feet shine along the sea.

Ah yet would God that stems and roots were bred
Out of my weary body and my head,
    That sleep were sealed upon me with a seal,
And I were as the least of all his dead.   60

Would God my blood were dew to feed the grass,
Mine ears made deaf and mine eyes blind as glass,
    My body broken as a turning wheel,
And my mouth stricken ere it saith Alas!

Ah God, that love were as a flower or flame,
That life were as the naming of a name,
    That death were not more pitiful than desire,
That these things were not one thing and the same!

Behold now, surely somewhere there is death:
For each man hath some space of years, he saith,   70

A little space of time ere time expire,
A little day, a little way of breath.

And lo, between the sundawn and the sun,
His day's work and his night's work are undone;
    And lo, between the nightfall and the light,
He is not, and none knoweth of such an one.

Ah God, that I were as all souls that be,
As any herb or leaf of any tree,
    As men that toil through hours of labouring night,
As bones of men under the deep sharp sea.   80

Outside it must be winter among men;
For at the gold bars of the gates again
    I heard all night and all the hours of it
The wind's wet wings and fingers drip with rain.

Knights gather, riding sharp for cold; I know
The ways and woods are strangled with the snow;
    And with short song the maidens spin and sit
Until Christ's birthnight, lily-like, arow.

The scent and shadow shed about me make
The very soul in all my senses ache;   90
    The hot hard night is fed upon my breath,
And sleep beholds me from afar awake.

Alas, but surely where the hills grow deep,
Or where the wild ways of the sea are steep,
    Or in strange places somewhere there is death,
And on death's face the scattered hair of sleep,

There lover-like with lips and limbs that meet
They lie, they pluck sweet fruit of life and eat;
    But me the hot and hungry days devour,
And in my mouth no fruit of theirs is sweet.   100

No fruit of theirs, but fruit of my desire,
For her love's sake whose lips through mine respire;

Her eyelids on her eyes like flower on flower,
Mine eyelids on mine eyes like fire on fire.

So lie we, not as sleep that lies by death,
With heavy kisses and with happy breath;
    Not as man lies by woman, when the bride
Laughs low for love's sake and the words he saith.

For she lies, laughing low with love; she lies
And turns his kisses on her lips to sighs,   110
    To sighing sound of lips unsatisfied,
And the sweet tears are tender with her eyes.

Ah, not as they, but as the souls that were
Slain in the old time, having found her fair;
    Who, sleeping with her lips upon their eyes,
Heard sudden serpents hiss across her hair.

Their blood runs round the roots of time like rain:
She casts them forth and gathers them again;
    With nerve and bone she weaves and multiplies
Exceeding pleasure out of extreme pain.   120

Her little chambers drip with flower-like red,
Her girdles, and the chaplets of her head,
    Her armlets and her anklets; with her feet
She tramples all that winepress of the dead.

Her gateways smoke with fume of flowers and fires,
With loves burnt out and unassuaged desires;
    Between her lips the steam of them is sweet,
The languor in her ears of many lyres.

Her beds are full of perfume and sad sound,
Her doors are made with music, and barred round   130
    With sighing and with laughter and with tears,
With tears whereby strong souls of men are bound.

There is the knight Adonis that was slain;
With flesh and blood she chains him for a chain;

The body and the spirit in her ears
Cry, for her lips divide him vein by vein.

Yea, all she slayeth; yea, every man save me;
Me, love, thy lover that must cleave to thee
   Till the ending of the days and ways of earth,
The shaking of the sources of the sea.   140

Me, most forsaken of all souls that fell;
Me, satiated with things insatiable;
   Me, for whose sake the extreme hell makes mirth,
Yea, laughter kindles at the heart of hell.

Alas thy beauty! for thy mouth's sweet sake
My soul is bitter to me, my limbs quake
   As water, as the flesh of men that weep,
As their heart's vein whose heart goes nigh to break.

Ah God, that sleep with flower-sweet finger-tips
Would crush the fruit of death upon my lips;   150
   Ah God, that death would tread the grapes of sleep
And wring their juice upon me as it drips.

There is no change of cheer for many days,
But change of chimes high up in the air, that sways
   Rung by the running fingers of the wind;
And singing sorrows heard on hidden ways.

Day smiteth day in twain, night sundereth night,
And on mine eyes the dark sits as the light;
   Yea, Lord, thou knowest I know not, having sinned,
If heaven be clean or unclean in thy sight.   160

Yea, as if earth were sprinkled over me,
Such chafed harsh earth as chokes a sandy sea,
   Each pore doth yearn, and the dried blood thereof
Gasps by sick fits, my heart swims heavily,

There is a feverish famine in my veins;
Below her bosom, where a crushed grape stains

The white and blue, there my lips caught and clove
An hour since, and what mark of me remains?

I dare not always touch her, lest the kiss
Leave my lips charred. Yea, Lord, a little bliss, 170
    Brief bitter bliss, one hath for a great sin;
Nathless thou knowest how sweet a thing it is.

Sin, is it sin whereby men's souls are thrust
Into the pit? yet had I a good trust
    To save my soul before it slipped therein,
Trod under by the fire-shod feet of lust.

For if mine eyes fail and my soul takes breath,
I look between the iron sides of death
    Into sad hell where all sweet love hath end,
All but the pain that never finisheth. 180

There are the naked faces of great kings,
The singing folk with all their lute-playings;
    There when one cometh he shall have to friend
The grave that covets and the worm that clings.

There sit the knights that were so great of hand,
The ladies that were queens of fair green land,
    Grown grey and black now, brought unto the dust,
Soiled, without raiment, clad about with sand.

There is one end for all of them; they sit
Naked and sad, they drink the dregs of it, 190
    Trodden as grapes in the wine-press of lust,
Trampled and trodden by the fiery feet.

I see the marvellous mouth whereby there fell
Cities and people whom the gods loved well,
    Yet for her sake on them the fire gat hold,
And for their sakes on her the fire of hell.

And softer than the Egyptian lote-leaf is,
The queen whose face was worth the world to kiss,

Wearing at breast a suckling snake of gold;
And large pale lips of strong Semiramis, 200

Curled like a tiger's that curl back to feed;
Red only where the last kiss made them bleed;
   Her hair most thick with many a carven gem,
Deep in the mane, great-chested, like a steed.

Yea, with red sin the faces of them shine;
But in all these there was no sin like mine;
   No, not in all the strange great sins of them
That made the wine-press froth and foam with wine.

For I was of Christ's choosing, I God's knight,
No blinkard heathen stumbling for scant light; 210
   I can well see, for all the dusty days
Gone past, the clean great time of goodly fight.

I smell the breathing battle sharp with blows,
With shriek of shafts and snapping short of bows;
   The fair pure sword smites out in subtle ways,
Sounds and long lights are shed between the rows

Of beautiful mailed men; the edged light slips,
Most like a snake that takes short breath and dips
   Sharp from the beautifully bending head,
With all its gracious body lithe as lips 220

That curl in touching you; right in this wise
My sword doth, seeming fire in mine own eyes,
   Leaving all colours in them brown and red
And flecked with death; then the keen breaths like sighs,

The caught-up choked dry laughters following them,
When all the fighting face is grown a flame
   For pleasure, and the pulse that stuns the ears,
And the heart's gladness of the goodly game.

Let me think yet a little; I do know
These things were sweet, but sweet such years ago, 230

Their savour is all turned now into tears;
Yea, ten years since, where the blue ripples blow,

The blue curled eddies of the blowing Rhine,
I felt the sharp wind shaking grass and vine
    Touch my blood too, and sting me with delight
Through all this waste and weary body of mine

That never feels clear air; right gladly then
I rode alone, a great way off my men,
    And heard the chiming bridle smite and smite,
And gave each rhyme thereof some rhyme again,   240

Till my song shifted to that iron one;
Seeing there rode up between me and the sun
    Some certain of my foe's men, for his three
White wolves across their painted coats did run.

The first red-bearded, with square cheeks—alack,
I made my knave's blood turn his beard to black;
    The slaying of him was a joy to see:
Perchance too, when at night he came not back,

Some woman fell a-weeping, whom this thief
Would beat when he had drunken; yet small grief   250
    Hath any for the ridding of such knaves;
Yea, if one wept, I doubt her teen was brief.

This bitter love is sorrow in all lands,
Draining of eyelids, wringing of drenched hands,
    Sighing of hearts and filling up of graves;
A sign across the head of the world he stands,

An one that hath a plague-mark on his brows;
Dust and spilt blood do track him to his house
    Down under earth; sweet smells of lip and cheek,
Like a sweet snake's breath made more poisonous   260

With chewing of some perfumed deadly grass,
Are shed all round his passage if he pass,

And their quenched savour leaves the whole soul weak,
Sick with keen guessing whence the perfume was.

As one who hidden in deep sedge and reeds
Smells the rare scent made where a panther feeds,
    And tracking ever slotwise the warm smell
Is snapped upon by the sweet mouth and bleeds,

His head far down the hot sweet throat of her—
So one tracks love, whose breath is deadlier,   270
    And lo, one springe and you are fast in hell,
Fast as the gin's grip of a wayfarer.

I think now, as the heavy hours decease
One after one, and bitter thoughts increase
    One upon one, of all sweet finished things;
The breaking of the battle; the long peace

Wherein we sat clothed softly, each man's hair
Crowned with green leaves beneath white hoods of vair;
    The sounds of sharp spears at great tourneyings,
And noise of singing in the late sweet air.   280

I sang of love too, knowing nought thereof;
'Sweeter,' I said, 'the little laugh of love
    Than tears out of the eyes of Magdalen,
Or any fallen feather of the Dove.

'The broken little laugh that spoils a kiss,
The ache of purple pulses, and the bliss
    Of blinded eyelids that expand again—
Love draws them open with those lips of his,

'Lips that cling hard till the kissed face has grown
Of one same fire and colour with his own;   290
    Then ere one sleep, appeased with sacrifice,
Where his lips wounded, there his lips atone.'

I sang these things long since and knew them not;
'Lo, here is love, or there is love, God wot,

This man and that finds favour in his eyes,'
I said, 'but I, what guerdon have I got?

'The dust of praise that is blown everywhere
In all men's faces with the common air;
    The bay-leaf that wants chafing to be sweet
Before they wind it in a singer's hair.'   300

So that one dawn I rode forth sorrowing;
I had no hope but of some evil thing,
    And so rode slowly past the windy wheat
And past the vineyard and the water-spring,

Up to the Horsel. A great elder-tree
Held back its heaps of flowers to let me see
    The ripe tall grass, and one that walked therein,
Naked, with hair shed over to the knee.

She walked between the blossom and the grass;
I knew the beauty of her, what she was,   310
    The beauty of her body and her sin,
And in my flesh the sin of hers, alas!

Alas! for sorrow is all the end of this.
O sad kissed mouth, how sorrowful it is!
    O breast whereat some suckling sorrow clings,
Red with the bitter blossom of a kiss!

Ah, with blind lips I felt for you, and found
About my neck your hands and hair enwound,
    The hands that stifle and the hair that stings,
I felt them fasten sharply without sound.   320

Yea, for my sin I had great store of bliss:
Rise up, make answer for me, let thy kiss
    Seal my lips hard from speaking of my sin,
Lest one go mad to hear how sweet it is.

Yet I waxed faint with fume of barren bowers,
And murmuring of the heavy-headed hours;

And let the dove's beak fret and peck within
My lips in vain, and Love shed fruitless flowers.

So that God looked upon me when your hands
Were hot about me; yea, God brake my bands
    To save my soul alive, and I came forth
Like a man blind and naked in strange lands

330

That hears men laugh and weep, and knows not whence
Nor wherefore, but is broken in his sense;
    Howbeit I met folk riding from the north
Towards Rome, to purge them of their souls' offence,

And rode with them, and spake to none; the day
Stunned me like lights upon some wizard way,
    And ate like fire mine eyes and mine eyesight;
So rode I, hearing all these chant and pray,

340

And marvelled; till before us rose and fell
White cursed hills, like outer skirts of hell
    Seen where men's eyes look through the day to night,
Like a jagged shell's lips, harsh, untunable,

Blown in between by devils' wrangling breath;
Nathless we won well past that hell and death,
    Down to the sweet land where all airs are good,
Even unto Rome where God's grace tarrieth.

Then came each man and worshipped at his knees
Who in the Lord God's likeness bears the keys
    To bind or loose, and called on Christ's shed blood,
And so the sweet-souled father gave him ease.

350

But when I came I fell down at his feet
Saying, 'Father, though the Lord's blood be right sweet,
    The spot it takes not off the panther's skin,
Nor shall an Ethiop's stain be bleached with it.

'Lo, I have sinned and have spat out at God,
Wherefore his hand is heavier and his rod

More sharp because of mine exceeding sin,
And all his raiment redder than bright blood   360

'Before mine eyes; yea, for my sake I wot
The heat of hell is waxen seven times hot
    Through my great sin.' Then spake he some sweet word,
Giving me cheer; which thing availed me not;

Yea, scarce I wist if such indeed were said;
For when I ceased—lo, as one newly dead
    Who hears a great cry out of hell, I heard
The crying of his voice across my head.

'Until this dry shred staff, that hath no whit
Of leaf nor bark, bear blossom and smell sweet,   370
    Seek thou not any mercy in God's sight,
For so long shalt thou be cast out from it.'

Yea, what if dried-up stems wax red and green,
Shall that thing be which is not nor has been?
    Yea, what if sapless bark wax green and white,
Shall any good fruit grow upon my sin?

Nay, though sweet fruit were plucked of a dry tree,
And though men drew sweet waters of the sea,
    There should not grow sweet leaves on this dead stem,
This waste wan body and shaken soul of me.   380

Yea, though God search it warily enough,
There is not one sound thing in all thereof;
    Though he search all my veins through, searching them
He shall find nothing whole therein but love.

For I came home right heavy, with small cheer,
And lo my love, mine own soul's heart, more dear
    Than mine own soul, more beautiful than God,
Who hath my being between the hands of her—

Fair still, but fair for no man saving me,
As when she came out of the naked sea   390

Making the foam as fire whereon she trod,
And as the inner flower of fire was she.

Yea, she laid hold upon me, and her mouth
Clove unto mine as soul to body doth,
   And, laughing, made her lips luxurious;
Her hair had smells of all the sunburnt south,

Strange spice and flower, strange savour of crushed fruit,
And perfume the swart kings tread underfoot
   For pleasure when their minds wax amorous,
Charred frankincense and grated sandal-root.   400

And I forgot fear and all weary things,
All ended prayers and perished thanksgivings,
   Feeling her face with all her eager hair
Cleave to me, clinging as a fire that clings

To the body and to the raiment, burning them;
As after death I know that such-like flame
   Shall cleave to me for ever; yea, what care,
Albeit I burn then, having felt the same?

Ah love, there is no better life than this;
To have known love, how bitter a thing it is,   410
   And afterward be cast out of God's sight;
Yea, these that know not, shall they have such bliss

High up in barren heaven before his face
As we twain in the heavy-hearted place,
   Remembering love and all the dead delight,
And all that time was sweet with for a space?

For till the thunder in the trumpet be,
Soul may divide from body, but not we
   One from another; I hold thee with my hand,
I let mine eyes have all their will of thee,   420

I seal myself upon thee with my might,
Abiding alway out of all men's sight

Until God loosen over sea and land
The thunder of the trumpets of the night.
                    Explicit Laus Veneris

THE TRIUMPH OF TIME

Before our lives divide for ever,
    While time is with us and hands are free,
(Time, swift to fasten and swift to sever
    Hand from hand, as we stand by the sea)
I will say no word that a man might say
Whose whole life's love goes down in a day;
For this could never have been; and never,
    Though the gods and the years relent, shall be.

Is it worth a tear, is it worth an hour,
    To think of things that are well outworn?
Of fruitless husk and fugitive flower,
    The dream foregone and the deed forborne?
Though joy be done with and grief be vain,
Time shall not sever us wholly in twain;
Earth is not spoilt for a single shower;
    But the rain has ruined the ungrown corn.

It will grow not again, this fruit of my heart,
    Smitten with sunbeams, ruined with rain.
The singing seasons divide and depart,
    Winter and summer depart in twain.
It will grow not again, it is ruined at root,
The bloodlike blossom, the dull red fruit;
Though the heart yet sickens, the lips yet smart,
    With sullen savour of poisonous pain.

I have given no man of my fruit to eat;
    I trod the grapes, I have drunken the wine.
Had you eaten and drunken and found it sweet,
    This wild new growth of the corn and vine,
This wine and bread without lees or leaven,
We had grown as gods, as the gods in heaven,

10

20

30

Souls fair to look upon, goodly to greet,
   One splendid spirit, your soul and mine.

In the change of years, in the coil of things,
   In the clamour and rumour of life to be,
We, drinking love at the furthest springs,
   Covered with love as a covering tree,
We had grown as gods, as the gods above,
Filled from the heart to the lips with love,
Held fast in his hands, clothed warm with his wings,
   O love, my love, had you loved but me!   40

We had stood as the sure stars stand, and moved
   As the moon moves, loving the world; and seen
Grief collapse as a thing disproved,
   Death consume as a thing unclean.
Twain halves of a perfect heart, made fast
Soul to soul while the years fell past;
Had you loved me once, as you have not loved;
   Had the chance been with us that has not been.

I have put my days and dreams out of mind,
   Days that are over, dreams that are done.   50
Though we seek life through, we shall surely find
   There is none of them clear to us now, not one.
But clear are these things; the grass and the sand,
Where, sure as the eyes reach, ever at hand,
With lips wide open and face burnt blind,
   The strong sea-daisies feast on the sun.

The low downs lean to the sea; the stream,
   One loose thin pulseless tremulous vein,
Rapid and vivid and dumb as a dream,
   Works downward, sick of the sun and the rain;   60
No wind is rough with the rank rare flowers;
The sweet sea, mother of loves and hours,
Shudders and shines as the grey winds gleam,
   Turning her smile to a fugitive pain.

Mother of loves that are swift to fade,
   Mother of mutable winds and hours.

A barren mother, a mother-maid,
    Cold and clean as her faint salt flowers.
I would we twain were even as she,
Lost in the night and the light of the sea,   70
Where faint sounds falter and wan beams wade,
    Break, and are broken, and shed into showers.

The loves and hours of the life of a man,
    They are swift and sad, being born of the sea.
Hours that rejoice and regret for a span,
    Born with a man's breath, mortal as he;
Loves that are lost ere they come to birth,
Weeds of the wave, without fruit upon earth.
I lose what I long for, save what I can,
    My love, my love, and no love for me!   80

It is not much that a man can save
    On the sands of life, in the straits of time,
Who swims in sight of the great third wave
    That never a swimmer shall cross or climb.
Some waif washed up with the strays and spars
That ebb-tide shows to the shore and the stars;
Weed from the water, grass from a grave,
    A broken blossom, a ruined rhyme.

There will no man do for your sake, I think,
    What I would have done for the least word said.   90
I had wrung life dry for your lips to drink,
    Broken it up for your daily bread:
Body for body and blood for blood,
As the flow of the full sea risen to flood
That yearns and trembles before it sink,
    I had given, and lain down for you, glad and dead.

Yea, hope at highest and all her fruit,
    And time at fullest and all his dower,
I had given you surely, and life to boot,
    Were we once made one for a single hour.   100
But now, you are twain, you are cloven apart,

Flesh of his flesh, but heart of my heart;
And deep in one is the bitter root,
    And sweet for one is the lifelong flower.

To have died if you cared I should die for you, clung
    To my life if you bade me, played my part
As it pleased you—these were the thoughts that stung,
    The dreams that smote with a keener dart
Than shafts of love or arrows of death;
These were but as fire is, dust, or breath,   110
Or poisonous foam on the tender tongue
    Of the little snakes that eat my heart.

I wish we were dead together to-day,
    Lost sight of, hidden away out of sight,
Clasped and clothed in the cloven clay,
    Out of the world's way, out of the light,
Out of the ages of worldly weather,
Forgotten of all men altogether,
As the world's first dead, taken wholly away,
    Made one with death, filled full of the night.   120

How we should slumber, how we should sleep,
    Far in the dark with the dreams and the dews!
And dreaming, grow to each other, and weep,
    Laugh low, live softly, murmur and muse;
Yea, and it may be, struck through by the dream,
Feel the dust quicken and quiver, and seem
Alive as of old to the lips, and leap
    Spirit to spirit as lovers use.

Sick dreams and sad of a dull delight;
    For what shall it profit when men are dead   130
To have dreamed, to have loved with the whole soul's might,
    To have looked for day when the day was fled?
Let come what will, there is one thing worth,
To have had fair love in the life upon earth:
To have held love safe till the day grew night,
    While skies had colour and lips were red.

Would I lose you now? would I take you then,
    If I lose you now that my heart has need?
And come what may after death to men,
    What thing worth this will the dead years breed?   140
Lose life, lose all; but at least I know,
O sweet life's love, having loved you so,
Had I reached you on earth, I should lose not again,
    In death nor life, nor in dream or deed.

Yea, I know this well: were you once sealed mine,
    Mine in the blood's beat, mine in the breath,
Mixed into me as honey in wine,
    Not time, that sayeth and gainsayeth,
Nor all strong things had severed us then;
Not wrath of gods, nor wisdom of men,   150
Nor all things earthly, nor all divine,
    Nor joy nor sorrow, nor life nor death.

I had grown pure as the dawn and the dew,
    You had grown strong as the sun or the sea.
But none shall triumph a whole life through:
    For death is one, and the fates are three.
At the door of life, by the gate of breath,
There are worse things waiting for men than death;
Death could not sever my soul and you,
    As these have severed your soul from me.   160

You have chosen and clung to the chance they sent you,
    Life sweet as perfume and pure as prayer.
But will it not one day in heaven repent you?
    Will they solace you wholly, the days that were?
Will you lift up your eyes between sadness and bliss,
Meet mine, and see where the great love is,
And tremble and turn and be changed? Content you;
    The gate is strait; I shall not be there.

But you, had you chosen, had you stretched hand,
    Had you seen good such a thing were done,   170
I too might have stood with the souls that stand
    In the sun's sight, clothed with the light of the sun;

But who now on earth need care how I live?
Have the high gods anything left to give,
Save dust and laurels and gold and sand?
   Which gifts are goodly; but I will none.

O all fair lovers about the world,
   There is none of you, none, that shall comfort me.
My thoughts are as dead things, wrecked and whirled
   Round and round in a gulf of the sea;   180
And still, through the sound and the straining stream,
Through the coil and chafe, they gleam in a dream,
The bright fine lips so cruelly curled,
   And strange swift eyes where the soul sits free.

Free, without pity, withheld from woe,
   Ignorant; fair as the eyes are fair.
Would I have you change now, change at a blow,
   Startled and stricken, awake and aware?
Yea, if I could, would I have you see
My very love of you filling me,   190
And know my soul to the quick, as I know
   The likeness and look of your throat and hair?

I shall not change you. Nay, though I might,
   Would I change my sweet one love with a word?
I had rather your hair should change in a night,
   Clear now as the plume of a black bright bird;
Your face fail suddenly, cease, turn grey,
Die as a leaf that dies in a day.
I will keep my soul in a place out of sight,
   Far off, where the pulse of it is not heard.   200

Far off it walks, in a bleak blown space,
   Full of the sound of the sorrow of years.
I have woven a veil for the weeping face,
   Whose lips have drunken the wine of tears;
I have found a way for the failing feet,
A place for slumber and sorrow to meet;
There is no rumour about the place,
   Nor light, nor any that sees or hears.

I have hidden my soul out of sight, and said
   'Let none take pity upon thee, none   210
Comfort thy crying: for lo, thou art dead,
   Lie still now, safe out of sight of the sun.
Have I not built thee a grave, and wrought
Thy grave-clothes on thee of grievous thought,
With soft spun verses and tears unshed,
   And sweet light visions of things undone?

'I have given thee garments and balm and myrrh,
   And gold, and beautiful burial things.
But thou, be at peace now, make no stir;
   Is not thy grave as a royal king's?   220
Fret not thyself though the end were sore;
Sleep, be patient, vex me no more.
Sleep; what hast thou to do with her?
   The eyes that weep, with the mouth that sings?'

Where the dead red leaves of the years lie rotten,
   The cold old crimes and the deeds thrown by,
The misconceived and the misbegotten,
   I would find a sin to do ere I die,
Sure to dissolve and destroy me all through,
That would set you higher in heaven, serve you   230
And leave you happy, when clean forgotten,
   As a dead man out of mind, am I.

Your lithe hands draw me, your face burns through me,
   I am swift to follow you, keen to see;
But love lacks might to redeem or undo me;
   As I have been, I know I shall surely be;
'What should such fellows as I do?' Nay,
My part were worse if I chose to play;
For the worst is this after all; if they knew me,
   Not a soul upon earth would pity me.   240

And I play not for pity of these; but you,
   If you saw with your soul what man am I,
You would praise me at least that my soul all through
   Clove to you, loathing the lives that lie;

The souls and lips that are bought and sold,
The smiles of silver and kisses of gold,
The lapdog loves that whine as they chew,
    The little lovers that curse and cry.

There are fairer women, I hear; that may be;
    But I, that I love you and find you fair,   250
Who are more than fair in my eyes if they be,
    Do the high gods know or the great gods care?
Though the swords in my heart for one were seven,
Would the iron hollow of doubtful heaven,
That knows not itself whether night-time or day be,
    Reverberate words and a foolish prayer?

I will go back to the great sweet mother,
    Mother and lover of men, the sea.
I will go down to her, I and none other,
    Close with her, kiss her and mix her with me;   260
Cling to her, strive with her, hold her fast;
O fair white mother, in days long past
Born without sister, born without brother,
    Set free my soul as thy soul is free.

O fair green-girdled mother of mine,
    Sea, that art clothed with the sun and the rain,
Thy sweet hard kisses are strong like wine,
    Thy large embraces are keen like pain.
Save me and hide me with all thy waves,
Find me one grave of thy thousand graves,   270
Those pure cold populous graves of thine
    Wrought without hand in a world without stain.

I shall sleep, and move with the moving ships,
    Change as the winds change, veer in the tide;
My lips will feast on the foam of thy lips,
    I shall rise with thy rising, with thee subside;
Sleep, and not know if she be, if she were,
Filled full with life to the eyes and hair,
As a rose is fulfilled to the roseleaf tips
    With splendid summer and perfume and pride.   280

This woven raiment of nights and days,
    Were it once cast off and unwound from me,
Naked and glad would I walk in thy ways,
    Alive and aware of thy ways and thee;
Clear of the whole world, hidden at home,
Clothed with the green and crowned with the foam,
A pulse of the life of thy straits and bays,
    A vein in the heart of the streams of the sea.

Fair mother, fed with the lives of men,
    Thou art subtle and cruel of heart, men say.   290
Thou hast taken, and shalt not render again;
    Thou art full of thy dead, and cold as they.
But death is the worst that comes of thee;
Thou art fed with our dead, O mother, O sea,
But when hast thou fed on our hearts? or when,
    Having given us love, hast thou taken away?

O tender-hearted, O perfect lover,
    Thy lips are bitter, and sweet thine heart.
The hopes that hurt and the dreams that hover,
    Shall they not vanish away and apart?   300
But thou, thou art sure, thou art older than earth;
Thou art strong for death and fruitful of birth;
Thy depths conceal and thy gulfs discover;
    From the first thou wert; in the end thou art.

And grief shall endure not for ever, I know.
    As things that are not shall these things be;
We shall live through seasons of sun and of snow,
    And none be grievous as this to me.
We shall hear, as one in a trance that hears,
The sound of time, the rhyme of the years;   310
Wrecked hope and passionate pain will grow
    As tender things of a spring-tide sea.

Sea-fruit that swings in the waves that hiss,
    Drowned gold and purple and royal rings.
And all time past, was it all for this?
    Times unforgotten, and treasures of things?

Swift years of liking and sweet long laughter,
That wist not well of the years thereafter
Till love woke, smitten at heart by a kiss,
    With lips that trembled and trailing wings?   320

There lived a singer in France of old
    By the tideless dolorous midland sea.
In a land of sand and ruin and gold
    There shone one woman, and none but she.
And finding life for her love's sake fail,
Being fain to see her, he bade her set sail,
Touched land, and saw her as life grew cold,
    And praised God, seeing; and so died he.

Died, praising God for his gift and grace:
    For she bowed down to him weeping, and said   330
'Live;' and her tears were shed on his face
    Or ever the life in his face was shed.
The sharp tears fell through her hair, and stung
Once, and her close lips touched him and clung
Once, and grew one with his lips for a space;
    And so drew back, and the man was dead.

O brother, the gods were good to you.
    Sleep, and be glad while the world endures.
Be well content as the years wear through;
    Give thanks for life, and the loves and lures;   340
Give thanks for life, O brother, and death,
For the sweet last sound of her feet, her breath,
For gifts she gave you, gracious and few,
    Tears and kisses, that lady of yours.

Rest, and be glad of the gods; but I,
    How shall I praise them or how take rest?
There is not room under all the sky
    For me that know not of worst or best,
Dream or desire of the days before,
Sweet things or bitterness, any more.   350
Love will not come to me now though I die,
    As love came close to you, breast to breast.

I shall never be friends again with roses;
   I shall loathe sweet tunes, where a note grown strong
Relents and recoils, and climbs and closes,
   As a wave of the sea turned back by song.
There are sounds where the soul's delight takes fire,
Face to face with its own desire;
A delight that rebels, a desire that reposes;
   I shall hate sweet music my whole life long.   360

The pulse of war and passion of wonder,
   The heavens that murmur, the sounds that shine,
The stars that sing and the loves that thunder,
   The music burning at heart like wine,
An armed archangel whose hands raise up
All senses mixed in the spirit's cup
Till flesh and spirit are molten in sunder—
   These things are over, and no more mine.

These were a part of the playing I heard
   Once, ere my love and my heart were at strife;   370
Love that sings and hath wings as a bird,
   Balm of the wound and heft of the knife.
Fairer than earth is the sea, and sleep
Than overwatching of eyes that weep,
Now time has done with his one sweet word,
   The wine and leaven of lovely life.

I shall go my ways, tread out my measure,
   Fill the days of my daily breath
With fugitive things not good to treasure,
   Do as the world doth, say as it saith;   380
But if we had loved each other—O sweet,
Had you felt, lying under the palms of your feet,
The heart of my heart, beating harder with pleasure
   To feel you tread it to dust and death—

Ah, had I not taken my life up and given
   All that life gives and the years let go,
The wine and honey, the balm and leaven,
   The dreams reared high and the hopes brought low?

Come life, come death, not a word be said;
Should I lose you living, and vex you dead?   390
I never shall tell you on earth; and in heaven,
    If I cry to you then, will you hear or know?

LES NOYADES

Whatever a man of the sons of men
    Shall say to his heart of the lords above,
They have shown man verily, once and again,
    Marvellous mercies and infinite love.

In the wild fifth year of the change of things,
    When France was glorious and blood-red, fair
With dust of battle and deaths of kings,
    A queen of men, with helmeted hair,

Carrier came down to the Loire and slew,
    Till all the ways and the waves waxed red: 10
Bound and drowned, slaying two by two,
    Maidens and young men, naked and wed.

They brought on a day to his judgment-place
    One rough with labour and red with fight,
And a lady noble by name and face,
    Faultless, a maiden, wonderful, white.

She knew not, being for shame's sake blind,
    If his eyes were hot on her face hard by.
And the judge bade strip and ship them, and bind
    Bosom to bosom, to drown and die.   20

The white girl winced and whitened; but he
    Caught fire, waxed bright as a great bright flame
Seen with thunder far out on the sea,
    Laughed hard as the glad blood went and came.

Twice his lips quailed with delight, then said,
    'I have but a word to you all, one word;

Bear with me; surely I am but dead;'
    And all they laughed and mocked him and heard.

'Judge, when they open the judgment-roll,
    I will stand upright before God and pray: 30
"Lord God, have mercy on one man's soul,
    For his mercy was great upon earth, I say.

' "Lord, if I loved thee—Lord, if I served—
    If these who darkened thy fair Son's face
I fought with, sparing not one, nor swerved
    A hand's-breadth, Lord, in the perilous place—

' "I pray thee say to this man, O Lord,
    Sit thou for him at my feet on a throne.
I will face thy wrath, though it bite as a sword,
    And my soul shall burn for his soul, and atone.   40

' "For, Lord, thou knowest, O God most wise,
    How gracious on earth were his deeds towards me.
Shall this be a small thing in thine eyes,
    That is greater in mine than the whole great sea?"

'I have loved this woman my whole life long,
    And even for love's sake when have I said
"I love you"? when have I done you wrong,
    Living? but now I shall have you dead.

'Yea, now, do I bid you love me, love?
    Love me or loathe, we are one not twain.   50
But God be praised in his heaven above
    For this my pleasure and that my pain!

'For never a man, being mean like me,
    Shall die like me till the whole world dies.
I shall drown with her, laughing for love; and she
    Mix with me, touching me, lips and eyes.

'Shall she not know me and see me all through,
    Me, on whose heart as a worm she trod?

You have given me, God requite it you,
    What man yet never was given of God.'   60

O sweet one love, O my life's delight,
    Dear, though the days have divided us,
Lost beyond hope, taken far out of sight,
    Not twice in the world shall the gods do thus.

Had it been so hard for my love? but I,
    Though the gods gave all that a god can give,
I had chosen rather the gift to die,
    Cease, and be glad above all that live.

For the Loire would have driven us down to the sea,
    And the sea would have pitched us from shoal to shoal;   70
And I should have held you, and you held me,
    As flesh holds flesh, and the soul the soul.

Could I change you, help you to love me, sweet,
    Could I give you the love that would sweeten death,
We should yield, go down, locked hands and feet,
    Die, drown together, and breath catch breath;

But you would have felt my soul in a kiss,
    And known that once if I loved you well;
And I would have given my soul for this
    To burn for ever in burning hell.   80

A LEAVE-TAKING

Let us go hence, my songs; she will not hear.
Let us go hence together without fear;
Keep silence now, for singing-time is over,
And over all old things and all things dear.
She loves not you nor me as all we love her.
Yea, though we sang as angels in her ear,
    She would not hear.

Let us rise up and part; she will not know.
Let us go seaward as the great winds go,
Full of blown sand and foam; what help is here?   10
There is no help, for all these things are so,
And all the world is bitter as a tear.
And how these things are, though ye strove to show,
     She would not know.

Let us go home and hence; she will not weep.
We gave love many dreams and days to keep,
Flowers without scent, and fruits that would not grow,
Saying 'If thou wilt, thrust in thy sickle and reap.'
All is reaped now; no grass is left to mow;
And we that sowed, though all we fell on sleep,
     She would not weep.

Let us go hence and rest; she will not love.
She shall not hear us if we sing hereof,
Nor see love's ways, how sore they are and steep.
Come hence, let be, lie still; it is enough.
Love is a barren sea, bitter and deep;
And though she saw all heaven in flower above,
     She would not love.

Let us give up, go down; she will not care.
Though all the stars made gold of all the air,   30
And the sea moving saw before it move
One moon-flower making all the foam-flowers fair;
Though all those waves went over us, and drove
Deep down the stifling lips and drowning hair,
     She would not care.

Let us go hence, go hence; she will not see.
Sing all once more together; surely she,
She too, remembering days and words that were,
Will turn a little toward us, sighing; but we,
We are hence, we are gone, as though we had not been there.   40
Nay, and though all men seeing had pity on me,
     She would not see.

ANACTORIA

τίνος αὖ τὺ πειθοῖ
μὰψ σαγηνεύσας φιλότατα

Sappho.

My life is bitter with thy love; thine eyes
Blind me, thy tresses burn me, thy sharp sighs
Divide my flesh and spirit with soft sound,
And my blood strengthens, and my veins abound.
I pray thee sigh not, speak not, draw not breath;
Let life burn down, and dream it is not death.
I would the sea had hidden us, the fire
(Wilt thou fear that, and fear not my desire?)
Severed the bones that bleach, the flesh that cleaves,
And let our sifted ashes drop like leaves.   10
I feel thy blood against my blood: my pain
Pains thee, and lips bruise lips, and vein stings vein.
Let fruit be crushed on fruit, let flower on flower,
Breast kindle breast, and either burn one hour.
Why wilt thou follow lesser loves? are thine
Too weak to bear these hands and lips of mine?
I charge thee for my life's sake, O too sweet
To crush love with thy cruel faultless feet,
I charge thee keep thy lips from hers or his,
Sweetest, till theirs be sweeter than my kiss: 20
Lest I too lure, a swallow for a dove,
Erotion or Erinna to my love.
I would my love could kill thee; I am satiated
With seeing thee live, and fain would have thee dead.
I would earth had thy body as fruit to eat,
And no mouth but some serpent's found thee sweet.
I would find grievous ways to have thee slain,
Intense device, and superflux of pain;
Vex thee with amorous agonies, and shake
Life at thy lips, and leave it there to ache;   30
Strain out thy soul with pangs too soft to kill,
Intolerable interludes, and infinite ill;
Relapse and reluctation of the breath,
Dumb tunes and shuddering semitones of death.

I am weary of all thy words and soft strange ways,
Of all love's fiery nights and all his days,
And all the broken kisses salt as brine
That shuddering lips make moist with waterish wine,
And eyes the bluer for all those hidden hours
That pleasure fills with tears and feeds from flowers,   40
Fierce at the heart with fire that half comes through,
But all the flowerlike white stained round with blue;
The fervent underlid, and that above
Lifted with laughter or abashed with love;
Thine amorous girdle, full of thee and fair,
And leavings of the lilies in thine hair.
Yea, all sweet words of thine and all thy ways,
And all the fruit of nights and flower of days,
And stinging lips wherein the hot sweet brine
That Love was born of burns and foams like wine,   50
And eyes insatiable of amorous hours,
Fervent as fire and delicate as flowers,
Coloured like night at heart, but cloven through
Like night with flame, dyed round like night with blue,
Clothed with deep eyelids under and above—
Yea, all thy beauty sickens me with love;
Thy girdle empty of thee and now not fair,
And ruinous lilies in thy languid hair.
Ah, take no thought for Love's sake; shall this be,
And she who loves thy lover not love thee?   60
Sweet soul, sweet mouth of all that laughs and lives,
Mine is she, very mine; and she forgives.
For I beheld in sleep the light that is
In her high place in Paphos, heard the kiss
Of body and soul that mix with eager tears
And laughter stinging through the eyes and ears;
Saw Love, as burning flame from crown to feet,
Imperishable, upon her storied seat;
Clear eyelids lifted toward the north and south,
A mind of many colours, and a mouth   70
Of many tunes and kisses; and she bowed,
With all her subtle face laughing aloud,
Bowed down upon me, saying, 'Who doth thee wrong,
Sappho?' but thou—thy body is the song,

Thy mouth the music; thou art more than I,
Though my voice die not till the whole world die;
Though men that hear it madden; though love weep,
Though nature change, though shame be charmed to sleep.
Ah, wilt thou slay me lest I kiss thee dead?
Yet the queen laughed from her sweet heart and said: 80
'Even she that flies shall follow for thy sake,
And she shall give thee gifts that would not take,
Shall kiss that would not kiss thee' (yea, kiss me)
'When thou wouldst not'—when I would not kiss thee!
Ah, more to me than all men as thou art,
Shall not my songs assuage her at the heart?
Ah, sweet to me as life seems sweet to death,
Why should her wrath fill thee with fearful breath?
Nay, sweet, for is she God alone? hath she
Made earth and all the centuries of the sea,   90
Taught the sun ways to travel, woven most fine
The moonbeams, shed the starbeams forth as wine,
Bound with her myrtles, beaten with her rods,
The young men and the maidens and the gods?
Have we not lips to love with, eyes for tears,
And summer and flower of women and of years?
Stars for the foot of morning, and for noon
Sunlight, and exaltation of the moon;
Waters that answer waters, fields that wear
Lilies, and languor of the Lesbian air?   100
Beyond those flying feet of fluttered doves,
Are there not other gods for other loves?
Yea, though she scourge thee, sweetest, for my sake,
Blossom not thorns and flowers not blood should break.
Ah that my lips were tuneless lips, but pressed
To the bruised blossom of thy scourged white breast!
Ah that my mouth for Muses' milk were fed
On the sweet blood thy sweet small wounds had bled!
That with my tongue I felt them, and could taste
The faint flakes from thy bosom to the waist!   110
That I could drink thy veins as wine, and eat
Thy breasts like honey! that from face to feet
Thy body were abolished and consumed,
And in my flesh thy very flesh entombed!

Ah, ah, thy beauty! like a beast it bites,
Stings like an adder, like an arrow smites.
Ah sweet, and sweet again, and seven times sweet,
The paces and the pauses of thy feet!
Ah sweeter than all sleep or summer air
The fallen fillets fragrant from thine hair!   120
Yea, though their alien kisses do me wrong,
Sweeter thy lips than mine with all their song;
Thy shoulders whiter than a fleece of white,
And flower-sweet fingers, good to bruise or bite
As honeycomb of the inmost honey-cells,
With almond-shaped and roseleaf-coloured shells
And blood like purple blossom at the tips
Quivering; and pain made perfect in thy lips
For my sake when I hurt thee; O that I
Durst crush thee out of life with love, and die,   130
Die of thy pain and my delight, and be
Mixed with thy blood and molten into thee!
Would I not plague thee dying overmuch?
Would I not hurt thee perfectly? not touch
Thy pores of sense with torture, and make bright
Thine eyes with bloodlike tears and grievous light?
Strike pang from pang as note is struck from note,
Catch the sob's middle music in thy throat,
Take thy limbs living, and new-mould with these
A lyre of many faultless agonies?   140
Feed thee with fever and famine and fine drouth,
With perfect pangs convulse thy perfect mouth,
Make thy life shudder in thee and burn afresh,
And wring thy very spirit through the flesh?
Cruel? but love makes all that love him well
As wise as heaven and crueller than hell.
Me hath love made more bitter toward thee
Than death toward man; but were I made as he
Who hath made all things to break them one by one,
If my feet trod upon the stars and sun   150
And souls of men as his have alway trod,
God knows I might be crueller than God.
For who shall change with prayers or thanksgivings
The mystery of the cruelty of things?

Or say what God above all gods and years
With offering and blood-sacrifice of tears,
With lamentation from strange lands, from graves
Where the snake pastures, from scarred mouths of slaves,
From prison, and from plunging prows of ships
Through flamelike foam of the sea's closing lips—   160
With thwartings of strange signs, and wind-blown hair
Of comets, desolating the dim air,
When darkness is made fast with seals and bars,
And fierce reluctance of disastrous stars,
Eclipse, and sound of shaken hills, and wings
Darkening, and blind inexpiable things—
With sorrow of labouring moons, and altering light
And travail of the planets of the night,
And weeping of the weary Pleiads seven,
Feeds the mute melancholy lust of heaven?   170
Is not his incense bitterness, his meat
Murder? his hidden face and iron feet
Hath not man known, and felt them on their way
Threaten and trample all things and every day?
Hath he not sent us hunger? who hath cursed
Spirit and flesh with longing? filled with thirst
Their lips who cried unto him? who bade exceed
The fervid will, fall short the feeble deed,
Bade sink the spirit and the flesh aspire,
Pain animate the dust of dead desire,   180
And life yield up her flower to violent fate?
Him would I reach, him smite, him desecrate,
Pierce the cold lips of God with human breath,
And mix his immortality with death.
Why hath he made us? what had all we done
That we should live and loathe the sterile sun,
And with the moon wax paler as she wanes,
And pulse by pulse feel time grow through our veins?
Thee too the years shall cover; thou shalt be
As the rose born of one same blood with thee,   190
As a song sung, as a word said, and fall
Flower-wise, and be not any more at all,
Nor any memory of thee anywhere;
For never Muse has bound above thine hair

The high Pierian flower whose graft outgrows
All summer kinship of the mortal rose
And colour of deciduous days, nor shed
Reflex and flush of heaven about thine head,
Nor reddened brows made pale by floral grief
With splendid shadow from that lordlier leaf.   200
Yea, thou shalt be forgotten like spilt wine,
Except these kisses of my lips on thine
Brand them with immortality; but me—
Men shall not see bright fire nor hear the sea,
Nor mix their hearts with music, nor behold
Cast forth of heaven, with feet of awful gold
And plumeless wings that make the bright air blind,
Lightning, with thunder for a hound behind
Hunting through fields unfurrowed and unsown,
But in the light and laughter, in the moan   210
And music, and in grasp of lip and hand
And shudder of water that makes felt on land
The immeasurable tremor of all the sea,
Memories shall mix and metaphors of me.
Like me shall be the shuddering calm of night,
When all the winds of the world for pure delight
Close lips that quiver and fold up wings that ache;
When nightingales are louder for love's sake,
And leaves tremble like lute-strings or like fire;
Like me the one star swooning with desire   220
Even at the cold lips of the sleepless moon,
As I at thine; like me the waste white noon,
Burnt through with barren sunlight; and like me
The land-stream and the tide-stream in the sea.
I am sick with time as these with ebb and flow,
And by the yearning in my veins I know
The yearning sound of waters; and mine eyes
Burn as that beamless fire which fills the skies
With troubled stars and travailing things of flame;
And in my heart the grief consuming them   230
Labours, and in my veins the thirst of these,
And all the summer travail of the trees
And all the winter sickness; and the earth,
Filled full with deadly works of death and birth,

Sore spent with hungry lusts of birth and death,
Has pain like mine in her divided breath;
Her spring of leaves is barren, and her fruit
Ashes; her boughs are burdened, and her root
Fibrous and gnarled with poison; underneath
Serpents have gnawn it through with tortuous teeth   240
Made sharp upon the bones of all the dead,
And wild birds rend her branches overhead.
These, woven as raiment for his word and thought,
These hath God made, and me as these, and wrought
Song, and hath lit it at my lips; and me
Earth shall not gather though she feed on thee.
As a shed tear shalt thou be shed; but I—
Lo, earth may labour, men live long and die,
Years change and stars, and the high God devise
New things, and old things wane before his eyes   250
Who wields and wrecks them, being more strong than they—
But, having made me, me he shall not slay.
Nor slay nor satiate, like those herds of his
Who laugh and live a little, and their kiss
Contents them, and their loves are swift and sweet,
And sure death grasps and gains them with slow feet,
Love they or hate they, strive or bow their knees—
And all these end; he hath his will of these.
Yea, but albeit he slay me, hating me—
Albeit he hide me in the deep dear sea   260
And cover me with cool wan foam, and ease
This soul of mine as any soul of these,
And give me water and great sweet waves, and make
The very sea's name lordlier for my sake,
The whole sea sweeter—albeit I die indeed
And hide myself and sleep and no man heed,
Of me the high God hath not all his will.
Blossom of branches, and on each high hill
Clear air and wind, and under in clamorous vales
Fierce noises of the fiery nightingales,   270
Buds burning in the sudden spring like fire,
The wan washed sand and the waves' vain desire,
Sails seen like blown white flowers at sea, and words
That bring tears swiftest, and long notes of birds

Violently singing till the whole world sings—
I Sappho shall be one with all these things,
With all high things for ever; and my face
Seen once, my songs once heard in a strange place,
Cleave to men's lives, and waste the days thereof
With gladness and much sadness and long love.   280
Yea, they shall say, earth's womb has borne in vain
New things, and never this best thing again;
Borne days and men, borne fruits and wars and wine,
Seasons and songs, but no song more like mine.
And they shall know me as ye who have known me here,
Last year when I loved Atthis, and this year
When I love thee; and they shall praise me, and say
'She hath all time as all we have our day,
Shall she not live and have her will?'—even I?
Yea, though thou diest, I say I shall not die.   290
For these shall give me of their souls, shall give
Life, and the days and loves wherewith I live,
Shall quicken me with loving, fill with breath,
Save me and serve me, strive for me with death.
Alas, that neither moon nor snow nor dew
Nor all cold things can purge me wholly through,
Assuage me nor allay me nor appease,
Till supreme sleep shall bring me bloodless ease;
Till time wax faint in all his periods;
Till fate undo the bondage of the gods,   300
And lay, to slake and satiate me all through,
Lotus and Lethe on my lips like dew,
And shed around and over and under me
Thick darkness and the insuperable sea.

HYMN TO PROSERPINE

(After the proclamation in Rome of the Christian faith)

Vicisti, Galilæe.

I have lived long enough, having seen one thing, that love hath an end;
Goddess and maiden and queen, be near me now and befriend.
Thou art more than the day or the morrow, the seasons that laugh or
    that weep;

For these give joy and sorrow; but thou, Proserpina, sleep.
Sweet is the treading of wine, and sweet the feet of the dove;
But a goodlier gift is thine than foam of the grapes or love.
Yea, is not even Apollo, with hair and harpstring of gold,
A bitter God to follow, a beautiful God to behold?
I am sick of singing: the bays burn deep and chafe: I am fain
To rest a little from praise and grievous pleasure and pain.   10
For the Gods we know not of, who give us our daily breath,
We know they are cruel as love or life, and lovely as death.
O Gods dethroned and deceased, cast forth, wiped out in a day!
From your wrath is the world released, redeemed from your chains, men
    say.
New Gods are crowned in the city; their flowers have broken your rods;
They are merciful, clothed with pity, the young compassionate Gods.
But for me their new device is barren, the days are bare;
Things long past over suffice, and men forgotten that were.
Time and the Gods are at strife; ye dwell in the midst thereof,
Draining a little life from the barren breasts of love.   20
I say to you, cease, take rest; yea, I say to you all, be at peace,
Till the bitter milk of her breast and the barren bosom shall cease.
Wilt thou yet take all, Galilean? but these thou shalt not take,
The laurels, the palms and the pæan, the breasts of the nymphs in the
    brake;
Breasts more soft than a dove's, that tremble with tenderer breath;
And all the wings of the Loves, and all the joy before death;
All the feet of the hours that sound as a single lyre,
Dropped and deep in the flowers, with strings that flicker like fire.
More than these wilt thou give, things fairer than all these things?
Nay, for a little we live, and life hath mutable wings.   30
A little while and we die; shall life not thrive as it may?
For no man under the sky lives twice, outliving his day.
And grief is a grievous thing, and a man hath enough of his tears:
Why should he labour, and bring fresh grief to blacken his years?
Thou hast conquered, O pale Galilean; the world has grown grey from
    thy breath;
We have drunken of things Lethean, and fed on the fullness of death.
Laurel is green for a season, and love is sweet for a day;
But love grows bitter with treason, and laurel outlives not May.
Sleep, shall we sleep after all? for the world is not sweet in the end;
For the old faiths loosen and fall, the new years ruin and rend.   40

Fate is a sea without shore, and the soul is a rock that abides;
But her ears are vexed with the roar and her face with the foam of
    the tides.
O lips that the live blood faints in, the leavings of racks and rods!
O ghastly glories of saints, dead limbs of gibbeted Gods!
Though all men abase them before you in spirit, and all knees bend,
I kneel not neither adore you, but standing, look to the end.
All delicate days and pleasant, all spirits and sorrows are cast
Far out with the foam of the present that sweeps to the surf of the past:
Where beyond the extreme sea-wall, and between the remote sea-gates,
Waste water washes, and tall ships founder, and deep death waits: 50
Where, mighty with deepening sides, clad about with the seas as with
    wings,
And impelled of invisible tides, and fulfilled of unspeakable things,
White-eyed and poisonous-finned, shark-toothed and serpentine-curled,
Rolls, under the whitening wind of the future, the wave of the world.
The depths stand naked in sunder behind it, the storms flee away;
In the hollow before it the thunder is taken and snared as a prey;
In its sides is the north-wind bound; and its salt is of all men's tears;
With light of ruin, and sound of changes, and pulse of years:
With travail of day after day, and with trouble of hour upon hour;
And bitter as blood is the spray; and the crests are as fangs that
    devour: 60
And its vapour and storm of its steam as the sighing of spirits to be;
And its noise as the noise in a dream; and its depth as the roots of the
    sea:
And the height of its heads as the height of the utmost stars of the air:
And the ends of the earth at the might thereof tremble, and time is
    made bare.
Will ye bridle the deep sea with reins, will ye chasten the high sea with
    rods?
Will ye take her to chain her with chains, who is older than all ye Gods?
All ye as a wind shall go by, as a fire shall ye pass and be past;
Ye are Gods, and behold, ye shall die, and the waves be upon you at last.
In the darkness of time, in the deeps of the years, in the changes of
    things,
Ye shall sleep as a slain man sleeps, and the world shall forget you for
    kings.   70
Though the feet of thine high priests tread where thy lords and our
    forefathers trod,

Though these that were Gods are dead, and thou being dead art a God,
Though before thee the throned Cytherean be fallen, and hidden her
      head,
Yet thy kingdom shall pass, Galilean, thy dead shall go down to thee
      dead.
Of the maiden thy mother men sing as a goddess with grace clad around;
Thou art throned where another was king; where another was queen she
      is crowned.
Yea, once we had sight of another: but now she is queen, say these.
Not as thine, not as thine was our mother, a blossom of flowering seas,
Clothed round with the world's desire as with raiment, and fair as the
      foam,
And fleeter than kindled fire, and a goddess, and mother of Rome.   80
For thine came pale and a maiden, and sister to sorrow; but ours,
Her deep hair heavily laden with odour and colour of flowers,
White rose of the rose-white water, a silver splendour, a flame,
Bent down unto us that besought her, and earth grew sweet with her
      name.
For thine came weeping, a slave among slaves, and rejected; but she
Came flushed from the full-flushed wave, and imperial, her foot on
      the sea.
And the wonderful waters knew her, the winds and the viewless ways,
And the roses grew rosier, and bluer the sea-blue stream of the bays.
Ye are fallen, our lords, by what token? we wist that ye should not fall.
Ye were all so fair that are broken; and one more fair than ye all.   90
But I turn to her still, having seen she shall surely abide in the end;
Goddess and maiden and queen, be near me now and befriend.
O daughter of earth, of my mother, her crown and blossom of birth,
I am also, I also, thy brother; I go as I came unto earth.
In the night where thine eyes are as moons are in heaven, the night where
      thou art,
Where the silence is more than all tunes, where sleep overflows from the
      heart,
Where the poppies are sweet as the rose in our world, and the red rose is
      white,
And the wind falls faint as it blows with the fume of the flowers of the
      night,
And the murmur of spirits that sleep in the shadow of Gods from afar
Grows dim in thine ears and deep as the deep dim soul of a star,   100
In the sweet low light of thy face, under heavens untrod by the sun,

Let my soul with their souls find place, and forget what is done and
    undone.
Thou art more than the Gods who number the days of our temporal
    breath;
For these give labour and slumber; but thou, Proserpina, death.
Therefore now at thy feet I abide for a season in silence. I know
I shall die as my fathers died, and sleep as they sleep; even so.
For the glass of the years is brittle wherein we gaze for a span;
A little soul for a little bears up this corpse which is man.[1]
So long I endure, no longer; and laugh not again, neither weep.
For there is no God found stronger than death; and death is a
    sleep.   110

[1]
$$\psi\upsilon\chi\acute{\alpha}\rho\iota o\nu \ \hat{\epsilon}\grave{\iota} \ \beta\alpha\sigma\tau\acute{\alpha}\zeta o\nu \ \nu\epsilon\kappa\rho\acute{o}\nu.$$
                                   EPICTETUS

A MATCH

If love were what the rose is,
    And I were like a leaf,
Our lives would grow together
In sad or singing weather,
Blown fields or flowerful closes,
    Green pleasure or grey grief;
If love were what the rose is,
    And I were like the leaf.

If I were what the words are,
    And love were like the tune,   10
With double sound and single
Delight our lips would mingle,
With kisses glad as birds are
    That get sweet rain at noon;
If I were what the words are,
    And love were like the tune.

If you were life, my darling,
    And I your love were death,
We'd shine and snow together

Ere March made sweet the weather   20
With daffodil and starling
   And hours of fruitful breath;
If you were life, my darling,
   And I your love were death.

If you were thrall to sorrow,
   And I were page to joy,
We'd play for lives and seasons
With loving looks and treasons
And tears of night and morrow
   And laughs of maid and boy;   30
If you were thrall to sorrow,
   And I were page to joy.

If you were April's lady,
   And I were lord in May,
We'd throw with leaves for hours
And draw for days with flowers,
Till day like night were shady
   And night were bright like day;
If you were April's lady,
   And I were lord in May.   40

If you were queen of pleasure,
   And I were king of pain,
We'd hunt down love together,
Pluck out his flying-feather,
And teach his feet a measure,
   And find his mouth a rein;
If you were queen of pleasure,
   And I were king of pain.

A CAMEO

There was a graven image of Desire
   Painted with red blood on a ground of gold
   Passing between the young men and the old,
And by him Pain, whose body shone like fire,

And Pleasure with gaunt hands that grasped their hire.
    Of his left wrist, with fingers clenched and cold,
    The insatiable Satiety kept hold,
Walking with feet unshod that pashed the mire.
The senses and the sorrows and the sins,
    And the strange loves that suck the breasts of Hate   10
Till lips and teeth bite in their sharp indenture,
Followed like beasts with flap of wings and fins.
    Death stood aloof behind a gaping grate,
Upon whose lock was written *Peradventure.*

DOLORES

(Notre-Dame des Sept Douleurs)

Cold eyelids that hide like a jewel
    Hard eyes that grow soft for an hour;
The heavy white limbs, and the cruel
    Red mouth like a venomous flower;
When these are gone by with their glories,
    What shall rest of thee then, what remain,
O mystic and sombre Dolores,
    Our Lady of Pain?

Seven sorrows the priests give their Virgin;
    But thy sins, which are seventy times seven,   10
Seven ages would fail thee to purge in,
    And then they would haunt thee in heaven:
Fierce midnights and famishing morrows.
    And the loves that complete and control
All the joys of the flesh, all the sorrows
    That wear out the soul.

O garment not golden but gilded,
    O garden where all men may dwell,
O tower not of ivory, but builded
    By hands that reach heaven from hell;   20
O mystical rose of the mire,
    O house not of gold but of gain,

O house of unquenchable fire,
   Our Lady of Pain!

O lips full of lust and of laughter,
   Curled snakes that are fed from my breast,
Bite hard, lest remembrance come after
   And press with new lips where you pressed.
For my heart too springs up at the pressure,
   Mine eyelids too moisten and burn;   30
Ah, feed me and fill me with pleasure,
   Ere pain come in turn.

In yesterday's reach and to-morrow's,
   Out of sight though they lie of to-day,
There have been and there yet shall be sorrows
   That smite not and bite not in play.
The life and the love thou despisest,
   These hurt us indeed, and in vain,
O wise among women, and wisest,
   Our Lady of Pain.   40

Who gave thee thy wisdom? what stories
   That stung thee, what visions that smote?
Wert thou pure and a maiden, Dolores,
   When desire took thee first by the throat?
What bud was the shell of a blossom
   That all men may smell to and pluck?
What milk fed thee first at what bosom?
   What sins gave thee suck?

We shift and bedeck and bedrape us,
   Thou art noble and nude and antique;   50
Libitina thy mother, Priapus
   Thy father, a Tuscan and Greek.
We play with light loves in the portal,
   And wince and relent and refrain;
Loves die, and we know thee immortal,
   Our Lady of Pain.

Fruits fail and love dies and time ranges;
   Thou art fed with perpetual breath,

And alive after infinite changes,
  And fresh from the kisses of death;
Of languors rekindled and rallied,
  Of barren delights and unclean,
Things monstrous and fruitless, a pallid
  And poisonous queen.

60

Could you hurt me, sweet lips, though I hurt you?
  Men touch them, and change in a trice
The lilies and languors of virtue
  For the raptures and roses of vice;
Those lie where thy foot on the floor is,
  These crown and caress thee and chain,
O splendid and sterile Dolores,
  Our Lady of Pain.

70

There are sins it may be to discover,
  There are deeds it may be to delight.
What new work wilt thou find for thy lover,
  What new passions for daytime or night?
What spells that they know not a word of
  Whose lives are as leaves overblown?
What tortures undreamt of, unheard of,
  Unwritten, unknown?

80

Ah beautiful passionate body
  That never has ached with a heart!
On thy mouth though the kisses are bloody,
  Though they sting till it shudder and smart,
More kind than the love we adore is,
  They hurt not the heart or the brain,
O bitter and tender Dolores,
  Our Lady of Pain.

As our kisses relax and redouble,
  From the lips and the foam and the fangs
Shall no new sin be born for men's trouble,
  No dream of impossible pangs?
With the sweet of the sins of old ages
  Wilt thou satiate thy soul as of yore?

90

Too sweet is the rind, say the sages,
     Too bitter the core.

Hast thou told all thy secrets the last time,
     And bared all thy beauties to one?
Ah, where shall we go then for pastime,
     If the worst that can be has been done?
But sweet as the rind was the core is;
     We are fain of thee still, we are fain,
O sanguine and subtle Dolores,
     Our Lady of Pain.

By the hunger of change and emotion,
     By the thirst of unbearable things,
By despair, the twin-born of devotion,
     By the pleasure that winces and stings,
The delight that consumes the desire,
     The desire that outruns the delight,
By the cruelty deaf as a fire
     And blind as the night,

By the ravenous teeth that have smitten
     Through the kisses that blossom and bud,
By the lips intertwisted and bitten
     Till the foam has a savour of blood,
By the pulse as it rises and falters,
     By the hands as they slacken and strain,
I adjure thee, respond from thine altars,
     Our Lady of Pain

Wilt thou smile as a woman disdaining
     The light fire in the veins of a boy?
But he comes to thee sad, without feigning,
     Who has wearied of sorrow and joy;
Less careful of labour and glory
     Than the elders whose hair has uncurled;
And young, but with fancies as hoary
     And grey as the world.

I have passed from the outermost portal
     To the shrine where a sin is a prayer;

100

110

120

130

What care though the service be mortal?
    O our Lady of Torture, what care?
All thine the last wine that I pour is,
    The last in the chalice we drain,
O fierce and luxurious Dolores,
    Our Lady of Pain.

All thine the new wine of desire,
    The fruit of four lips as they clung
Till the hair and the eyelids took fire,
    The foam of a serpentine tongue,   140
The froth of the serpents of pleasure,
    More salt than the foam of the sea,
Now felt as a flame, now at leisure
    As wine shed for me.

Ah thy people, thy children, thy chosen,
    Marked cross from the womb and perverse!
They have found out the secrets to cozen
    The gods that constrain us and curse;
They alone, they are wise, and none other;
    Give me place, even me, in their train,
O my sister, my spouse, and my mother,   150
    Our Lady of Pain.

For the crown of our life as it closes
    Is darkness, the fruit thereof dust;
No thorns go as deep as a rose's,
    And love is more cruel than lust.
Time turns the old days to derision,
    Our loves into corpses or wives;
And marriage and death and division
    Make barren our lives.   160

And pale from the past we draw nigh thee,
    And satiate with comfortless hours;
And we know thee, how all men belie thee,
    And we gather the fruit of thy flowers;
The passion that slays and recovers,
    The pangs and the kisses that rain

On the lips and the limbs of thy lovers,
   Our Lady of Pain.

The desire of thy furious embraces
   Is more than the wisdom of years,   170
On the blossom though blood lie in traces,
   Though the foliage be sodden with tears.
For the lords in whose keeping the door is
   That opens on all who draw breath
Gave the cypress to love, my Dolores,
   The myrtle to death.

And they laughed, changing hands in the measure.
   And they mixed and made peace after strife;
Pain melted in tears, and was pleasure;
   Death tingled with blood, and was life.   180
Like lovers they melted and tingled,
   In the dusk of thine innermost fane;
In the darkness they murmured and mingled,
   Our Lady of Pain.

In a twilight where virtues are vices,
   In thy chapels, unknown of the sun,
To a tune that enthralls and entices,
   They were wed, and the twain were as one.
For the tune from thine altar hath sounded
   Since God bade the world's work begin,   190
And the fume of thine incense abounded,
   To sweeten the sin.

Love listens, and paler than ashes,
   Through his curls as the crown on them slips,
Lifts languid wet eyelids and lashes,
   And laughs with insatiable lips.
Thou shalt hush him with heavy caresses,
   With music that scares the profane;
Thou shalt darken his eyes with thy tresses,
   Our Lady of Pain.   200

Thou shalt blind his bright eyes though he wrestle,
    Thou shalt chain his light limbs though he strive;
In his lips all thy serpents shall nestle,
    In his hands all thy cruelties thrive.
In the daytime thy voice shall go through him,
    In his dreams he shall feel thee and ache;
Thou shalt kindle by night and subdue him
    Asleep and awake.

Thou shalt touch and make redder his roses
    With juice not of fruit nor of bud;   210
When the sense in the spirit reposes,
    Thou shalt quicken the soul through the blood.
Thine, thine the one grace we implore is,
    Who would live and not languish or feign,
O sleepless and deadly Dolores,
    Our Lady of Pain.

Dost thou dream, in a respite of slumber,
    In a lull of the fires of thy life,
Of the days without name, without number,
    When thy will stung the world into strife;   220
When, a goddess, the pulse of thy passion
    Smote kings as they revelled in Rome;
And they hailed thee re-risen, O Thalassian,
    Foam-white, from the foam?

When thy lips had such lovers to flatter;
    When the city lay red from thy rods,
And thine hands were as arrows to scatter
    The children of change and their gods;
When the blood of thy foemen made fervent
    A sand never moist from the main,   230
As one smote them, their lord and thy servant,
    Our Lady of Pain.

On sands by the storm never shaken,
    Nor wet from the washing of tides;
Nor by foam of the waves overtaken,
    Nor winds that the thunder bestrides;

But red from the print of thy paces,
    Made smooth for the world and its lords,
Ringed round with a flame of fair faces,
    And splendid with swords.   240

There the gladiator, pale for thy pleasure,
    Drew bitter and perilous breath;
There torments laid hold on the treasure
    Of limbs too delicious for death;
When thy gardens were lit with live torches;
    When the world was a steed for thy rein;
When the nations lay prone in thy porches,
    Our Lady of Pain.

When, with flame all around him aspirant,
    Stood flushed, as a harp-player stands,   250
The implacable beautiful tyrant,
    Rose-crowned, having death in his hands;
And a sound as the sound of loud water
    Smote far through the flight of the fires,
And mixed with the lightning of slaughter
    A thunder of lyres.

Dost thou dream of what was and no more is,
    The old kingdoms of earth and the kings?
Dost thou hunger for these things, Dolores,
For these, in a world of new things?   260
But thy bosom no fasts could emaciate,
    No hunger compel to complain
Those lips that no bloodshed could satiate,
    Our Lady of Pain.

As of old when the world's heart was lighter,
    Through thy garments the grace of thee glows,
The white wealth of thy body made whiter
    By the blushes of amorous blows,
And seamed with sharp lips and fierce fingers,
    And branded by kisses that bruise;   270
When all shall be gone that now lingers,
    Ah, what shall we lose?

Thou wert fair in the fearless old fashion,
    And thy limbs are as melodies yet,
And move to the music of passion
    With lithe and lascivious regret.
What ailed us, O gods, to desert you
    For creeds that refuse and restrain?
Come down and redeem us from virtue,
    Our Lady of Pain.   280

All shrines that were Vestal are flameless,
    But the flame has not fallen from this;
Though obscure be the god, and though nameless
    The eyes and the hair that we kiss;
Low fires that love sits by and forges
    Fresh heads for his arrows and thine;
Hair loosened and soiled in mid orgies
    With kisses and wine.

Thy skin changes country and colour,
    And shrivels or swells to a snake's.   290
Let it brighten and bloat and grow duller,
    We know it, the flames and the flakes,
Red brands on it smitten and bitten,
    Round skies where a star is a stain,
And the leaves with thy litanies written,
    Our Lady of Pain.

On thy bosom though many a kiss be,
    There are none such as knew it of old.
Was it Alciphron once or Arisbe,
    Male ringlets or feminine gold,   300
That thy lips met with under the statue,
    Whence a look shot out sharp after thieves
From the eyes of the garden-god at you
    Across the fig-leaves?

Then still, through dry seasons and moister,
    One god hath a wreath to his shrine;
Then love was the pearl of his oyster,*
    And Venus rose red out of wine.

We have all done amiss, choosing rather
   Such loves as the wise gods disdain;   310
Intercede for us thou with thy father,
   Our Lady of Pain.

In spring he had crowns of his garden,
   Red corn in the heat of the year,
Then hoary green olives that harden
   When the grape-blossom freezes with fear;
And milk-budded myrtles with Venus
   And vine-leaves with Bacchus he trod;
And ye said, 'We have seen, he hath seen us,
   A visible God.'   320

What broke off the garlands that girt you?
   What sundered you spirit and clay?
Weak sins yet alive are as virtue
   To the strength of the sins of that day.
For dried is the blood of thy lover,
   Ipsithilla, contracted the vein;
Cry aloud, 'Will he rise and recover,
   Our Lady of Pain?'

Cry aloud; for the old word is broken:
   Cry out; for the Phrygian is priest,   330
And rears not the bountiful token
   And spreads not the fatherly feast.
From the midmost of Ida, from shady
   Recesses that murmur at morn,
They have brought and baptized her, Our Lady,
   A goddess new-born.

And the chaplets of old are above us,
   And the oyster-bed teems out of reach;
Old poets outsing and outlove us,
   And Catullus makes mouths at our speech.   340
Who shall kiss, in thy father's own city,
   With such lips as he sang with, again?
Intercede for us all of thy pity,
   Our Lady of Pain.

Out of Dindymus heavily laden
    Her lions draw bound and unfed
A mother, a mortal, a maiden,
    A queen over death and the dead.
She is cold, and her habit is lowly,
    Her temple of branches and sods;   350
Most fruitful and virginal, holy,
    A mother of gods.

She hath wasted with fire thine high places,
    She hath hidden and marred and made sad
The fair limbs of the Loves, the fair faces
    Of gods that were goodly and glad.
She slays, and her hands are not bloody;
    She moves as a moon in the wane,
White-robed, and thy raiment is ruddy,
    Our Lady of Pain.   360

They shall pass and their places be taken,
    The gods and the priests that are pure.
They shall pass, and shalt thou not be shaken?
    They shall perish, and shalt thou endure?
Death laughs, breathing close and relentless
    In the nostrils and eyelids of lust,
With a pinch in his fingers of scentless
    And delicate dust.

But the worm shall revive thee with kisses;
    Thou shalt change and transmute as a god,   370
As the rod to a serpent that hisses,
    As the serpent again to a rod.
Thy life shall not cease though thou doff it;
    Thou shalt live until evil be slain,
And good shall die first, said thy prophet,
    Our Lady of Pain.

Did he lie? did he laugh? does he know it,
    Now he lies out of reach, out of breath,
Thy prophet, thy preacher, thy poet,
    Sin's child by incestuous Death?   380

Did he find out in fire at his waking,
    Or discern as his eyelids lost light,
When the bands of the body were breaking
    And all came in sight?

Who has known all the evil before us,
    Or the tyrannous secrets of time?
Though we match not the dead men that bore us
    At a song, at a kiss, at a crime—
Though the heathen outface and outlive us,
    And our lives and our longings are twain—   390
Ah, forgive us our virtues, forgive us,
    Our Lady of Pain.

Who are we that embalm and embrace thee
    With spices and savours of song?
What is time, that his children should face thee?
    What am I, that my lips do thee wrong?
I could hurt thee—but pain would delight thee;
    Or caress thee—but love would repel;
And the lovers whose lips would excite thee
    Are serpents in hell.   400

Who now shall content thee as they did,
    Thy lovers, when temples were built
And the hair of the sacrifice braided
    And the blood of the sacrifice spilt,
In Lampsacus fervent with faces,
    In Aphaca red from thy reign,
Who embraced thee with awful embraces,
    Our Lady of Pain?

Where are they, Cotytto or Venus,
    Astarte or Ashtaroth, where?   410
Do their hands as we touch come between us?
    Is the breath of them hot in thy hair?
From their lips have thy lips taken fever,
    With the blood of their bodies grown red?
Hast thou left upon earth a believer
    If these men are dead?

They were purple of raiment and golden,
  Filled full of thee, fiery with wine,
Thy lovers, in haunts unbeholden,
  In marvellous chambers of thine.   420
They are fled, and their footprints escape us,
  Who appraise thee, adore, and abstain,
O daughter of Death and Priapus,
  Our Lady of Pain.

What ails us to fear overmeasure,
  To praise thee with timorous breath,
O mistress and mother of pleasure,
  The one thing as certain as death?
We shall change as the things that we cherish,
  Shall fade as they faded before,   430
As foam upon water shall perish,
  As sand upon shore.

We shall know what the darkness discovers,
  If the grave-pit be shallow or deep;
And our fathers of old, and our lovers,
  We shall know if they sleep not or sleep.
We shall see whether hell be not heaven,
  Find out whether tares be not grain,
And the joys of thee seventy times seven,
  Our Lady of Pain.   440

* Nam te praecipue in suis urbibus colit ora
  Hellespontia, ceteris ostreosior oris.
                              Catull. *Carm*. xviii.

THE GARDEN OF PROSERPINE

Here, where the world is quiet;
  Here, where all trouble seems
Dead winds' and spent waves' riot
  In doubtful dreams of dreams;
I watch the green field growing

For reaping folk and sowing,
For harvest-time and mowing,
   A sleepy world of streams.

I am tired of tears and laughter,
   And men that laugh and weep;
Of what may come hereafter
   For men that sow to reap:
I am weary of days and hours,
Blown buds of barren flowers,
Desires and dreams and powers
   And everything but sleep.

Here life has death for neighbour,
   And far from eye or ear
Wan waves and wet winds labour,
   Weak ships and spirits steer;
They drive adrift, and whither
They wot not who make thither;
But no such winds blow hither,
   And no such things grow here.

No growth of moor or coppice,
   No heather-flower or vine,
But bloomless buds of poppies,
   Green grapes of Proserpine,
Pale beds of blowing rushes
Where no leaf blooms or blushes
Save this whereout she crushes
   For dead men deadly wine.

Pale, without name or number,
   In fruitless fields of corn,
They bow themselves and slumber
   All night till light is born;
And like a soul belated,
In hell and heaven unmated,
By cloud and mist abated
   Comes out of darkness morn.

10

20

30

40

Though one were strong as seven,
    He too with death shall dwell,
Nor wake with wings in heaven,
    Nor weep for pains in hell;
Though one were fair as roses,
His beauty clouds and closes;
And well though love reposes,
    In the end it is not well.

Pale, beyond porch and portal,
    Crowned with calm leaves, she stands   50
Who gathers all things mortal
    With cold immortal hands;
Her languid lips are sweeter
Than love's who fears to greet her
To men that mix and meet her
    From many times and lands.

She waits for each and other,
    She waits for all men born;
Forgets the earth her mother,
    The life of fruits and corn;   60
And spring and seed and swallow
Take wing for her and follow
Where summer song rings hollow
    And flowers are put to scorn.

There go the loves that wither,
    The old loves with wearier wings;
And all dead years draw thither,
    And all disastrous things;
Dead dreams of days forsaken,
Blind buds that snows have shaken,   70
Wild leaves that winds have taken,
    Red strays of ruined springs.

We are not sure of sorrow,
    And joy was never sure;
To-day will die to-morrow;
    Time stoops to no man's lure;

And love, grown faint and fretful,
With lips but half regretful
Sighs, and with eyes forgetful
 Weeps that no loves endure.   80

From too much love of living,
 From hope and fear set free,
We thank with brief thanksgiving
 Whatever gods may be
That no life lives for ever;
That dead men rise up never;
That even the weariest river
 Winds somewhere safe to sea.

Then star nor sun shall waken,
 Nor any change of light: 90
Nor sound of waters shaken,
 Nor any sound or sight:
Nor wintry leaves nor vernal,
Nor days nor things diurnal;
Only the sleep eternal
 In an eternal night.

THE SUNDEW

A little marsh-plant, yellow green,
And pricked at lip with tender red.
Tread close, and either way you tread
Some faint black water jets between
Lest you should bruise the curious head.

A live thing maybe; who shall know?
The summer knows and suffers it;
For the cool moss is thick and sweet
Each side, and saves the blossom so
That it lives out the long June heat.   10

The deep scent of the heather burns
About it; breathless though it be,

Bow down and worship; more than we
Is the least flower whose life returns,
Least weed renascent in the sea.

We are vexed and cumbered in earth's sight
With wants, with many memories;
These see their mother what she is,
Glad-growing, till August leave more bright
The apple-coloured cranberries.   20

Wind blows and bleaches the strong grass,
Blown all one way to shelter it
From trample of strayed kine, with feet
Felt heavier than the moorhen was,
Strayed up past patches of wild wheat.

You call it sundew: how it grows,
If with its colour it have breath,
If life taste sweet to it, if death
Pain its soft petal, no man knows:
Man has no sight or sense that saith.   30

My sundew, grown of gentle days,
In these green miles the spring begun
Thy growth ere April had half done
With the soft secret of her ways
Or June made ready for the sun.

O red-lipped mouth of marsh-flower,
I have a secret halved with thee.
The name that is love's name to me
Thou knowest, and the face of her
Who is my festival to see.   40

The hard sun, as thy petals knew,
Coloured the heavy moss-water:
Thou wert not worth green midsummer
Nor fit to live to August blue,
O sundew, not remembering her.

FELISE

Mais où sont les neiges d'antan?

What shall be said between us here
    Among the downs, between the trees,
In fields that knew our feet last year,
    In sight of quiet sands and seas,
      This year, Félise?

Who knows what word were best to say?
    For last year's leaves lie dead and red
On this sweet day, in this green May,
    And barren corn makes bitter bread.
      What shall be said?   10

Here as last year the fields begin,
    A fire of flowers and glowing grass;
The old fields we laughed and lingered in,
    Seeing each our souls in last year's glass,
      Félise, alas!

Shall we not laugh, shall we not weep,
    Not we, though this be as it is?
For love awake or love asleep
    Ends in a laugh, a dream, a kiss,
      A song like this.   20

I that have slept awake, and you
    Sleep, who last year were well awake.
Though love do all that love can do,
    My heart will never ache or break
      For your heart's sake.

The great sea, faultless as a flower,
    Throbs, trembling under beam and breeze,
And laughs with love of the amorous hour.
    I found you fairer once, Félise,
      Than flowers or seas.   30

We played at bondsman and at queen;
    But as the days change men change too;
I find the grey sea's notes of green,
    The green sea's fervent flakes of blue,
      More fair than you.

Your beauty is not over fair
    Now in mine eyes, who am grown up wise.
The smell of flowers in all your hair
    Allures not now; no sigh replies
      If your heart sighs.   40

But you sigh seldom, you sleep sound,
    You find love's new name good enough.
Less sweet I find it than I found
    The sweetest name that ever love
      Grew weary of.

My snake with bright bland eyes, my snake
    Grown tame and glad to be caressed,
With lips athirst for mine to slake
    Their tender fever! who had guessed
      You loved me best?   50

I had died for this last year, to know
    You loved me. Who shall turn on fate?
I care not if love come or go
    Now, though your love seek mine for mate.
      It is too late.

The dust of many strange desires
    Lies deep between us; in our eyes
Dead smoke of perishable fires
    Flickers, a fume in air and skies,
      A steam of sighs.   60

You loved me and you loved me not;
    A little, much, and overmuch.
Will you forget as I forgot?
    Let all dead things lie dead; none such
      Are soft to touch.

I love you and I do not love,
    Too much, a little, not at all;
Too much, and never yet enough.
    Birds quick to fledge and fly at call
    Are quick to fall.   70

And these love longer now than men,
    And larger loves than ours are these.
No diver brings up love again
    Dropped once, my beautiful Félise,
    In such cold seas.

Gone deeper than all plummets sound,
    Where in the dim green dayless day
The life of such dead things lies bound
    As the sea feeds on, wreck and stray
    And castaway.   80

Can I forget? yea, that can I,
    And that can all men; so will you,
Alive, or later, when you die.
    Ah, but the love you plead was true?
    Was mine not too?

I loved you for that name of yours
    Long ere we met, and long enough.
Now that one thing of all endures—
    The sweetest name that ever love
    Waxed weary of.   90

Like colours in the sea, like flowers,
    Like a cat's splendid circled eyes
That wax and wane with love for hours,
    Green as green flame, blue-grey like skies,
    And soft like sighs—

And all these only like your name,
    And your name full of all of these.
I say it, and it sounds the same—
    Save that I say it now at ease,
    Your name, Félise.   100

I said 'she must be swift and white,
   And subtly warm, and half perverse,
And sweet like sharp soft fruit to bite,
   And like a snake's love lithe and fierce.'
   Men have guessed worse.

What was the song I made of you
   Here where the grass forgets our feet
As afternoon forgets the dew?
   Ah that such sweet things should be fleet,
   Such fleet things sweet!   110

As afternoon forgets the dew,
   As time in time forgets all men,
As our old place forgets us two,
   Who might have turned to one thing then,
   But not again.

      O lips that mine have grown into
         Like April's kissing May,
      O fervent eyelids letting through
      Those eyes the greenest of things blue,
         The bluest of things grey,   120

      If you were I and I were you,
         How could I love you, say?
      How could the roseleaf love the rue,
      The day love nightfall and her dew,
         Though night may love the day?

You loved it may be more than I;
   We know not; love is hard to seize.
And all things are not good to try;
   And lifelong loves the worst of these
   For us, Félise.   130

Ah, take the season and have done,
   Love well the hour and let it go: .
Two souls may sleep and wake up one,
   Or dream they wake and find it so,
   And then—you know.

Kiss me once hard as though a flame
   Lay on my lips and made them fire;
The same lips now, and not the same;
   What breath shall fill and re-inspire
   A dead desire?   140

The old song sounds hollower in mine ear
   Than thin keen sounds of dead men's speech—
A noise one hears and would not hear;
   Too strong to die, too weak to reach
   From wave to beach.

We stand on either side the sea,
   Stretch hands, blow kisses, laugh and lean
I toward you, you toward me;
   But what hears either save the keen
   Grey sea between?   150

A year divides us, love from love,
   Though you love now, though I loved then.
The gulf is strait, but deep enough;
   Who shall recross, who among men
   Shall cross again?

Love was a jest last year, you said,
   And what lives surely, surely dies.
Even so; but now that love is dead,
   Shall love rekindle from wet eyes,
   From subtle sighs?   160

For many loves are good to see;
   Mutable loves, and loves perverse;
But there is nothing, nor shall be,
   So sweet, so wicked, but my verse
   Can dream of worse.

For we that sing and you that love
   Know that which man may, only we.
The rest live under us; above,
   Live the great gods in heaven, and see
   What things shall be.   170

So this thing is and must be so;
   For man dies, and love also dies.
Though yet love's ghost moves to and fro
   The sea-green mirrors of your eyes,
   And laughs, and lies.

Eyes coloured like a water-flower,
   And deeper than the green sea's glass;
Eyes that remember one sweet hour—
   In vain we swore it should not pass;
   In vain, alas!   180

Ah my Félise, if love or sin,
   If shame or fear could hold it fast,
Should we not hold it? Love wears thin,
   And they laugh well who laugh the last.
   Is it not past?

The gods, the gods are stronger; time
   Falls down before them, all men's knees
Bow, all men's prayers and sorrows climb
   Like incense towards them; yea, for these
   Are gods, Félise.   190

Immortal are they, clothed with powers,
   Not to be comforted at all;
Lords over all the fruitless hours;
   Too great to appease, too high to appal,
   Too far to call.

For none shall move the most high gods,
   Who are most sad, being cruel; none
Shall break or take away the rods
   Wherewith they scourge us, not as one
   That smites a son.   200

By many a name of many a creed
   We have called upon them, since the sands
Fell through time's hour-glass first, a seed
   Of life; and out of many lands
   Have we stretched hands.

When have they heard us? who hath known
   Their faces, climbed unto their feet,
Felt them and found them? Laugh or groan,
   Doth heaven remurmur and repeat
   Sad sounds or sweet? 210

Do the stars answer? in the night
   Have ye found comfort? or by day
Have ye seen gods? What hope, what light,
   Falls from the farthest starriest way
   On you that pray?

Are the skies wet because we weep,
   Or fair because of any mirth?
Cry out; they are gods; perchance they sleep;
   Cry; thou shalt know what prayers are worth,
   Thou dust and earth. 220

O earth, thou art fair; O dust, thou art great;
   O laughing lips and lips that mourn,
Pray, till ye feel the exceeding weight
   Of God's intolerable scorn,
   Not to be borne.

Behold, there is no grief like this;
   The barren blossom of thy prayer,
Thou shalt find out how sweet it is.
   O fools and blind, what seek ye there,
   High up in the air? 230

Ye must have gods, the friends of men,
   Merciful gods, compassionate,
And these shall answer you again.
   Will ye beat always at the gate,
   Ye fools of fate?

Ye fools and blind; for this is sure,
   That all ye shall not live, but die.
Lo, what thing have ye found endure?
   Or what thing have ye found on high
   Past the blind sky? 240

The ghosts of words and dusty dreams,
    Old memories, faiths infirm and dead.
Ye fools; for which among you deems
    His prayer can alter green to red
    Or stones to bread?

Why should ye bear with hopes and fears
    Till all these things be drawn in one,
The sound of iron-footed years,
    And all the oppression that is done
    Under the sun?   250

Ye might end surely, surely pass
    Out of the multitude of things,
Under the dust, beneath the grass,
    Deep in dim death, where no thought stings,
    No record clings.

No memory more of love or hate,
    No trouble, nothing that aspires,
No sleepless labour thwarting fate,
    And thwarted; where no travail tires,
    Where no faith fires.   260

All passes, nought that has been is,
    Things good and evil have one end.
Can anything be otherwise
    Though all men swear all things would mend
    With God to friend?

Can ye beat off one wave with prayer
    Can ye move mountains? bid the flower
Take flight and turn to a bird in the air?
    Can ye hold fast for shine or shower
    One wingless hour?   270

Ah sweet, and we too, can we bring
    One sigh back, bid one smile revive?
Can God restore one ruined thing,
    Or he who slays our souls alive
    Make dead things thrive?

Two gifts perforce he has given us yet,
 Though sad things stay and glad things fly;
Two gifts he has given us, to forget
 All glad and sad things that go by,
 And then to die.   280

We know not whether death be good,
 But life at least it will not be:
Men will stand saddening as we stood,
 Watch the same fields and skies as we
 And the same sea.

Let this be said between us here,
 One love grows green when one turns grey;
This year knows nothing of last year;
 To-morrow has no more to say
 To yesterday.   290

Live and let live, as I will do,
 Love and let love, and so will I.
But, sweet, for me no more with you:
 Not while I live, not though I die.
 Goodnight, goodbye.

HENDECASYLLABICS

In the month of the long decline of roses
I, beholding the summer dead before me,
Set my face to the sea and journeyed silent,
Gazing eagerly where above the sea-mark
Flame as fierce as the fervid eyes of lions
Half divided the eyelids of the sunset;
Till I heard as it were a noise of waters
Moving tremulous under feet of angels
Multitudinous, out of all the heavens;
Knew the fluttering wind, the fluttered foliage,   10
Shaken fitfully, full of sound and shadow;
And saw, trodden upon by noiseless angels,
Long mysterious reaches fed with moonlight,

Sweet sad straits in a soft subsiding channel,
Blown about by the lips of winds I knew not,
Winds not born in the north nor any quarter,
Winds not warm with the south nor any sunshine;
Heard between them a voice of exultation,
'Lo, the summer is dead, the sun is faded,
Even like as a leaf the year is withered, 20
All the fruits of the day from all her branches
Gathered, neither is any left to gather.
All the flowers are dead, the tender blossoms,
All are taken away; the season wasted,
Like an ember among the fallen ashes.
Now with light of the winter days, with moonlight,
Light of snow, and the bitter light of hoarfrost,
We bring flowers that fade not after autumn,
Pale white chaplets and crowns of latter seasons,
Fair false leaves (but the summer leaves were falser), 30
Woven under the eyes of stars and planets
When low light was upon the windy reaches
Where the flower of foam was blown, a lily
Dropt among the sonorous fruitless furrows
And green fields of the sea that make no pasture:
Since the winter begins, the weeping winter,
All whose flowers are tears, and round his temples
Iron blossom of frost is bound for ever.'

SAPPHICS

All the night sleep came not upon my eyelids,
Shed not dew, nor shook nor unclosed a feather,
Yet with lips shut close and with eyes of iron
  Stood and beheld me.

Then to me so lying awake a vision
Came without sleep over the seas and touched me,
Softly touched mine eyelids and lips; and I too,
  Full of the vision,

Saw the white implacable Aphrodite,
Saw the hair unbound and the feet unsandalled   10
Shine as fire of sunset on western waters;
   Saw the reluctant

Feet, the straining plumes of the doves that drew her,
Looking always, looking with necks reverted,
Back to Lesbos, back to the hills whereunder
   Shone Mitylene;

Heard the flying feet of the Loves behind her
Make a sudden thunder upon the waters,
As the thunder flung from the strong unclosing
   Wings of a great wind.   20

So the goddess fled from her place, with awful
Sound of feet and thunder of wings around her;
While behind a clamour of singing women
   Severed the twilight.

Ah the singing, ah the delight, the passion!
All the Loves wept, listening; sick with anguish,
Stood the crowned nine Muses about Apollo;
   Fear was upon them,

While the tenth sang wonderful things they knew not.
Ah the tenth, the Lesbian! the nine were silent,   30
None endured the sound of her song for weeping;
   Laurel by laurel,

Faded all their crowns; but about her forehead,
Round her woven tresses and ashen temples
White as dead snow, paler than grass in summer,
   Ravaged with kisses,

Shone a light of fire as a crown for ever.
Yea, almost the implacable Aphrodite
Paused, and almost wept; such a song was that song.
   Yea, by her name too   40

Called her, saying, 'Turn to me, O my Sappho;'
Yet she turned her face from the Loves, she saw not
Tears for laughter darken immortal eyelids,
    Heard not about her

Fearful fitful wings of the doves departing,
Saw not how the bosom of Aphrodite
Shook with weeping, saw not her shaken raiment,
    Saw not her hands wrung;

Saw the Lesbians kissing across their smitten
Lutes with lips more sweet than the sound of lute-strings,   50
Mouth to mouth and hand upon hand, her chosen,
    Fairer than all men;

Only saw the beautiful lips and fingers,
Full of songs and kisses and little whispers,
Full of music; only beheld among them
    Soar, as a bird soars

Newly fledged, her visible song, a marvel,
Made of perfect sound and exceeding passion,
Sweetly shapen, terrible, full of thunders,
    Clothed with the wind's wings.   60

Then rejoiced she, laughing with love, and scattered
Roses, awful roses of holy blossom;
Then the Loves thronged sadly with hidden faces
    Round Aphrodite,

Then the Muses, stricken at heart, were silent;
Yea, the gods waxed pale; such a song was that song.
All reluctant, all with a fresh repulsion,
    Fled from before her.

All withdrew long since, and the land was barren,
Full of fruitless women and music only.   70
Now perchance, when winds are assuaged at sunset,
    Lulled at the dewfall,

By the grey sea-side, unassuaged, unheard of,
Unbeloved, unseen in the ebb of twilight,
Ghosts of outcast women return lamenting,
    Purged not in Lethe,

Clothed about with flame and with tears, and singing
Songs that move the heart of the shaken heaven,
Songs that break the heart of the earth with pity,
    Hearing, to hear them.   80

DEDICATION

1865

The sea gives her shells to the shingle,
    The earth gives her streams to the sea;
They are many, but my gift is single,
    My verses, the firstfruits of me.
Let the wind take the green and the grey leaf,
    Cast forth without fruit upon air;
Take rose-leaf and vine-leaf and bay-leaf
    Blown loose from the hair.

The night shakes them round me in legions,
    Dawn drives them before her like dreams;   10
Time sheds them like snows on strange regions,
    Swept shoreward on infinite streams;
Leaves pallid and sombre and ruddy,
    Dead fruits of the fugitive years;
Some stained as with wine and made bloody,
    And some as with tears.

Some scattered in seven years' traces,
    As they fell from the boy that was then;
Long left among idle green places,
Or gathered but now among men;   20
On seas full of wonder and peril,
    Blown white round the capes of the north;
Or in islands where myrtles are sterile
    And loves bring not forth.

O daughters of dreams and of stories
    That life is not wearied of yet,
Faustine, Fragoletta, Dolores,
    Félise and Yolande and Juliette,
Shall I find you not still, shall I miss you,
    When sleep, that is true or that seems,   30
Comes back to me hopeless to kiss you,
    O daughters of dreams?

They are past as a slumber that passes,
    As the dew of a dawn of old time;
More frail than the shadows on glasses,
    More fleet than a wave or a rhyme.
As the waves after ebb drawing seaward,
    When their hollows are full of the night,
So the birds that flew singing to me-ward
    Recede out of sight.   40

The songs of dead seasons, that wander
    On wings of articulate words;
Lost leaves that the shore-wind may squander,
    Light flocks of untameable birds;
Some sang to me dreaming in class-time
    And truant in hand as in tongue;
For the youngest were born of boy's pastime,
    The eldest are young.

Is there shelter while life in them lingers,
    Is there hearing for songs that recede,   50
Tunes touched from a harp with man's fingers
    Or blown with boy's mouth in a reed?
Is there place in the land of your labour,
    Is there room in your world of delight,
Where change has not sorrow for neighbour
    And day has not night?

In their wings though the sea-wind yet quivers,
    Will you spare not a space for them there
Made green with the running of rivers
    And gracious with temperate air;   60

In the fields and the turreted cities,
    That cover from sunshine and rain
Fair passions and bountiful pities
    And loves without stain?

In a land of clear colours and stories,
    In a region of shadowless hours,
Where earth has a garment of glories
    And a murmur of musical flowers;
In woods where the spring half uncovers
    The flush of her amorous face,   70
By the waters that listen for lovers,
    For these is there place?

For the song-birds of sorrow, that muffle
    Their music as clouds do their fire:
For the storm-birds of passion, that ruffle
    Wild wings in a wind of desire;
In the stream of the storm as it settles
    Blown seaward, borne far from the sun,
Shaken loose on the darkness like petals
    Dropt one after one?   80

Though the world of your hands be more gracious
    And lovelier in lordship of things
Clothed round by sweet art with the spacious
    Warm heaven of her imminent wings,
Let them enter, unfledged and nigh fainting,
    For the love of old loves and lost times;
And receive in your palace of painting
    This revel of rhymes.

Though the seasons of man full of losses
    Make empty the years full of youth,   90
If but one thing be constant in crosses,
    Change lays not her hand upon truth;
Hopes die, and their tombs are for token
    That the grief as the joy of them ends
Ere time that breaks all men has broken
    The faith between friends.

Though the many lights dwindle to one light,
   There is help if the heaven has one;
Though the skies be discrowned of the sunlight
   And the earth dispossessed of the sun.   100
They have moonlight and sleep for repayment,
   When, refreshed as a bride and set free,
With stars and sea-winds in her raiment,
   Night sinks on the sea.

from SONGS BEFORE SUNRISE

THE EVE OF REVOLUTION

1

The trumpets of the four winds of the world
   From the ends of the earth blow battle; the night heaves,
With breasts palpitating and wings refurled,
   With passion of couched limbs, as one who grieves
Sleeping, and in her sleep she sees uncurled
   Dreams serpent-shaped, such as sickness weaves,
Down the wild wind of vision caught and whirled,
     Dead leaves of sleep, thicker than autumn leaves,
       Shadows of storm-shaped things,
       Flights of dim tribes of kings,   10
     The reaping men that reap men for their sheaves,
       And, without grain to yield,
       Their scythe-swept harvest-field
     Thronged thick with men pursuing and fugitives,
       Dead foliage of the tree of sleep,
Leaves blood-coloured and golden, blown from deep to deep.

2

I hear the midnight on the mountains cry
   With many tongues of thunders, and I hear
Sound and resound the hollow shield of sky
   With trumpet-throated winds that charge and cheer,   20
And through the roar of the hours that fighting fly,
   Through flight and fight and all the fluctuant fear,
A sound sublimer than the heavens are high,

A voice more instant than the winds are clear,
    Say to my spirit, 'Take
    Thy trumpet too, and make
A rallying music in the void night's ear,
    Till the storm lose its track,
    And all the night go back;
Till, as through sleep false life knows true life near,   30
    Thou know the morning through the night,
And through the thunder silence, and through darkness light.'

    3
I set the trumpet to my lips and blow.
    The height of night is shaken, the skies break,
The winds and stars and waters come and go
    By fits of breath and light and sound, that wake
As out of sleep, and perish as the show
    Built up of sleep, when all her strengths forsake
The sense-compelling spirit; the depths glow,
    The heights flash, and the roots and summits shake   40
    Of earth in all her mountains,
    And the inner foamless fountains
And wellsprings of her fast-bound forces quake;
    Yea, the whole air of life
    Is set on fire of strife,
Till change unmake things made and love remake;
    Reason and love, whose names are one,
Seeing reason is the sunlight shed from love the sun.

    4
The night is broken eastward ; is it day,
    Or but the watchfires trembling here and there,   50
Like hopes on memory's devastated way,
    In moonless wastes of planet-stricken air?
O many-childed mother great and grey,
    O multitudinous bosom, and breasts that bare
Our fathers' generations, whereat lay
    The weanling peoples and the tribes that were,
    Whose new-born mouths long dead
    Those ninefold nipples fed,
    Dim face with deathless eyes and withered hair,

Fostress of obscure lands,   60
    Whose multiplying hands
  Wove the world's web with divers races fair
    And cast it waif-wise on the stream,
The waters of the centuries, where thou sat'st to dream;

    5

O many-minded mother and visionary,
    Asia, that sawest their westering waters sweep
With all the ships and spoils of time to carry
    And all the fears and hopes of life to keep,
Thy vesture wrought of ages legendary
    Hides usward thine impenetrable sleep,   70
And thy veiled head, night's oldest tributary,
    We know not if it speak or smile or weep.
        But where for us began
        The first live light of man
    And first-born fire of deeds to burn and leap,
        The first war fair as peace
        To shine and lighten Greece,
    And the first freedom moved upon the deep,
        God's breath upon the face of time
Moving, a present spirit, seen of men sublime;   80

    6

There where our east looks always to thy west,
    Our mornings to thine evenings, Greece to thee,
These lights that catch the mountains crest by crest,
    Are they of stars or beacons that we see?
Taygetus takes here the winds abreast,
    And there the sun resumes Thermopylae;
The light is Athens where those remnants rest,
    And Salamis the sea-wall of that sea.
        The grass men tread upon
        Is very Marathon,   90
    The leaves are of that time-unstricken tree
        That storm nor sun can fret
        Nor wind, since she that set
    Made it her sign to men whose shield was she;
        Here, as dead time his deathless things,
Eurotas and Cephisus keep their sleepless springs.

7

O hills of Crete, are these things dead? O waves,
    O many-mouthèd streams, are these springs dry?
Earth, dost thou feed and hide now none but slaves?
    Heaven, hast thou heard of men that would not die?   100
Is the land thick with only such men's graves
    As were ashamed to look upon the sky?
Ye dead, whose name outfaces and outbraves
    Death is the seed of such as you gone by?
      Sea, have thy ports not heard
      Some Marathonian word
    Rise up to landward and to Godward fly?
      No thunder, that the skies
      Sent not upon us, rise
    With fire and earthquake and a cleaving cry?   110
      Nay, light is here, and shall be light,
Though all the face of the hour be overborne with night.

8

I set the trumpet to my lips and blow.
    The night is broken northward; the pale plains
And footless fields of sun-forgotten snow
    Feel through their creviced lips and iron veins
Such quick breath labour and such clean blood flow
    As summer-stricken spring feels in her pains
When dying May bears June, too young to know
    The fruit that waxes from the flower that wanes;   120
      Strange tyrannies and vast,
      Tribes frost-bound to their past,
    Lands that are loud all through their length with chains,
      Wastes where the wind's wings break,
      Displumed by daylong ache
And anguish of blind snows and rack-blown rains,
    And ice that seals the White Sea's lips,
Whose monstrous weights crush flat the sides of shrieking ships;

9

Horrible sights and sounds of the unreached pole,
    And shrill fierce climes of inconsolable air,   130
Shining below the beamless aureole
    That hangs about the north-wind's hurtling hair,

A comet-lighted lamp, sublime and sole
   Dawn of the dayless heaven where suns despair;
Earth, skies, and waters, smitten into soul,
   Feel the hard veil that iron centuries wear
      Rent as with hands in sunder,
      Such hands as make the thunder
   And clothe with form all substance and strip bare;
     Shapes, shadows, sounds and lights   140
      Of their dead days and nights
   Take soul of life too keen for death to bear;
    Life, conscience, forethought, will, desire,
Flood men's inanimate eyes and dry-drawn hearts with fire.

10

Light, light and light! to break and melt in sunder
   All clouds and chains that in one bondage bind
Eyes, hands, and spirits, forged by fear and wonder
   And sleek fierce fraud with hidden knife behind;
There goes no fire from heaven before their thunder,
   Nor are the links not malleable that wind   150
Round the snared limbs and souls that ache thereunder;
   The hands are mighty, were the head not blind.
      Priest is the staff of king,
      And chains and clouds one thing,
   And fettered flesh with devastated mind.
      Open thy soul to see,
      Slave, and thy feet are free;
   Thy bonds and thy beliefs are one in kind,
    And of thy fears thine irons wrought
Hang weights upon thee fashioned out of thine own thought.   160

11

O soul, O God, O glory of liberty,
   To night and day their lightning and their light!
With heat of heart thou kindlest the quick sea,
   And the dead earth takes spirit from thy sight;
The natural body of things is warm with thee,
   And the world's weakness parcel of thy might;
Thou seest us feeble and forceless, fit to be
   Slaves of the years that drive us left and right,

      Drowned under hours like waves
       Wherethrough we row like slaves;   170
   But if thy finger touch us, these take flight.
      If but one sovereign word
       Of thy live lips be heard,
   What man shall stop us, and what God shall smite?
     Do thou but look in our dead eyes,
They are stars that light each other till thy sundawn rise.

    12

Thou art the eye of this blind body of man,
   The tongue of this dumb people; shalt thou not   ·
See, shalt thou speak not for them? Time is wan
   And hope is weak with waiting, and swift thought   180
Hath lost the wings at heel wherewith he ran,
   And on the red pit's edge sits down distraught
To talk with death of days republican
   And dreams and fights long since dreamt out and fought;
     Of the last hope that drew
      To that red edge anew
The firewhite faith of Poland without spot;
     Of the blind Russian might,
      And fire that is not light;
Of the green Rhineland where thy spirit wrought;   190
    But though time, hope, and memory tire,
Canst thou wax dark as they do, thou whose light is fire?

    13

I set the trumpet to my lips and blow.
   The night is broken westward; the wide sea
That makes immortal motion to and fro
   From world's end unto world's end, and shall be
When nought now grafted of men's hands shall grow
   And as the weed in last year's waves are we
Or spray the sea-wind shook a year ago
   From its sharp tresses down the storm to lee,   200
     The moving god that hides
      Time in its timeless tides
   Wherein time dead seems live eternity,
     That breaks and makes again

Much mightier things than men,
Doth it not hear change coming, or not see?
Are the deeps deaf and dead and blind,
To catch no light or sound from landward of mankind?

14

O thou, clothed round with raiment of white waves,
Thy brave brows lightening through the grey wet air,   210
Thou, lulled with sea-sounds of a thousand caves,
And lit with sea-shine to thine inland lair,
Whose freedom clothed the naked souls of slaves
And stripped the muffled souls of tyrants bare,
O, by the centuries of thy glorious graves,
By the live light of the earth that was thy care,
Live, thou must not be dead,
Live; let thine armèd head
Lift itself up to sunward and the fair
Daylight of time and man,   220
Thine head republican,
With the same splendour on thine helmless hair
That in his eyes kept up a light
Who on thy glory gazed away their sacred sight;

15

Who loved and looked their sense to death on thee;
Who taught thy lips imperishable things,
And in thine ears outsang thy singing sea;
Who made thy foot firm on the necks of kings
And thy soul somewhile steadfast—woe are we
It was but for a while, and all the strings   230
Were broken of thy spirit; yet had he
Set to such tunes and clothed it with such wings
It seemed for his sole sake
Impossible to break,
And woundless of the worm that waits and stings,
The golden-headed worm
Made headless for a term,
The king-snake whose life kindles with the spring's,
To breathe his soul upon her bloom,
And while she marks not turn her temple to her tomb.   240

16

By those eyes blinded and that heavenly head
   And the secluded soul adorable,
O Milton's land, what ails thee to be dead?
   Thine ears are yet sonorous with his shell
That all the songs of all thy sea-line fed
   With motive sound of spring-tides at mid swell,
And through thine heart his thought as blood is shed,
     Requickening thee with wisdom to do well;
       Such sons were of thy womb,
       England, for love of whom   250
     Thy name is not yet writ with theirs that fell,
       But, till thou quite forget
       What were thy children, yet
     On the pale lips of hope is as a spell;
      And Shelley's heart and Landor's mind
Lit thee with latter watch-fires; why wilt thou be blind?

17

Though all were else indifferent, all that live
   Spiritless shapes of nations; though time wait
In vain on hope till these have help to give,
     And faith and love crawl famished from the gate;   260
Canst thou sit shamed and self-contemplative
   With soulless eyes on thy secluded fate?
Though time forgive them, thee shall he forgive,
     Whose choice was in thine hand to be so great?
       Who cast out of thy mind
       The passion of man's kind,
     And made thee and thine old name separate?
       Now when time looks to see
       New names and old and thee
     Build up our one Republic state by state,   270
      England with France, and France with Spain,
And Spain with sovereign Italy strike hands and reign.

18

O known and unknown fountain-heads that fill
   Our dear life-springs of England! O bright race
Of streams and waters that bear witness still

To the earth her sons were made of! O fair face
Of England, watched of eyes death cannot kill,
How should the soul that lit you for a space
Fall through sick weakness of a broken will
To the dead cold damnation of disgrace?   280
Such wind of memory stirs
On all green hills of hers,
Such breath of record from so high a place,
From years whose tongues of flame
Prophesied in her name
Her feet should keep truth's bright and burning trace,
We needs must have her heart with us,
Whose hearts are one with man's; she must be dead or thus.

19

Who is against us? who is on our side?
Whose heart of all men's hearts is one with man's?   290
Where art thou that wast prophetess and bride,
When truth and thou trod under time and chance?
What latter light of what new hope shall guide
Out of the snares of hell thy feet, O France?
What heel shall bruise these heads that hiss and glide,
What wind blow out these fen-born fires that dance
Before thee to thy death?
No light, no life, no breath,
From thy dead eyes and lips shall take the trance,
Till on that deadliest crime   300
Reddening the feet of time
Who treads through blood and passes, time shall glance
Pardon, and Italy forgive,
And Rome arise up whom thou slewest, and bid thee live.

20

I set the trumpet to my lips and blow.
The night is broken southward; the springs run,
The daysprings and the watersprings that flow
Forth with one will from where their source was one,
Out of the might of morning: high and low,
The hungering hills feed full upon the sun,   310
The thirsting valleys drink of him and glow

As a heart burns with some divine thing done,
    Or as blood burns again
    In the bruised heart of Spain,
A rose renewed with red new life begun,
    Dragged down with thorns and briers,
    That puts forth buds like fires
Till the whole tree take flower in unison,
    And prince that clogs and priest that slings
Be cast as weeds upon the dunghill of dead things.   320

21

Ah heaven, bow down, be nearer! This is she,
    Italia, the world's wonder, the world's care,
Free in her heart ere quite her hands be free,
    And lovelier than her loveliest robe of air.
The earth hath voice, and speech is in the sea,
    Sounds of great joy, too beautiful to bear;
All things are glad because of her, but we
    Most glad, who loved her when the worst days were.
        O sweetest, fairest, first,
        O flower, when times were worst,   330
    Thou hadst no stripe wherein we had no share.
        Have not our hearts held close,
        Kept fast the whole world's rose?
Have we not worn thee at heart whom none would wear?
    First love and last love, light of lands,
Shall we not touch thee full-blown with our lips and hands?

22

O too much loved, what shall we say of thee?
    What shall we make of our heart's burning fire,
The passion in our lives that fain would be
    Made each a brand to pile into the pyre   340
That shall burn up thy foemen, and set free
    The flame whence thy sun-shadowing wings aspire?
Love of our life, what more than men are we,
    That this our breath for thy sake should expire,
        For whom to joyous death
        Glad gods might yield their breath,
    Great gods drop down from heaven to serve for hire?

We are but men, are we,
   And thou art Italy;
What shall we do for thee with our desire?   350
  What gift shall we deserve to give?
How shall we die to do thee service, or how live?

23

The very thought in us how much we love thee
  Makes the throat sob with love and blinds the eyes.
How should love bear thee, to behold above thee
  His own light burning from reverberate skies?
They give thee light, but the light given them of thee
  Makes faint the wheeling fires that fall and rise.
What love, what life, what death of man's should move thee,
  What face that lingers or what foot that flies?   360
    It is not heaven that lights
    Thee with such days and nights,
  But thou that heaven is lit from in such wise.
    O thou her dearest birth,
    Turn thee to lighten earth,
  Earth too that bore thee and yearns to thee and cries;
    Stand up, shine, lighten, become flame,
Till as the sun's name through all nations be thy name.

24

I take the trumpet from my lips and sing.
  O life immeasurable and imminent love,   370
And fear like winter leading hope like spring,
  Whose flower-bright brows the day-star sits above,
Whose hand unweariable and untiring wing
  Strike music from a world that wailed and strove,
Each bright soul born and every glorious thing,
  From very freedom to man's joy thereof,
    O time, O change and death,
    Whose now not hateful breath
  But gives the music swifter feet to move
    Through sharp remeasuring tones   380
    Of refluent antiphones
  More tender-tuned than heart or throat or dove,
    Soul into soul, song into song,
Life changing into life, by laws that work not wrong;

25

O natural force in spirit and sense, that art
   One thing in all things, fruit of thine own fruit,
O thought illimitable and infinite heart
   Whose blood is life in limbs indissolute
That still keeps hurtless thine invisible part
   And inextirpable thy viewless root   390
Whence all sweet shafts of green and each thy dart
   Of sharpening leaf and bud resundering shoot;
      Hills that the day-star hails,
      Heights that the first beam scales,
   And heights that souls outshining suns salute,
      Valleys for each mouth born
      Free now of plenteous corn,
  Waters and woodlands musical or mute;
    Free winds that brighten brows as free,
And thunder and laughter and lightning of the sovereign sea;   400

26

Rivers and springs, and storms that seek your prey;
   With strong wings ravening through the skies by night;
Spirits and stars that hold one choral way;
   O light of heaven, and thou the heavenlier light
Aflame above the souls of men that sway
   All generations of all years with might;
O sunrise of the repossessing day,
   And sunrise of all-renovating right;
      And thou, whose trackless foot
      Mocks hope's or fear's pursuit,   410
  Swift Revolution, changing depth with height;
      And thou, whose mouth makes one
      All songs that seek the sun,
  Serene Republic of a world made white;
    Thou, Freedom, whence the soul's springs ran;
Praise earth for man's sake living, and for earth's sake man.

27

Make yourselves wings, O tarrying feet of fate,
   And hidden hour that hast our hope to bear,
A child-god, through the morning-coloured gate

That lets love in upon the golden air,   420
Dead on whose threshold lies heart-broken hate,
  Dead discord, dead injustice, dead despair;
O love long looked for, wherefore wilt thou wait,
    And shew not yet the dawn on thy bright hair.
      Not yet thine hand released
      Refreshing the faint east,
  Thine hand reconquering heaven, to seat man there?
      Come forth, be born and live,
      Thou that hast help to give
And light to make man's day of manhood fair: 430
  With flight outflying the spherèd sun,
Hasten thine hour and halt not, till thy work be done.

HERTHA

      I am that which began;
        Out of me the years roll;
      Out of me God and man;
        I am equal and whole;
God changes, and man, and the form of them bodily; I am the soul.

      Before ever land was,
        Before ever the sea,
      Or soft hair of the grass,
        Or fair limbs of the tree,
Or the flesh-coloured fruit of my branches, I was, and thy soul was
    in me.   10

      First life on my sources
        First drifted and swam;
      Out of me are the forces
        That save it or damn;
Out of me man and woman, and wild-beast and bird; before God was,
    I am.

      Beside or above me
        Nought is there to go;
      Love or unlove me,

Unknow me or know,
I am that which unloves me and loves; I am stricken, and I am
    the blow.   20

    I the mark that is missed
        And the arrows that miss,
    I the mouth that is kissed
        And the breath in the kiss,
The search, and the sought, and the seeker, the soul and the body that is.

    I am that thing which blesses
        My spirit elate;
    That which caresses
        With hands uncreate
My limbs unbegotten that measure the length of the measure of fate.   30

    But what thing dost thou now,
        Looking Godward, to cry
    'I am I, thou art thou,
        I am low, thou are high'?
I am thou, whom thou seekest to find him; find thou but thyself, thou
    art I.

    I the grain and the furrow,
        The plough-cloven clod
    And the ploughshare drawn thorough,
        The germ and the sod,
The deed and the doer, the seed and the sower, the dust which
    is God.   40

    Hast thou known how I fashioned thee,
        Child, underground?
    Fire that impassioned thee,
        Iron that bound,
Dim changes of water, what thing of all these hast thou known of or
    found?

    Canst thou say in thine heart
        Thou hast seen with thine eyes
    With what cunning of art

Thou wast wrought in what wise,
By what force of what stuff thou wast shapen, and shown on my breast
    to the skies?   50

Who hath given, who hath sold it thee,
    Knowledge of me?
Hath the wilderness told it thee?
    Hast thou learnt of the sea?
Hast thou communed in spirit with night? have the winds taken counsel
    with thee?

Have I set such a star
    To show light on thy brow
That thou sawest from afar
    What I show to thee now?
Have ye spoken as brethren together, the sun and the mountains
    and thou?   60

What is here, dost thou know it?
    What was, hast thou known?
Prophet nor poet
    Nor tripod nor throne
Nor spirit nor flesh can make answer, but only thy mother alone.

Mother, not maker,
    Born, and not made;
Though her children forsake her,
    Allured or afraid,
Praying prayers to the God of their fashion, she stirs not for all that
    have prayed.   70

A creed is a rod,
    And a crown is of night;
But this thing is God,
    To be man with thy might,
To grow straight in the strength of thy spirit, and live out thy life as
    the light.

I am in thee to save thee
    As my soul in thee saith;

Give thou as I gave thee,
Thy life-blood and breath,
Green leaves of thy labour, white flowers of thy thought, and red fruit
of thy death.   80

Be the ways of thy giving
As mine were to thee;
The free life of thy living,
Be the gift of it free;
Not as servant to lord, nor as master to slave, shalt thou give thee to me.

O children of banishment,
Souls overcast,
Were the lights ye see vanish meant
Alway to last,
Ye would know not the sun overshining the shadows and stars
overpast.   90

I that saw where ye trod
The dim paths of the night
Set the shadow called God
In your skies to give light;
But the morning of manhood is risen, and the shadowless soul is in sight.

The tree many-rooted
That swells to the sky
With frondage red-fruited,
The life-tree am I;
In the buds of your lives is the sap of my leaves: ye shall live and not
die.   100

But the Gods of your fashion
That take and that give,
In their pity and passion
That scourge and forgive,
They are worms that are bred in the bark that falls off; they shall die
and not live.

My own blood is what stanches
The wounds in my bark;

Stars caught in my branches
Make day of the dark,
And are worshipped as suns till the sunrise shall tread out their fires
as a spark.   110

Where dead ages hide under
The live roots of the tree,
In my darkness the thunder
Makes utterance of me;
In the clash of my boughs with each other ye hear the waves sound
of the sea.

That noise is of Time,
As his feathers are spread
And his feet set to climb
Through the boughs overhead,
And my foliage rings round him and rustles, and branches are bent
with his tread.   120

The storm-winds of ages
Blow through me and cease,
The war-wind that rages,
The spring-wind of peace,
Ere the breath of them roughen my tresses, ere one of my blossoms
increase.

All sounds of all changes,
All shadows and lights
On the world's mountain-ranges
And stream-riven heights,
Whose tongue is the wind's tongue and language of storm-clouds on
earth-shaking nights;   130

All forms of all faces,
All works of all hands
In unsearchable places
Of time-stricken lands,
All death and all life, and all reigns and all ruins, drop through me as
sands.

Though sore be my burden
   And more than ye know,
And my growth have no guerdon
   But only to grow,
Yet I fail not of growing for lightnings above me or deathworms
   below.   140

These too have their part in me,
   As I too in these;
Such fire is at heart in me,
   Such sap is this tree's,
Which hath in it all sounds and all secrets of infinite lands and of seas.

In the spring-coloured hours
   When my mind was as May's,
There brake forth of me flowers
   By centuries of days,
Strong blossoms with perfume of manhood, shot out from my spirit
   as rays.   150

And the sound of them springing
   And smell of their shoots
Were as warmth and sweet singing
   And strength to my roots;
And the lives of my children made perfect with freedom of soul were
   my fruits.

I bid you but be;
   I have need not of prayer;
I have need of you free
   As your mouths of mine air;
That my heart may be greater within me, beholding the fruits of me
   fair.   160

More fair than strange fruit is
   Of faiths ye espouse;
In me only the root is
   That blooms in your boughs;
Behold now your God that ye made you, to feed him with faith of
   your vows.

In the darkening and whitening
    Abysses adored,
With dayspring and lightning
    For lamp and for sword,
God thunders in heaven, and his angels are red with the wrath of
    the Lord.   170

O my sons, O too dutiful
    Toward Gods not of me,
Was not I enough beautiful?
    Was it hard to be free?
For behold, I am with you, am in you and of you; look forth now
    and see.

Lo, winged with world's wonders,
    With miracles shod,
With the fires of his thunders
    For raiment and rod,
God trembles in heaven, and his angels are white with the terror of
    God.   180

For his twilight is come on him,
    His anguish is here;
And his spirits gaze dumb on him,
    Grown grey from his fear;
And his hour taketh hold on him stricken, the last of his infinite year.

Thought made him and breaks him,
    Truth slays and forgives;
But to you, as time takes him,
    This new thing it gives,
Even love, the beloved Republic, that feeds upon freedom and lives. 190

For truth only is living,
    Truth only is whole,
And the love of his giving
    Man's polestar and pole;
Man, pulse of my centre, and fruit of my body, and seed of my soul.

One birth of my bosom;
    One beam of mine eye;
  One topmost blossom
    That scales the sky;
Man, equal and one with me, man that is made of me, man that is I.   200

GENESIS

In the outer world that was before this earth,
    That was before all shape or space was born,
Before the blind first hour of time had birth,
    Before night knew the moonlight or the morn;

Yea, before any world had any light,
    Or anything called God or man drew breath,
Slowly the strong sides of the heaving night
    Moved, and brought forth the strength of life and death.

And the sad shapeless horror increate
    That was all things and one thing, without fruit,   10
Limit, or law; where love was none, nor hate,
    Where no leaf came to blossom from no root;

The very darkness that time knew not of,
    Nor God laid hand on, nor was man found there,
Ceased, and was cloven in several shapes; above
    Light, and night under, and fire, earth, water, and air.

Sunbeams and starbeams, and all coloured things,
    All forms and all similitudes began;
And death, the shadow cast by life's wide wings,
    And God, the shade cast by the soul of man.   20

Then between shadow and substance, night and light,
    Then between birth and death, and deeds and days,
The illimitable embrace and the amorous fight
    That of itself begets, bears, rears, and slays,

The immortal war of mortal things, that is
    Labour and life and growth and good and ill,

The mild antiphonies that melt and kiss,
   The violent symphonies that meet and kill,

All nature of all things began to be.
   But chiefliest in the spirit (beast or man,   30
Planet of heaven or blossom of earth or sea)
   The divine contraries of life began.

For the great labour of growth, being many, is one;
   One thing the white death and the ruddy birth;
The invisible air and the all-beholden sun,
   And barren water and many-childed earth.

And these things are made manifest in men
   From the beginning forth unto this day:
Time writes and life records them, and again
   Death seals them lest the record pass away.   40

For if death were not, then should growth not be,
   Change, nor the life of good nor evil things;
Nor were there night at all nor light to see,
   Nor water of sweet nor water of bitter springs.

For in each man and each year that is born
   Are sown the twin seeds of the strong twin powers;
The white seed of the fruitful helpful morn,
   The black seed of the barren hurtful hours.

And he that of the black seed eateth fruit,
   To him the savour as honey shall be sweet;   50
And he in whom the white seed hath struck root,
   He shall have sorrow and trouble and tears for meat.

And him whose lips the sweet fruit hath made red
   In the end men loathe and make his name a rod;
And him whose mouth on the unsweet fruit hath fed
   In the end men follow and know for very God.

And of these twain, the black seed and the white,
   All things come forth, endured of men and done;

And still the day is great with child of night,
    And still the black night labours with the sun.   60

And each man and each year that lives on earth
    Turns hither or thither, and hence or thence is fed;
And as a man before was from his birth,
    So shall a man be after among the dead.

MATER DOLOROSA

Citoyen, lui dit Enjolras, ma mère, c'est la République.

                                            Les Misérables.

Who is this that sits by the way, by the wild wayside,
In a rent stained raiment, the robe of a cast-off bride,
In the dust, in the rainfall sitting, with soiled feet bare,
With the night for a garment upon her, with torn wet hair?
She is fairer of face than the daughters of men, and her eyes,
Worn through with her tears, are deep as the depth of skies.

This is she for whose sake being fallen, for whose abject sake,
Earth groans in the blackness of darkness, and men's hearts break.
This is she for whose love, having seen her, the men that were
Poured life out as water, and shed their souls upon air.   10
This is she for whose glory their years were counted as foam;
Whose face was a light upon Greece, was a fire upon Rome.

Is it now not surely a vain thing, a foolish and vain,
To sit down by her, mourn to her, serve her, partake in the pain?
She is grey with the dust of time on his manifold ways,
Where her faint feet stumble and falter through year-long days.
Shall she help us at all, O fools, give fruit or give fame,
Who herself is a name despised, a rejected name?

We have not served her for guerdon. If any do so,
That his mouth may be sweet with such honey, we care not to know.   20
We have drunk from a wine-unsweetened, a perilous cup,
A draught very bitter. The kings of the earth stood up,
And the rulers took counsel together to smite her and slay;
And the blood of her wounds is given us to drink today.

Can these bones live? or the leaves that are dead leaves bud?
Or the dead blood drawn from her veins be in your veins blood?
Will ye gather up water again that was drawn and shed?
In the blood is the life of the veins, and her veins are dead.
For the lives that are over are over, and past things past;
She had her day, and it is not; was first, and is last   30

Is it nothing unto you then, all ye that pass by,
If her breath be left in her lips, if she live now or die?
Behold now, O people, and say if she be not fair,
Whom your fathers followed to find her, with praise and prayer,
And rejoiced, having found her, though roof they had none nor bread;
But ye care not; what is it to you if her day be dead?

It was well with our fathers; their sound was in all men's lands;
There was fire in their hearts , and the hunger of fight in their hands.
Naked and strong they went forth in her strength like flame,
For her love's and her name's sake of old, her republican name.   40
But their children, by kings made quiet, by priests made wise,
Love better the heat of their hearths than the light of her eyes.

Are they children of these thy children indeed, who have sold,
O golden goddess, the light of thy face for gold?
Are they sons indeed of the sons of thy dayspring of hope,
Whose lives are in fief of an emperor, whose souls of a Pope?
Hide then thine head, O belovèd; thy time is done;
Thy kingdom is broken in heaven, and blind thy sun.

What sleep is upon you, to dream she indeed shall rise,
When the hopes are dead in her heart as the tears in her eyes?   50
If ye sing of her dead, will she stir? if ye weep for her, weep?
Come away now, leave her; what hath she to do but sleep?
But ye that mourn are alive, and have years to be;
And life is good, and the world is wiser than we.

Yea, wise is the world and mighty, with years to give,
And years to promise; but how long now shall it live?
And foolish and poor is faith, and her ways are bare,
Till she find the way of the sun, and the morning air.
In that hour shall this dead face shine as the face of the sun,
And the soul of man and her soul and the world's be one.   60

TIRESIAS

Part I

It is an hour before the hour of dawn.
    Set in mine hand my staff and leave me here
    Outside the hollow house that blind men fear,
More blind than I who live on life withdrawn
    And feel on eyes that see not but foresee
    The shadow of death which clothes Antigone.

Here lay her living body that here lies
    Dead, if man living know what thing is death,
    If life be all made up of blood and breath,
And no sense be save as of ears and eyes.   10
    But heart there is not, tongue there is not found,
       To think or sing what verge hath life or bound.

In the beginning when the powers that made
    The young child man a little loved him, seeing
    His joy of life and fair face of his being,
And bland and laughing with the man-child played,
    As friends they saw on our divine one day
    King Cadmus take to queen Harmonia.

The strength of soul that builds up as with hands
    Walls spiritual and towers and towns of thought   20
    Which only fate, not force, can bring to nought,
Took then to wife the light of all men's lands,
    War's child and love's, most sweet and wise and strong.
    Order of things and rule and guiding song.

It was long since: yea, even the sun that saw
    Remembers hardly what was, nor how long.
    And now the wise heart of the worldly song
Is perished, and the holy hand of law
    Can set no tune on time, nor help again
    The power of thought to build up life for men.   30

Yea, surely are they now transformed or dead,
    And sleep below this world, where no sun warms,

Or move about it now in formless forms
Incognizable, and all their lordship fled;
    And where they stood up singing crawl and hiss,
    With fangs that kill behind their lips that kiss.

Yet though her marriage-garment, seeming fair,
    Was dyed in sin and woven of jealousy
    To turn their seed to poison, time shall see
The gods reissue from them, and repair   40
    Their broken stamp of godhead, and again
    Thought and wise love sing words of law to men.

I, Tiresias the prophet, seeing in Thebes
    Much evil, and the misery of men's hands
    Who sow with fruitless wheat the stones and sands,
With fruitful thorns the fallows and warm glebes,
    Bade their hands hold lest worse hap came to pass;
    But which of you had heed of Tiresias?

I am as Time's self in mine own wearied mind,
    Whom the strong heavy-footed years have led   50
    From night to night and dead men unto dead,
And from the blind hope to the memory blind;
    For each man's life is woven, as Time's life is,
    Of blind young hopes and old blind memories.

I am a soul outside of death and birth.
    I see before me and afterward I see,
    O child, O corpse, the live dead face of thee,
Whose life and death are one thing upon earth
    Where day kills night and night again kills day
    And dies; but where is that Harmonia?   60

O all-beholden light not seen of me,
    Air, and warm winds that under the sun's eye
    Stretch your strong wings at morning; and thou, sky,
Whose hollow circle engirdling earth and sea
    All night the set stars limit, and all day
    The moving sun remeasures; ye, I say,

Ye heights of hills, and thou Dircean spring
   Inviolable, and ye towers that saw cast down
   Seven kings keen-sighted toward your seven-faced town
And quenched the red seed of one sightless king;   70
   And thou, for death less dreadful than for birth,
   Whose wild leaves hide the horror of the earth,

O mountain whereon gods made chase of kings,
   Cithaeron, thou that sawest on Pentheus dead
   Fangs of a mother fasten and wax red
And satiate with a son thy swollen springs,
   And heardst her cry fright all thine eyries' nests ·
   Who gave death suck at sanguine-suckling breasts;

Yea, and a grief more grievous, without name,
   A curse too grievous for the name of grief,   80
   Thou sawest, and heardst the rumour scare belief
Even unto death and madness, when the flame
   Was lit whose ashes dropped about the pyre
   That of two brethren made one sundering fire;

O bitter nurse, that on thine hard bare knees
   Rear'dst for his fate the bloody-footed child
   Whose hands should be more bloodily defiled
And the old blind feet walk wearier ways than these,
   Whose seed, brought forth in darkness unto doom,
   Should break as fire out of his mother's womb;   90

I bear you witness as ye bear to me,
   Time, day, night, sun, stars, life, death, air, sea, earth,
   And ye that round the human house of birth
Watch with veiled heads and weaponed hands, and see
   Good things and evil, strengthless yet and dumb,
   Sit in the clouds with cloudlike hours to come;

Ye forces without form and viewless powers
   That have the keys of all our years in hold,
   That prophesy too late with tongues of gold,
In a strange speech whose words are perished hours,   100
   I witness to you what good things ye give
   As ye to me what evil while I live.

What should I do to blame you, what to praise,
    For floral hours and hours funereal?
    What should I do to curse or bless at all
For winter-woven or summer-coloured days?
    Curse he that will and bless you whoso can,
    I have no common part in you with man.

I hear a springing water, whose quick sound
    Makes softer the soft sunless patient air,   110
    And the wind's hand is laid on my thin hair
Light as a lover's, and the grasses round
    Have odours in them of green bloom and rain
    Sweet as the kiss wherewith sleep kisses pain.

I hear the low sound of the spring of time
    Still beating as the low live throb of blood,
    And where its waters gather head and flood
I hear change moving on them, and the chime
    Across them of reverberate wings of hours
    Sounding, and feel the future air of flowers.   120

The wind of change is soft as snow, and sweet
    The sense thereof as roses in the sun,
    The faint wind springing with the springs that run,
The dim sweet smell of flowering hopes, and heat
    Of unbeholden sunrise; yet how long
    I know not, till the morning put forth song.

I prophesy of life, who live with death;
    Of joy, being sad; of sunlight, who am blind;   130
    Of man, whose ways are alien from mankind
And his lips are not parted with man's breath;
    I am a word out of the speechless years,
    The tongue of time, that no man sleeps who hears.

I stand a shadow across the door of doom,
    Athwart the lintel of death's house, and wait;
    Nor quick nor dead, nor flexible by fate,
Nor quite of earth nor wholly of the tomb;
    A voice, a vision, light as fire or air,
    Driven between days that shall be and that were.   140

I prophesy, with feet upon a grave,
   Of death cast out and life devouring death
   As flame doth wood and stubble with a breath;
Of freedom, though all manhood were one slave;
   Of truth, though all the world were liar; of love,
   That time nor hate can raze the witness of.

Life that was given for love's sake and his law's
   Their powers have no more power on; they divide
   Spoils wrung from lust or wrath of man or pride,
And keen oblivion without pity or pause   150
   Sets them on fire and scatters them on air
   Like ashes shaken from a suppliant's hair.

But life they lay no hand on; life once given
   No force of theirs hath competence to take;
   Life that was given for some divine thing's sake,
To mix the bitterness of earth with heaven,
   Light with man's night, and music with his breath,
   Dies not, but makes its living food of death.

I have seen this, who live where men are not,
   In the high starless air of fruitful night   160
   On that serenest and obscurest height
Where dead and unborn things are one in thought
   And whence the live unconquerable springs
   Feed full of force the torrents of new things.

I have seen this, who saw long since, being man,
   As now I know not if indeed I be,
   The fair bare body of Wisdom, good to see
And evil, whence my light and night began;
   Light on the goal and darkness on the way,
   Light all through night and darkness all through day.   170

Mother, that by that Pegasean spring
   Didst fold round in thine arms thy blinded son,
   Weeping 'O holiest, what thing hast thou done,
What, to my child? woe's me that see the thing!
   Is this thy love to me-ward, and hereof
   Must I take sample how the gods can love?

'O child, thou hast seen indeed, poor child of mine,
    The breasts and flanks of Pallas bare in sight,
    But never shalt see more the dear sun's light;
O Helicon, how great a pay is thine   180
    For some poor antelopes and wild-deer dead,
    My child's eyes hast thou taken in their stead—'

Mother, thou knewest not what she had to give,
    Thy goddess, though then angered, for mine eyes;
    Fame and foreknowledge, and to be most wise,
And centuries of high-thoughted life to live,
    And in mine hand this guiding staff to be
    As eyesight to the feet of men that see.

Perchance I shall not die at all, nor pass
    The general door and lintel of men dead;   190
    Yet even the very tongue of wisdom said
What grace should come with death to Tiresias,
    What special honour that God's hand accord
    Who gathers all men's nations as their lord.

And sometimes when the secret eye of thought
    Is changed with obscuration, and the sense
    Aches with long pain of hollow prescience,
And fiery foresight with foresuffering bought
    Seems even to infect my spirit and consume,
    Hunger and thirst come on me for the tomb.   200

I could be fain to drink my death and sleep,
    And no more wrapped about with bitter dreams
    Talk with the stars and with the winds and streams
And with the inevitable years, and weep;
    For how should he who communes with the years
    Be sometime not a living spring of tears?

O child, that guided of thine only will
    Didst set thy maiden foot against the gate
    To strike it open ere thine hour of fate,
Antigone, men say not thou didst ill,   210
    For love's sake and the reverence of his awe
    Divinely dying, slain by mortal law;

For love is awful as immortal death.
    And through thee surely hath thy brother won
    Rest, out of sight of our world-weary sun,
And in the dead land where ye ghosts draw breath
    A royal place and honour; so wast thou
    Happy, though earth have hold of thee too now.

So hast thou life and name inviolable
    And joy it may be, sacred and severe,   220
    Joy secret-souled beyond all hope or fear,
A monumental joy wherein to dwell
    Secluse and silent, a selected state,
    Serene possession of thy proper fate.

Thou art not dead as these are dead who live
    Full of blind years, a sorrow-shaken kind,
    Nor as these are am I the prophet blind;
They have not life that have not heart to give
    Life, nor have eyesight who lack heart to see
    When to be not is better than to be.   230

O ye whom time but bears with for a span,
    How long will ye be blind and dead, how long
    Make your own souls part of your own soul's wrong?
Son of the word of the most high gods, man,
    Why wilt thou make thine hour of light and breath
    Emptier of all but shame than very death?

Fool, wilt thou live for ever? though thou care
    With all thine heart for life to keep it fast,
    Shall not thine hand forego it at the last?
Lo, thy sure hour shall take thee by the hair   240
    Sleeping, or when thou knowest not, or wouldst fly;
    And as men died much mightier shalt thou die.

Yea, they are dead, men much more worth than thou;
    The savour of heroic lives that were,
    Is it not mixed into thy common air?
The sense of them is shed about thee now:
    Feel not thy brows a wind blowing from far?
    Aches not thy forehead with a future star?

The light that thou may'st make out of thy name
    Is in the wind of this same hour that drives,   250
    Blown within reach but once of all men's lives;
And he that puts forth hand upon the flame
    Shall have it for a garland on his head
    To sign him for a king among the dead.

But these men that the lessening years behold,
    Who sit the most part without flame or crown,
    And brawl and sleep and wear their life-days down
With joys and griefs ignobler than of old,
    And care not if the better day shall be—
    Are these or art thou dead, Antigone?   260

Part II

As when one wakes out of a waning dream
    And sees with instant eyes the naked thought
    Whereof the vision as a web was wrought,
I saw beneath a heaven of cloud and gleam,
    Ere yet the heart of the young sun waxed brave,
    One like a prophet standing by a grave.

In the hoar heaven was hardly beam or breath,
    And all the coloured hills and fields were grey,
    And the wind wandered seeking for the day,
And wailed as though he had found her done to death   270
    And this grey hour had built to bury her
    The hollow twilight for a sepulchre.

But in my soul I saw as in a glass
    A pale and living body full of grace
    There lying, and over it the prophet's face
Fixed; and the face was not of Tiresias,
    For such a starry fire was in his eyes
    As though their light it was that made the skies.

Such eyes should God's have been when very love
    Looked forth of them and set the sun aflame,   280
    And such his lips that called the light by name

And bade the morning forth at sound thereof;
  His face was sad and masterful as fate,
  And like a star's his look compassionate.

Like a star's gazed on of sad eyes so long
  It seems to yearn with pity, and all its fire
  As a man's heart to tremble with desire
And heave as though the light would bring forth song;
  Yet from his face flashed lightning on the land,
  And like the thunder-bearer's was his hand.   290

The steepness of strange stairs had tired his feet,
  And his lips yet seemed sick of that salt bread
  Wherewith the lips of banishment are fed;
But nothing was there in the world so sweet
  As the most bitter love, like God's own grace,
  Wherewith he gazed on that fair buried face.

Grief and glad pride and passion and sharp shame,
  Wrath and remembrance, faith and hope and hate
  And pitiless pity of days degenerate,
Were in his eyes as an incorporate flame   300
  That burned about her, and the heart thereof
  And central flower was very fire of love.

But all about her grave wherein she slept
  Were noises of the wild wind-footed years
  Whose footprints flying were full of blood and tears,
Shrieks as of Mænads on their hills that leapt
  And yelled as beasts of ravin, and their meat
  Was the rent flesh of their own sons to eat:

And fiery shadows passing with strange cries,
  And Sphinx-like shapes about the ruined lands,   310
  And the red reek of parricidal hands
And intermixture of incestuous eyes,
  And light as of that self-divided flame
  Which made an end of the Cadmean name.

And I beheld again, and lo the grave,
  And the bright body laid therein as dead,

And the same shadow across another head
That bowed down silent on that sleeping slave
    Who was the lady of empire from her birth
    And light of all the kingdoms of the earth.   320

Within the compass of the watcher's hand
    All strengths of other men and divers powers
    Were held at ease and gathered up as flowers;
His heart was as the heart of his whole land,
    And at his feet as natural servants lay
    Twilight and dawn and night and labouring day.

He was most awful of the sons of God.
    Even now men seeing seemed at his lips to see
    The trumpet of the judgment that should be,
And in his right hand terror for a rod,   330
    And in the breath that made the mountains bow
    The horned fire of Moses on his brow.

The strong wind of the coming of the Lord
    Had blown as flame upon him, and brought down
    On his bare head from heaven fire for a crown,
And fire was girt upon him as a sword
    To smite and lighten, and on what ways he trod
    There fell from him the shadow of a God.

Pale, with the whole world's judgment in his eyes,
    He stood and saw the grief and shame endure   340
    That he, though highest of angels, might not cure,
And the same sins done under the same skies,
    And the same slaves to the same tyrants thrown,
    And fain he would have slept, and fain been stone.

But with unslumbering eyes he watched the sleep
    That sealed her sense whose eyes were suns of old;
    And the night shut and opened, and behold,
The same grave where those prophets came to weep,
    But she that lay therein had moved and stirred,
    And where those twain had watched her stood a third.   350

The tripled rhyme that closed in Paradise
    With Love's name sealing up its starry speech—
    The tripled might of hand that found in reach
All crowns beheld far off of all men's eyes,
    Song, colour, carven wonders of live stone—
    These were not, but the very soul alone.

The living spirit, the good gift of grace,
    The faith which takes of its own blood to give
    That the dead veins of buried hope may live,
Came on her sleeping, face to naked face,   360
    And from a soul more sweet than all the south
    Breathed love upon her sealed and breathless mouth.

Between her lips the breath was blown as fire,
    And through her flushed veins leapt the liquid life,
    And with sore passion and ambiguous strife
The new birth rent her and the new desire,
    The will to live, the competence to be,
    The sense to hearken and the soul to see.

And the third prophet standing by her grave
    Stretched forth his hand and touched her, and her eyes   370
    Opened as sudden suns in heaven might rise,
And her soul caught from his the faith to save;
    Faith above creeds, faith beyond records, born
    Of the pure, naked, fruitful, awful morn.

For in the daybreak now that night was dead
    The light, the shadow, the delight, the pain,
    The purpose and the passion of those twain,
Seemed gathered on that third prophetic head,
    And all their crowns were as one crown, and one
    His face with her face in the living sun.   380

For even with that communion of their eyes
    His whole soul passed into her and made her strong;
    And all the sounds and shows of shame and wrong,
The hand that slays, the lip that mocks and lies,
    Temples and thrones that yet men seem to see—
    Are these dead or art thou dead, Italy?

ON THE DOWNS

A faint sea without wind or sun;
A sky like flameless vapour dun;
　　A valley like an unsealed grave
That no man cares to weep upon,
　　Bare, without boon to crave,
　　　Or flower to save.

And on the lip's edge of the down,
Here where the bent-grass burns to brown
　　In the dry sea-wind, and the heath
Crawls to the cliff-side and looks down,　　　　　10
　　I watch, and hear beneath
　　　The low tide breathe.

Along the long lines of the cliff,
Down the flat sea-line without skiff
　　Or sail or back-blown fume for mark,
Through wind-worn heads of heath and stiff
　　Stems blossomless and stark
　　　With dry sprays dark,

I send my eyes out as for news
Of comfort that all these refuse,　　　　　　　　20
　　Tidings of light or living air
From windward where the low clouds muse
　　And the sea blind and bare
　　　Seems full of care.

So is it now as it was then,
And as men have been such are men.
　　There as I stood I seem to stand,
Here sitting chambered, and again
　　Feel spread on either hand
　　　Sky, sea, and land.　　　　　　　　　　　30

As a queen taken and stripped and bound
Sat earth, discoloured and discrowned;
　　As a king's palace empty and dead

The sky was, without light or sound;
  And on the summer's head
    Were ashes shed.

Scarce wind enough was on the sea,
Scarce hope enough there moved in me,
  To sow with live blown flowers of white
The green plain's sad serenity,   40
  Or with stray thoughts of light
    Touch my soul's sight.

By footless ways and sterile went
My thought unsatisfied, and bent
  With blank unspeculative eyes
On the untracked sands of discontent
  Where, watched of helpless skies,
    Life hopeless lies.

East and west went my soul to find.
Light, and the world was bare and blind   50
  And the soil herbless where she trod
And saw men laughing scourge mankind,
  Unsmitten by the rod
    Of any God.

Out of time's blind old eyes were shed
Tears that were mortal, and left dead
  The heart and spirit of the years,
And on man's fallen and helmless head
  Time's disanointing tears
    Fell cold as fears.   60

Hope flowering had but strength to bear
The fruitless fruitage of despair;
  Grief trod the grapes of joy for wine,
Whereof love drinking unaware
  Died as one undivine
    And made no sign.

And soul and body dwelt apart;
And weary wisdom without heart

Stared on the dead round heaven and sighed,
'Is death too hollow as thou art,   70
    Or as man's living pride?'
        And saying so died.

And my soul heard the songs and groans
That are about and under thrones,
    And felt through all time's murmur thrill
Fate's old imperious semitones
    That made of good and ill
        One same tune still.

Then 'Where is God? and where is aid?
Or what good end of these?' she said;   80
    'Is there no God or end at all,
Nor reason with unreason weighed,
    Nor force to disenthral
        Weak feet that fall?

'No light to lighten and no rod
To chasten men? Is there no God?'
    So girt with anguish, iron-zoned,
Went my soul weeping as she trod
    Between the men enthroned
        And men that groaned.   90

O fool, that for brute cries of wrong
Heard not the grey glad mother's song
    Ring response from the hills and waves,
But heard harsh noises all day long
    Of spirits that were slaves
        And dwelt in graves.

The wise word of the secret earth
Who knows what life and death are worth,
    And how no help and no control
Can speed or stay things come to birth,   100
    Nor all worlds' wheels that roll
        Crush one born soul.

With all her tongues of life and death,
With all her bloom and blood and breath,
   From all years dead and all things done,
In the ear of man the mother saith,
    'There is no God, O son,
      If thou be none.'

So my soul sick with watching heard
That day the wonder of that word,   110
   And as one springs out of a dream
Sprang, and the stagnant wells were stirred
   Whence flows through gloom and gleam
      Thought's soundless stream.

Out of pale cliff and sunburnt heath,
Out of the low sea curled beneath
   In the land's bending arm embayed,
Out of all lives that thought hears breathe
   Life within life inlaid,
      Was answer made.   120

A multitudinous monotone
Of dust and flower and seed and stone,
   In the deep sea-rock's mid-sea sloth,
In the live water's trembling zone,
   In all men love and loathe,
      One God at growth.

One forceful nature uncreate
That feeds itself with death and fate,
   Evil and good, and change and time,
That within all men lies at wait   130
   Till the hour shall bid them climb
      And live sublime.

For all things come by fate to flower
At their unconquerable hour,
   And time brings truth, and truth makes free,
And freedom fills time's veins with power,
   As, brooding on that sea,
      My thought filled me.

And the sun smote the clouds and slew
And from the sun the sea's breath blew, 140
    And white waves laughed and turned and fled
The long green heaving sea-field through,
      And on them overhead
        The sky burnt red.

Like a furled flag that wind sets free,
On the swift summer-coloured sea
    Shook out the red lines of the light,
The live sun's standard, blown to lee
      Across the live sea's white
        And green delight. 150

And with divine triumphant awe
My spirit moved within me saw,
    With burning passion of stretched eyes,
Clear as the light's own firstborn law,
      In windless wastes of skies
        Time's deep dawn rise.

'NON DOLET'

It does not hurt. She looked along the knife
    Smiling, and watched the thick drops mix and run
    Down the sheer blade; not that which had been done
Could hurt the sweet sense of the Roman wife,
But that which was to do yet ere the strife
    Could end for each for ever, and the sun:
    Nor was the palm yet nor was peace yet won
While pain had power upon her husband's life.

It does not hurt, Italia. Thou art more
    Than bride to bridegroom; how shalt thou not take
    The gift love's blood has reddened for thy sake?
Was not thy lifeblood given for us before?
    And if love's heartblood can avail thy need,
    And thou not die, how should it hurt indeed?

EURYDICE

to Victor Hugo

Orpheus, the night is full of tears and cries,
   And hardly for the storm and ruin shed
   Can even thine eyes be certain of her head
Who never passed out of thy spirit's eyes,
But stood and shone before them in such wise
   As when with love her lips and hands were fed,
   And with mute mouth out of the dusty dead
Strove to make answer when thou bad'st her rise.

Yet viper-stricken must her lifeblood feel
   The fang that stung her sleeping, the foul germ
   Even when she wakes of hell's most poisonous worm,
Though now it writhe beneath her wounded heel.
   Turn yet, she will not fade nor fly from thee;
   Wait, and see hell yield up Eurydice.

from BOTHWELL

NELSON
                         Sir, what dreams?
DARNLEY
No matter what: I'll tell thee yet some part,
That thou may'st know I shrink not for no cause.
I dreamed this bed here was a boat adrift
Wherein one sat with me who played and sang,
Yet of his cittern I could hear no note
Nor in what speech he sang inaudibly,
But watched his working fingers and quick lips
As with a passionate and loathing fear,
And could not speak nor smite him; and methought   10
That this was David; and he knew my heart,
How fain I would have smitten him, and laughed
As 'twere to mock my helpless hands and hate.
So drove we toward a rock whereon one sat
Singing, that all the highest air of heaven
Was kindled into light therewith, and shone

As with a double dawn; stars east and west
Lightened with love to hear her, and the sky
Brake in red bloom as leaf-buds break in spring,
But these bore fires for blossoms: then awhile   20
My heart too kindled and sprang up and sang
And made sweet music in me, to keep time
With that swift singing; then as fire drops down
Dropped, and was quenched, and in joy's stead I felt
Fear ache in me like hunger; and I saw
These were not stars nor overhead was heaven,
But a blind vault more thick and gross than earth,
The nether firmament that roofs in hell,
And those hot lights were of lost souls, and this
The sea of tears and fire below the world   30
That still must wash and cleanse not of one curse
The far foul strands with all its wandering brine:
And as we drove I felt the shallop's sides,
Sapped by the burning water, plank from plank
Severing; and fain I would have cried on God,
But that the rank air took me by the throat;
And ever she that sat on the sea-rock
Sang, and about her all the reefs were white
With bones of men whose souls were turned to fire;
And if she were or were not what I thought   40
Meseemed we drew not near enough to know;
For ere we came to split upon that reef
The sundering planks opened, and through their breach
Swarmed in the dense surf of the dolorous sea
With hands that plucked and tongues thrust out at us,
And fastened on me flamelike, that my flesh
Was molten as with earthly fire, and dropped
From naked bone and sinew; but mine eyes
The hot surf seared not, nor put out my sense;
For I beheld and heard out of the surge   50
Voices that shrieked and heads that rose, and knew
Whose all they were, and whence their wrath at me;
For all these cried upon me that mine ears
Rang, and my brain was like as beaten brass,
Vibrating; and the froth of that foul tide
Was as their spittle shot in my full face

That burnt it; and with breast and flanks distent
I strained myself to curse them back, and lacked
Breath; the sore surge throttled my tongueless speech,
Though its weight buoyed my dipping chin, that sank   60
No lower than where my lips were burnt with brine
And my throat clenched fast of the strangling sea,
Till I swam short with sick strokes, as one might
Whose hands were maimed; then mine ill spirit of sleep
Shifted, and showed me as a garden walled,
Wherein I stood naked, a shipwrecked man,
Stunned yet and staggered from the sea, and soiled
With all the weed and scurf of the gross wave
Whose breach had cast me broken on that shore:
And one came like a god in woman's flesh   70
And took mine eyes with hers, and gave me fruit
As red as fire, but full of worms within
That crawled and gendered; and she gave me wine
But in the cup a toad was; and she said,
Eat, and I ate, and *Drink*, and I did drink,
And sickened; then came one with spur on heel
Red from his horse o'erridden, smeared with dust,
And took my hand to lead me as to rest,
Being bruised yet from the sea-breach; and his hand
Was as of molten iron wherein mine   80
Was as a brand in fire; and at his feet
The earth split, and I saw within the gulf
As in clear water mine own writhen face,
Eaten of worms and living; then I woke.

from ERECTHEUS

    O son of the rose-red morning, O God twin-born with
        the day,   *[Str.6.*
    O wind with the young sun waking, and winged for the same wide way,
Give up not the house of thy kin to the host thou hast marshalled from
        northward for prey.
    From the cold of thy cradle in Thrace, from the mists of the fountains
        of night,   *[Ant.6.*

From the bride-bed of dawn whence day leaps laughing, on fire
   for his flight,
Come down with their doom in thine hand on the ships thou has brought
   up against us to fight.
For now not in word but in deed is the harvest of spears begun,   *[Str.7.*
And its clamour outbellows the thunder, its lightning outlightens the sun.
From the springs of the morning it thunders and lightens across and afar
To the wave where the moonset ends and the fall of the last low star.   10
With a trampling of drenched red hoofs and an earth quake of men that
   meet,
Strong war sets hand to the scythe, and the furrows take fire from his
   feet.
Earth groans from her great rent heart, and the hollows of rocks are
   afraid,
And the mountains are moved, and the valleys as waves in a storm-wind
   swayed.
From the roots of the hills to the plain's dim verge and the dark loud
   shore,
Air shudders with shrill spears crossing, and hurtling of wheels that
   roar.
As the grinding of teeth in the jaws of a lion that foam as they gnash
Is the shriek of the axles that loosen, the shock of the poles that crash.
The dense manes darken and glitter, the mouths of the mad steeds
   champ,
Their heads flash blind through the battle, and death's foot rings in
   their tramp.   20
For a fourfold host upon earth and in heaven is arrayed for the fight,
Clouds ruining in thunder and armies encountering as clouds in the night.
Mine ears are amazed with the terror of trumpets, with darkness mine
   eyes,
At the sound of the sea's host charging that deafens the roar of the sky's.
White frontlet is dashed upon frontlet, and horse against horse reels
   hurled,
And the gorge of the gulfs of the battle is wide for the spoil of the world.
And the meadows are cumbered with shipwreck of chariots that founder
   on land,   *[Ant.7.*
And the horsemen are broken with breach as of breakers, and scattered
   as sand.
Through the roar and recoil of the charges that mingle their cries and
   confound.

Like fire are the notes of the trumpets that flash through the darkness
    of sound.   30
As the swing of the sea churned yellow that sways with the wind as it
    swells
Is the lift and relapse of the wave of the chargers that clash with their
    bells;
And the clang of the sharp shrill brass through the burst of the wave as
    it shocks
Rings clean as the clear wind's cry through the roar of the surge on the
    rocks:
And the heads of the steeds in their headgear of war, and their corsleted
    breasts,
Gleam broad as the brows of the billows that brighten the storm with
    their crests,
Gleam dread as their bosoms that heave to the ship-wrecking wind as
    they rise,
Filled full of the terror and thunder of water, that slays as it dies.
So dire is the glare of their foreheads, so fearful the fire of their breath,
And the light of their eyeballs enkindled so bright with the lightnings
    of death;   40
And the foam of their mouths as the sea's when the jaws of its gulf are
    as graves,
And the ridge of their necks as the wind-shaken mane on the ridges of
    waves:
And their fetlocks afire as they rear drip thick with a dewfall of blood
As the lips of the rearing breaker with froth of the manslaying flood.
And the whole plain reels and resounds as the fields of the sea by night
When the stroke of the wind falls darkling, and death is the seafarer's light.

from POEMS AND BALLADS, SECOND SERIES

THE LAST ORACLE
(A.D. 361)

> εἴπατε τῷ βασιλῆϊ, χαμαὶ πέσε δαίδαλος αὐλά·
> οὐκέτι Φοῖβος ἔχει καλύβαν, οὐ μάντιδα δάφνην,
> οὐ παγὰν λαλέουσαν· ἀπέσβετο καὶ λάλον ὕδωρ.

Years have risen and fallen in darkness or in twilight,
    Ages waxed and waned that knew not thee nor thine,

While the world sought light by night and sought not thy light,
   Since the sad last pilgrim left thy dark mid shrine.
Dark the shrine and dumb the fount of song thence welling,
   Save for words more sad than tears of blood, that said;
Tell the king, on earth has fallen the glorious dwelling,
   And the watersprings that spake are quenched and dead.
Not a cell is left the God, no roof, no cover
   In his hand the prophet laurel flowers no more.   10
And the great king's high sad heart, thy true last lover,
   Felt thine answer pierce and cleave it to the core.
     And he bowed down his hopeless head
        In the drift of the wild world's tide,
     And dying, *Thou hast conquered*, he said,
        Galilean; he said it, and died.
     And the world that was thine and was ours
        When the Graces took hands with the Hours
     Grew cold as a winter wave
        In the wind from a wide-mouthed grave,   20
     As a gulf wide open to swallow
        The light that the world held dear.
   O father of all of us, Paian, Apollo,
        Destroyer and healer, hear!

Age on age thy mouth was mute, thy face was hidden,
   And the lips and eyes that loved thee blind and dumb;
Song forsook their tongues that held thy name forbidden,
   Light their eyes that saw the strange God's kingdom come.
Fire for light and hell for heaven and psalms for pæans
   Filled the clearest eyes and lips most sweet of song,   30
When for chant of Greeks the wail of Galileans
   Made the whole world moan with hymns of wrath and wrong.
Yea, not yet we see thee, father, as they saw thee,
   They that worshipped when the world was theirs and thine,
They whose words had power by thine own power to draw thee
   Down from heaven till earth seemed more than heaven divine.
     For the shades are about us that hover
        When darkness is half withdrawn
     And the skirts of the dead night cover
        The face of the live new dawn.   40
     For the past is not utterly past

Though the word on its lips be the last,
And the time be gone by with its creed
When men were as beasts that bleed,
As sheep or as swine that wallow,
    In the shambles of faith and of fear.
O father of all of us, Paian, Apollo,
    Destroyer and healer, hear!

Yet it may be, lord and father, could we know it,
    We that love thee for our darkness shall have light   50
More than ever prophet hailed of old or poet
    Standing crowned and robed and sovereign in thy sight.
To the likeness of one God their dreams enthralled thee,
    Who wast greater than all Gods that waned and grew;
Son of God the shining son of Time they called thee,
    Who wast older, O our father, than they knew.
For no thought of man made Gods to love or honour
    Ere the song within the silent soul began,
Nor might earth in dream or deed take heaven upon her
    Till the word was clothed with speech by lips of man.   60
    And the word and the life wast thou,
        The spirit of man and the breath;
    And before thee the Gods that bow
        Take life at thine hands and death.
    For these are as ghosts that wane,
    That are gone in an age or twain;
    Harsh, merciful, passionate, pure,
    They perish, but thou shalt endure;
    Be their flight with the swan or the swallow,
        They pass as the flight of a year.   70
    O father of all of us, Paian, Apollo,
        Destroyer and healer, hear!

Thou the word, the light, the life, the breath, the glory,
    Strong to help and heal, to lighten and to slay,
Thine is all the song of man, the world's whole story;
    Not of morning and of evening is thy day.
Old and younger Gods are buried or begotten
    From uprising to downsetting of thy sun,
Risen from eastward, fallen to westward and forgotten,

And their springs are many, but their end is one.   80
Divers births of godheads find one death appointed,
   As the soul whence each was born makes room for each;
God by God goes out, discrowned and disanointed,
   But the soul stands fast that gave them shape and speech.
     Is the sun yet cast out of heaven?
       Is the song yet cast out of man?
     Life that had song for its leaven
       To quicken the blood that ran
     Through the veins of the songless years
     More bitter and cold than tears,   90
     Heaven that had thee for its one
     Light, life, word, witness, O sun,
     Are they soundless and sightless and hollow,
       Without eye, without speech, without ear?
  O father of all of us, Paian, Apollo,
     Destroyer and healer, hear!

Time arose and smote thee silent at his warning,
   Change and darkness fell on men that fell from thee;
Dark thou satest, veiled with light, behind the morning,
   Till the soul of man should lift up eyes and see.   100
Till the blind mute soul get speech again and eye-sight,
   Man may worship not the light of life within;
In his sight the stars whose fires grow dark in thy sight
   Shine as sunbeams on the night of death and sin.
Time again is risen with mightier word of warning,
   Change hath blown again a blast of louder breath;
Clothed with clouds and stars and dreams that melt in morning,
   Lo, the Gods that ruled by grace of sin and death!
     They are conquered, they break, they are stricken,
       Whose might made the whole world pale;   110
     They are dust that shall rise not or quicken
       Though the world for their death's sake wail.
     As a hound on a wild beast's trace,
     So time has their godhead in chase;
     As wolves when the hunt makes head,
     They are scattered, they fly, they are fled;
     They are fled beyond hail, beyond hollo.

And the cry of the chase, and the cheer.
O father of all of us, Paian, Apollo,
Destroyer and healer, hear!   120

Day by day thy shadow shines in heaven beholden,
Even the sun, the shining shadow of thy face:
King, the ways of heaven before thy feet grow golden;
God, the soul of earth is kindled with thy grace.
In thy lips the speech of man whence Gods were fashioned,
In thy soul the thought that makes them and unmakes;
By thy light and heat incarnate and impassioned,
Soul to soul of man gives light for light and takes.
As they knew thy name of old time could we know it,
Healer called of sickness, slayer invoked of wrong,   130
Light of eyes that saw thy light, God, king, priest, poet,
Song should bring thee back to heal us with thy song.
For thy kingdom is past not away,
Nor thy power from the place thereof hurled;
Out of heaven they shall cast not the day,
They shall cast not out song from the world.
By the song and the light they give
We know thy works that they live;
With the gift thou hast given us of speech
We praise, we adore, we beseech,   140
We arise at thy bidding and follow,
We cry to thee, answer, appear,
O father of all of us, Paian, Apollo,
Destroyer and healer, hear!

IN THE BAY

I

Beyond the hollow sunset, ere a star
Take heart in heaven from eastward, while the west,
Fulfilled of watery resonance and rest,
Is as a port with clouds for harbour bar
To fold the fleet in of the winds from far
That stir no plume now of the bland sea's breast:

II

Above the soft sweep of the breathless bay
Southwestward, far past flight of night and day,
Lower than the sunken sunset sinks, and higher
Than dawn can freak the front of heaven with fire,   10
My thought with eyes and wings made wide makes way
To find the place of souls that I desire.

III

If any place for any soul there be,
Disrobed and disentrammelled; if the might,
The fire and force that filled with ardent light
The souls whose shadow is half the light we see,
Survive and be suppressed not of the night;
This hour should show what all day hid from me.

IV

Night knows not, neither is it shown to day,
By sunlight nor by starlight is it shown, ·   20
Nor to the full moon's eye nor footfall known,
Their world's untrodden and unkindled way.
Nor is the breath nor music of it blown
With sounds of winter or with winds of May.

V

But here, where light and darkness reconciled
Hold earth between them as a weanling child
Between the balanced hands of death and birth,
Even as they held the new-born shape of earth
When first life trembled in her limbs and smiled,
Here hope might think to find what hope were worth.   30

VI

Past Hades, past Elysium, past the long
Slow smooth strong lapse of Lethe—past the toil
Wherein all souls are taken as a spoil,
The Stygian web of waters—if your song
Be quenched not, O our brethren, but be strong
As ere ye too shook off our temporal coil;

VII

If yet these twain survive your worldly breath,
Joy trampling sorrow, life devouring death,
If perfect life possess your life all through
And like your words your souls be deathless too,   40
To-night, of all whom night encompasseth,
My soul would commune with one soul of you.

VIII

Above the sunset might I see thine eyes
That were above the sundawn in our skies,
Son of the songs of morning,—thine that were
First lights to lighten that rekindling air
Wherethrough men saw the front of England rise
And heard thine loudest of the lyre-notes there—

IX

If yet thy fire have not one spark the less,
O Titan, born of her a Titaness,   50
Across the sunrise and the sunset's mark
Send of thy lyre one sound, thy fire one spark,
To change this face of our unworthiness,
Across this hour dividing light from dark.

X

To change this face of our chill time, that hears
No song like thine of all that crowd its ears,
Of all its lights that lighten all day long
Sees none like thy most fleet and fiery sphere's
Outlightening Sirius—in its twilight throng
No thunder and no sunrise like thy song.   60

XI

Hath not the sea-wind swept the sea-line bare
To pave with stainless fire through stainless air
A passage for thine heavenlier feet to tread
Ungrieved of earthly floor-work? hath it spread
No covering splendid as the sun-god's hair
To veil or to reveal thy lordlier head?

XII

Hath not the sunset strewn across the sea
A way majestical enough for thee?
What hour save this should be thine hour—and mine,
If thou have care of any less divine   70
Than thine own soul; if thou take thought of me,
Marlowe, as all my soul takes thought of thine?

XIII

Before the moon's face as before the sun
The morning star and evening star are one
For all men's lands as England. O, if night
Hang hard upon us,—ere our day take flight,
Shed thou some comfort from the day long done
On us pale children of the latter light!

XIV

For surely, brother and master and lord and king,
Where'er thy footfall and thy face make spring   80
In all souls' eyes that meet thee wheresoe'er,
And have thy soul for sunshine and sweet air—
Some late love of thine old live land should cling,
Some living love of England, round thee there.

XV

Here from her shore across her sunniest sea
My soul makes question of the sun for thee,
And waves and beams make answer. When thy feet
Made her ways flowerier and their flowers more sweet
With childlike passage of a god to be,
Like spray these waves cast off her foemen's fleet.   90

XVI

Like foam they flung it from her, and like weed
Its wrecks were washed from scornful shoal to shoal,
From rock to rock reverberate; and the whole
Sea laughed and lightened with a deathless deed
That sowed our enemies in her field for seed
And made her shores fit harbourage for thy soul.

XVII

Then in her green south fields, a poor man's child,
Thou hadst thy short sweet fill of half-blown joy,
That ripens all of us for time to cloy
With full-blown pain and passion; ere the wild   100
World caught thee by the fiery heart, and smiled
To make so swift end of the godlike boy.

XVIII

For thou, if ever godlike foot there trod
These fields of ours, wert surely like a god.
Who knows what splendour of strange dreams was shed
With sacred shadow and glimmer of gold and red
From hallowed windows, over stone and sod,
On thine unbowed bright insubmissive head?

XIX

The shadow stayed not, but the splendour stays,
Our brother, till the last of English days.   110
No day nor night on English earth shall be
For ever, spring nor summer, Junes nor Mays,
But somewhat as a sound or gleam of thee
Shall come on us like morning from the sea.

XX

Like sunrise never wholly risen, nor yet
Quenched; or like sunset never wholly set,
A light to lighten as from living eyes
The cold unlit close lids of one that lies
Dead, or a ray returned from death's far skies
To fire us living lest our lives forget.   120

XXI

For in that heaven what light of lights may be,
What splendour of what stars, what spheres of flame
Sounding, that none may number nor may name,
We know not, even thy brethren; yea, not we
Whose eyes desire the light that lightened thee,
Whose ways and thine are one way and the same.

XXII

But if the riddles that in sleep we read,
And trust them not, be flattering truth indeed,
As he that rose our mightiest called them,—he,
Much higher than thou as thou much higher than we—   130
There, might we say, all flower of all our seed,
All singing souls are as one sounding sea.

XXIII

All those that here were of thy kind and kin,
Beside thee and below thee, full of love,
Full-souled for song,—and one alone above
Whose only light folds all your glories in—
With all birds' notes from nightingale to dove
Fill the world whither we too fain would win.

XXIV

The world that sees in heaven the sovereign light
Of sunlike Shakespeare, and the fiery night   140
Whose stars were watched of Webster; and beneath,
The twin-souled brethren of the single wreath,
Grown in kings' gardens, plucked from pastoral heath,
Wrought with all flowers for all men's heart's delight.

XXV

And that fixed fervour, iron-red like Mars,
In the mid moving tide of tenderer stars,
That burned on loves and deeds the darkest done,
Athwart the incestuous prisoner's bride-house bars;
And thine, most highest of all their fires but one,
Our morning star, sole risen before the sun.   150

XXVI

And one light risen since theirs to run such race
Thou hast seen, O Phosphor, from thy pride of place.
Thou hast seen Shelley, him that was to thee
As light to fire or dawn to lightning; me,
Me likewise, O our brother, shalt thou see,
And I behold thee, face to glorious face?

XXVII

You twain the same swift year of manhood swept
Down the steep darkness, and our father wept.
And from the gleam of Apollonian tears
A holier aureole rounds your memories, kept   160
Most fervent-fresh of all the singing spheres,
And April-coloured through all months and years.

XXVIII

You twain fate spared not half your fiery span;
The longer date fulfils the lesser man.
Ye from beyond the dark dividing date
Stand smiling, crowned as gods with foot on fate.
For stronger was your blessing than his ban,
And earliest whom he struck, he struck too late.

XXIX

Yet love and loathing, faith and unfaith yet
Bind less to greater souls in unison,   170
And one desire that makes three spirits as one
Takes great and small as in one spiritual net
Woven out of hope toward what shall yet be done
Ere hate or love remember or forget.

XXX

Woven out of faith and hope and love too great
To bear the bonds of life and death and fate:
Woven out of love and hope and faith too dear
To take the print of doubt and change and fear:
And interwoven with lines of wrath and hate
Blood-red with soils of many a sanguine year.   180

XXXI

Who cannot hate, can love not; if he grieve,
His tears are barren as the unfruitful rain
That rears no harvest from the green sea's plain,
And as thorns crackling this man's laugh is vain.
Nor can belief touch, kindle, smite, reprieve
His heart who has not heart to disbelieve.

XXXII

But you, most perfect in your hate and love,
Our great twin-spirited brethren; you that stand
Head by head glittering, hand made fast in hand,
And underfoot the fang-drawn worm that strove   190
To wound you living; from so far above,
Look to love, not scorn, on ours that was your land.

XXXIII

For love we lack, and help and heat and light
To clothe us and to comfort us with might.
What help is ours to take or give? but ye—
O, more than sunrise to the blind cold sea,
That wailed aloud with all her waves all night,
Much more, being much more glorious, should you be.

XXXIV

As fire to frost, as ease to toil, as dew
To flowerless fields, as sleep to slackening pain,   200
As hope to souls long weaned from hope again
Returning, or as blood revived anew
To dry-drawn limbs and every pulseless vein,
Even so toward us should no man be but you.

XXXV

One rose before the sunrise was, and one
Before the sunset, lovelier than the sun.
And now the heaven is dark and bright and loud
With wind and starry drift and moon and cloud,
And night's cry rings in straining sheet and shroud,
What help is ours if hope like yours be none?   210

XXXVI

O well-beloved, our brethren, if ye be,
Then are we not forsaken. This kind earth
Made fragrant once for all time with your birth,
And bright for all men with your love, and worth
The clasp and kiss and wedlock of the sea,
Were not your mother if not your brethren we.

XXXVII

Because the days were dark with gods and kings
And in time's hand the old hours of time as rods,
When force and fear set hope and faith at odds,
Ye failed not nor abased your plum-plucked wings;   220
And we that front not more disastrous things,
How should we fail in face of kings and gods?

XXXVIII

For now the deep dense plumes of night are thinned
Surely with winnowing of the glimmering wind
Whose feet are fledged with morning; and the breath
Begins in heaven that sings the dark to death.
And all the night wherein men groaned and sinned
Sickens at heart to hear what sundawn saith.

XXXIX

O first-born sons of hope and fairest, ye
Whose prows first clove the thought-unsounded sea   230
Whence all the dark dead centuries rose to bar
The spirit of man lest truth should make him free,
The sunrise and the sunset, seeing one star,
Take heart as we to know you that ye are.

XL

Ye rise not and ye set not; we that say
Ye rise and set like hopes that set and rise
Look yet but seaward from a land-locked bay;
But where at last the sea's line is the sky's
And truth and hope one sunlight in your eyes,
No sunrise and no sunset marks their day.   240

A FORSAKEN GARDEN

In a coign of the cliff between lowland and highland,
    At the sea-down's edge between windward and lee,
Walled round with rocks as an inland island,
    The ghost of a garden fronts the sea.

A girdle of brushwood and thorn encloses
    The steep square slope of the blossomless bed
Where the weeds that grew green from the graves of its roses
        Now lie dead.

The fields fall southward, abrupt and broken,
    To the low last edge of the long lone land.   10
If a step should sound or a word be spoken,
    Would a ghost not rise at the strange guest's hand?
So long have the grey bare walks lain guestless,
    Through branches and briars if a man make way,
He shall find no life but the sea-wind's, restless
        Night and day.

The dense hard passage is blind and stifled
    That crawls by a track none turn to climb
To the strait waste place that the years have rifled
    Of all but the thorns that are touched not of time.   20
The thorns he spares when the rose is taken;
    The rocks are left when he wastes the plain.
The wind that wanders, the weeds wind-shaken,
        These remain.

Not a flower to be pressed of the foot that falls not;
    As the heart of a dead man the seed-plots are dry;
From the thicket of thorns whence the nightingale calls not,
    Could she call, there were never a rose to reply.
Over the meadows that blossom and wither
    Rings but the note of a sea-bird's song;   30
Only the sun and the rain come hither
        All year long.

The sun burns sere and the rain dishevels
    One gaunt bleak blossom of scentless breath.
Only the wind here hovers and revels
    In a round where life seems barren as death.
Here there was laughing of old, there was weeping,
    Haply, of lovers none ever will know,
Whose eyes went seaward a hundred sleeping
        Years ago.   40

Heart handfast in heart as they stood, 'Look thither,'
    Did he whisper? 'look forth from the flowers to the sea;
For the foam-flowers endure when the rose-blossoms wither,
    And men that love lightly may die—but we?'
And the same wind sang and the same waves whitened,
    And or ever the garden's last petals were shed,
In the lips that had whispered, the eyes that had lightened,
        Love was dead.

Or they loved their life through, and then went whither?
    And were one to the end—but what end who knows?   50
Love deep as the sea as a rose must wither,
    As the rose-red seaweed that mocks the rose.
Shall the dead take thought for the dead to love them?
    What love was ever as deep as a grave?
They are loveless now as the grass above them
        Or the wave.

All are at one now, roses and lovers,
    Not known of the cliffs and the fields and the sea.
Not a breath of the time that has been hovers
    In the air now soft with a summer to be.   60
Not a breath shall there sweeten the seasons hereafter
    Of the flowers or the lovers that laugh now or weep,
When as they that are free now of weeping and laughter
        We shall sleep.

Here death may deal not again for ever;
    Here change may come not till all change end.
From the graves they have made they shall rise up never,
    Who have left nought living to ravage and rend.
Earth, stones, and thorns of the wild ground growing,
    While the sun and the rain live, these shall be;   70
Till a last wind's breath upon all these blowing
        Roll the sea.

Till the slow sea rise and the sheer cliff crumble,
    Till terrace and meadow the deep gulfs drink,
Till the strength of the waves of the high tides humble
    The fields that lessen, the rocks that shrink,

Here now in his triumph where all things falter,
   Stretched out on the spoils that his own hand spread,
As a god self-slain on his own strange altar,
       Death lies dead.   80

RELICS

This flower that smells of honey and the sea,
White laurustine, seems in my hand to be
   A white star made of memory long ago
Lit in the heaven of dear times dead to me.

A star out of the skies love used to know
Here held in hand, a stray left yet to show
   What flowers my heart was full of in the days
That are long since gone down dead memory's flow.

Dead memory that revives on doubtful ways,
Half hearkening what the buried season says   10
   Out of the world of the unapparent dead
Where the lost Aprils are, and the lost Mays.

Flower, once I knew thy star-white brethren bred
Nigh where the last of all the land made head
   Against the sea, a keen-faced promontory,
Flowers on salt wind and sprinkled sea-dews fed.

Their hearts were glad of the free place's glory;
The wind that sang them all his stormy story
   Had talked all winter to the sleepless spray,
And as the sea's their hues were hard and hoary.   20

Like things born of the sea and the bright day,
They laughed out at the years that could not slay,
   Live sons and joyous of unquiet hours,
And stronger than all storms that range for prey.

And in the close indomitable flowers
A keen-edged odour of the sun and showers
   Was as the smell of the fresh honeycomb
Made sweet for mouths of none but paramours.

Out of the hard green wall of leaves that clomb
They showed like windfalls of the snow-soft foam,   30
   Or feathers from the weary south-wind's wing,
Fair as the spray that it came shoreward from.

And thou, as white, what word hast thou to bring?
If my heart hearken, whereof wilt thou sing?
   For some sign surely thou too hast to bear,
Some word far south was taught thee of the spring.

White like a white rose, not like these that were
Taught of the wind's mouth and the winter air,
   Poor tender thing of soft Italian bloom,
Where once thou grewest, what else for me grew there?   40

Born in what spring and on what city's tomb,
By whose hand wast thou reached, and plucked for whom?
   There hangs about thee, could the soul's sense tell,
An odour as of love and of love's doom.

Of days more sweet than thou wast sweet to smell,
Of flower-soft thoughts that came to flower and fell,
   Of loves that lived a lily's life and died,
Of dreams now dwelling where dead roses dwell.

O white birth of the golden mountain-side
That for the sun's love makes its bosom wide   50
   At sunrise, and with all its woods and flowers
Takes in the morning to its heart of pride!

Thou hast a word of that one land of ours,
And of the fair town called of the Fair Towers,
   A word for me of my San Gimignan,
A word of April's greenest-girdled hours.

Of the old breached walls whereon the wallflowers ran
Called of Saint Fina, breachless now of man,
 Though time with soft feet break them stone by stone,
Who breaks down hour by hour his own reign's span.   60

Of the old cliff overcome and overgrown
That all that flowerage clothed as flesh clothes bone,
 That garment of acacias made for May,
Whereof here lies one witness overblown.

The fair brave trees with all their flowers at play,
How king-like they stood up into the day!
 How sweet the day was with them, and the night!
Such words of message have dead flowers to say.

This that the winter and the wind made bright,
And this that lived upon Italian light,   70
 Before I throw them and these words away,
Who knows but I what memories too take flight?

AT A MONTH'S END

The night last night was strange and shaken:
 More strange the change of you and me.
Once more, for the old love's love forsaken,
 We went out once more toward the sea.

For the old love's love-sake dead and buried,
 One last time, one more and no more,
We watched the waves set in, the serried
 Spears of the tide storming the shore.

Hardly we saw the high moon hanging,
 Heard hardly through the windy night   10
Far waters ringing, low reefs clanging,
 Under wan skies and waste white light.

With chafe and change of surges chiming,
 The clashing channels rocked and rang

Large music, wave to wild wave timing,
   And all the choral water sang.

Faint lights fell this way, that way floated,
   Quick sparks of sea-fire keen like eyes
From the rolled surf that flashed, and noted
   Shores and faint cliffs and bays and skies.   20

The ghost of sea that shrank up sighing
   At the sand's edge, a short sad breath
Trembling to touch the goal, and dying
   With weak heart heaved up once in death—

The rustling sand and shingle shaken
   With light sweet touches and small sound—
These could not move us, could not waken
   Hearts to look forth, eyes to look round.

Silent we went an hour together,
   Under grey skies by waters white.   30
Our hearts were full of windy weather,
   Clouds and blown stars and broken light.

Full of cold clouds and moonbeams drifted
   And streaming storms and straying fires,
Our souls in us were stirred and shifted
   By doubts and dreams and foiled desires.

Across, aslant, a scudding sea-mew
   Swam, dipped, and dropped, and grazed the sea:
And one with me I could not dream you;
   And one with you I could not be.   40

As the white wing the white wave's fringes
   Touched and slid over and flashed past—
As a pale cloud a pale flame tinges
   From the moon's lowest light and last—

As a star feels the sun and falters,
   Touched to death by diviner eyes—

As on the old gods' untended altars
   The old fire of withered worship dies—

(Once only, once the shrine relighted
   Sees the last fiery shadow shine,   50
Last shadow of flame and faith benighted,
   Sees falter and flutter and fail the shrine)

So once with fiery breath and flying
   Your winged heart touched mine and went,
And the swift spirits kissed, and sighing,
   Sundered and smiled and were content.

That only touch, that feeling only,
   Enough we found, we found too much;
For the unlit shrine is hardly lonely
   As one the old fire forgets to touch.   60

Slight as the sea's sight of the sea-mew,
   Slight as the sun's sight of the star:
Enough to show one must not deem you
   For love's sake other than you are.

Who snares and tames with fear and danger
   A bright beast of a fiery kin,
Only to mar, only to change her
   Sleek supple soul and splendid skin?

Easy with blows to mar and maim her,
   Easy with bonds to bind and bruise;   70
What profit, if she yield her tamer
   The limbs to mar, the soul to lose?

Best leave or take the perfect creature,
   Take all she is or leave complete;
Transmute you will not form or feature,
   Change feet for wings or wings for feet.

Strange eyes, new limbs, can no man give her;
   Sweet is the sweet thing as it is.

No soul she hath, we see, to outlive her;
    Hath she for that no lips to kiss?   80

So may one read his weird, and reason,
    And with vain drugs assuage no pain.
For each man in his loving season
    Fools and is fooled of these in vain.

Charms that allay not any longing,
    Spells that appease not any grief,
Time brings us all by handfuls, wronging
    All hurts with nothing of relief.

Ah, too soon shot, the fool's bolt misses!
    What help? the world is full of loves;   90
Night after night of running kisses,
    Chirp after chirp of changing doves.

Should Love disown or disesteem you
    For loving one man more or less?
You could not tame your light white sea-mew,
    Nor I my sleek black pantheress.

For a new soul let whoso please pray,
    We are what life made us, and shall be.
For you the jungle and me the sea-spray,
    And south for you and north for me.   100

But this one broken foam-white feather
    I throw you off the hither wing.
Splashed stiff with sea-scurf and salt weather,
    This song for sleep to learn and sing—

Sing in your ear when, daytime over,
    You couched at long length on hot sand
With some sleek sun-discoloured lover,
    Wince from his breath as from a brand:

Till the acrid hour aches out and ceases,
    And the sheathed eyeball sleepier swims,   110
The deep flank smoothes its dimpling creases,
    And passion loosens all the limbs:

Till dreams of sharp grey north-sea weather
    Fall faint upon your fiery sleep,
As on strange sands a strayed bird's feather
    The wind may choose to lose or keep.

But I, who leave my queen of panthers,
    As a tired honey-heavy bee
Gilt with sweet dust from gold-grained anthers
    Leaves the rose-chalice, what for me?   120

From the ardours of the chaliced centre,
    From the amorous anthers' golden grime,
That scorch and smutch all wings that enter,
    I fly forth hot from honey-time.

But as to a bee's gilt thighs and winglets
    The flower-dust with the flower-smell clings;
As a snake's mobile rampant ringlets
    Leave the sand marked with print of rings;

So to my soul in surer fashion
    Your savage stamp and savour hangs;   130
The print and perfume of old passion,
    The wild-beast mark of panther's fangs.

AVE ATQUE VALE

In memory of Charles Baudelaire

Nous devrions pourtant lui porter quelques fleurs;
Les morts, les pauvres morts, ont de grandes douleurs,
Et quand Octobre souffle, émondeur des vieux arbres,
Son vent mélancolique à l'entour de leurs marbres,
Certe, ils doivent trouver les vivants bien ingrats.

Les Fleurs du Mal

I

Shall I strew on thee rose or rue or laurel,
    Brother, on this that was the veil of thee?
    Or quiet sea-flower moulded by the sea,
Or simplest growth of meadow-sweet or sorrel,
    Such as the summer-sleepy Dryads weave,
    Waked up by snow-soft sudden rains at eve?
Or wilt thou rather, as on earth before,
    Half-faded fiery blossoms, pale with heat
    And full of bitter summer, but more sweet
To thee than gleanings of a northern shore   10
    Trod by no tropic feet?

II

For always thee the fervid languid glories
    Allured of heavier suns in mightier skies;
    Thine ears knew all the wandering watery sighs
Where the sea sobs round Lesbian promontories,
    The barren kiss of piteous wave to wave
    That knows not where is that Leucadian grave
Which hides too deep the supreme head of song.
    Ah, salt and sterile as her kisses were,
    The wild sea winds her and the green gulfs bear   20
Hither and thither, and vex and work her wrong,
    Blind gods than cannot spare.

III

Thou sawest, in thine old singing season, brother,
    Secrets and sorrow unbeheld of us:
    Fierce loves, and lovely leaf-buds poisonous,

Bare to thy subtler eye, but for none other
    Blowing by night in some unbreathed-in clime;
    The hidden harvest of luxurious time,
Sin without shape, and pleasure without speech;
    And where strange dreams in a tumultuous sleep   30
    Make the shut eyes of stricken spirits weep;
And with each face thou sawest the shadow on each,
    Seeing as men sow men reap.

IV

O sleepless heart and sombre soul unsleeping,
    That were athirst for sleep and no more life
    And no more love, for peace and no more strife!
Now the dim gods of death have in their keeping
    Spirit and body and all the springs of song,
    Is it well now where love can do no wrong,
Where stingless pleasure has no foam or fang   40
    Behind the unopening closure of her lips?
    Is it not well where soul from body slips
And flesh from bone divides without a pang
    As dew from flower-bell drips?

V

It is enough; the end and the beginning
    Are one thing to thee, who art past the end.
    O hand unclasped of unbeholden friend,
For thee no fruits to pluck, no palms for winning,
    No triumph and no labour and no lust,
    Only dead yew-leaves and a little dust.   50
O quiet eyes wherein the light saith nought,
    Whereto the day is dumb, nor any night
    With obscure finger silences your sight,
Nor in your speech the sudden soul speaks thought,
    Sleep, and have sleep for light.

VI

Now all strange hours and all strange loves are over,
    Dreams and desires and sombre songs and sweet,
    Hast thou found place at the great knees and feet
Of some pale Titan-woman like a lover,

Such as thy vision here solicited,   60
   Under the shadow of her fair vast head,
The deep division of prodigious breasts,
   The solemn slope of mighty limbs asleep,
   The weight of awful tresses that still keep
The savour and shade of old-world pine-forests
   Where the wet hill-winds weep?

VIII

Hast thou found any likeness for thy vision?
   O gardener of strange flowers, what bud, what bloom,
   Hast thou found sown, what gathered in the gloom?
What of despair, of rapture, of derision,   70
   What of life is there, what of ill or good?
   Are the fruits grey like dust or bright like blood?
Does the dim ground grow any seed of ours,
   The faint fields quicken any terrene root,
   In low lands where the sun and moon are mute
And all the stars keep silence? Are there flowers
   At all, or any fruit?

VIII

Alas, but though my flying song flies after,
   O sweet strange elder singer, thy more fleet
   Singing, and footprints of thy fleeter feet,   80
Some dim derision of mysterious laughter
   From the blind tongueless warders of the dead,
   Some gainless glimpse of Proserpine's veiled head,
Some little sound of unregarded tears
   Wept by effaced unprofitable eyes,
   And from pale mouths some cadence of dead sighs—
These only, these the hearkening spirit hears,
   Sees only such things rise.

IX

Thou art far too far for wings of words to follow,
   Far too far off for thought or any prayer.   90
   What ails us with thee, who art wind and air?
What ails us gazing where all seen is hollow?
   Yet with some fancy, yet with some desire,

Dreams pursue death as winds a flying fire,
Our dreams pursue our dead and do not find.
    Still, and more swift than they, the thin flame flies,
    The low light fails us in elusive skies,
Still the foiled earnest ear is deaf, and blind
    Are still the eluded eyes.

    X
Not thee, O never thee, in all time's changes,   100
    Not thee, but this the sound of thy sad soul,
    The shadow of thy swift spirit, this shut scroll
I lay my hand on, and not death estranges
    My spirit from communion of thy song—
    These memories and these melodies that throng
Veiled porches of a Muse funereal—
    These I salute, these touch, these clasp and fold
    As though a hand were in my hand to hold,
Or through mine ears a mourning musical
    Of many mourners rolled.   110

    XI
I among these, I also, in such station
    As when the pyre was charred, and piled the sods,
    And offering to the dead made, and their gods,
The old mourners had, standing to make libation,
    I stand, and to the gods and to the dead
    Do reverence without prayer or praise, and shed
Offering to these unknown, the gods of gloom,
    And what of honey and spice my seedlands bear,
    And what I may of fruits in this chilled air,
And lay, Orestes-like, across the tomb   120
    A curl of severed hair.

    XII
But by no hand nor any treason stricken,
    Not like the low-lying head of Him, the King,
    The flame that made of Troy a ruinous thing,
Thou liest, and on this dust no tears could quicken
    There fall no tears like theirs that all men hear
    Fall tear by sweet imperishable tear

Down the opening leaves of holy poets' pages.
 Thee not Orestes, not Electra mourns;
  But bending us-ward with memorial urns   130
The most high Muses that fulfil all ages
 Weep, and our God's heart yearns.

  XIII

For, sparing of his sacred strength, not often
 Among us darkling here the lord of light
 Makes manifest his music and his might
In hearts that open and in lips that soften
 With the soft flame and heat of songs that shine.
 Thy lips indeed he touched with bitter wine,
  Yet surely from his hand thy soul's food came,   140
 The fire that scarred thy spirit at his flame
Was lighted, and thine hungering heart he fed
 Who feeds our hearts with fame.

  XIV

Therefore he too now at thy soul's sunsetting,
 God of all suns and songs, he too bends down
 To mix his laurel with thy cypress crown,
And save thy dust from blame and from forgetting.
 Therefore he too, seeing all thou wert and art,
 Compassionate, with sad and sacred heart,
Mourns thee of many his children the last dead,   150
 And hallows with strange tears and alien sighs
 Thine unmelodious mouth and sunless eyes,
And over thine irrevocable head.
 Sheds light from the under skies.

  XV

And one weeps with him in the ways Lethean,
 And stains with tears her changing bosom chill:
 That obscure Venus of the hollow hill,
That thing transformed which was the Cytherean,
 With lips that lost their Grecian laugh divine
 Long since, and face no more called Erycine;   160
A ghost, a bitter and luxurious god.
 Thee also with fair flesh and singing spell

Did she, a sad and second prey, compel
Into the footless places once more trod,
    And shadows hot from hell.

   XVI

And now no sacred staff shall break in blossom,
    No choral salutation lure to light
    A spirit sick with perfume and sweet night
And love's tired eyes and hands and barren bosom.
    There is no help for these things; none to mend   170
    And none to mar; not all our songs, O friend,
Will make death clear or make life durable.
    Howbeit with rose and ivy and wild vine
    And with wild notes about this dust of thine
At least I fill the place where white dreams dwell
    And wreathe an unseen shrine.

   XVII

Sleep; and if life was bitter to thee, pardon,
    If sweet, give thanks; thou hast no more to live;
    And to give thanks is good, and to forgive.
Out of the mystic and the mournful garden   180
    Where all day through thine hands in barren braid
    Wove the sick flowers of secrecy and shade,
Green buds of sorrow and sin, and remnants grey,
    Sweet-smelling, pale with poison, sanguine-hearted,
    Passions that sprang from sleep and thoughts that started,
Shall death not bring us all as thee one day
    Among the days departed?

   XVIII

For thee, O now a·silent soul, my brother,
    Take at my hands this garland, and farewell.
    Thin is the leaf, and chill the wintry smell,   190
And chill the solemn earth, a fatal mother,
    With sadder than the Niobean womb,
    And in the hollow of her breasts a tomb.
Content thee, howsoe'er, whose days are done;
    There lies not any troublous thing before,
    Nor sight nor sound to war against thee more,
For whom all winds are quiet as the sun,
    All waters as the shore.

SONNET

(With a copy of *Mademoiselle de Maupin*)

This is the golden book of spirit and sense,
    The holy writ of beauty; he that wrought
    Made it with dreams and faultless words and thought
That seeks and finds and loses in the dense
Dim air of life that beauty's excellence
    Wherewith love makes one hour of life distraught
    And all hours after follow and find not aught.
Here is that height of all love's eminence
Where man may breathe but for a breathing-space
    And feel his soul burn as an altar-fire
    To the unknown God of unachieved desire,
And from the middle mystery of the place
    Watch lights that break, hear sounds as of a quire,
But see not twice unveiled the veiled God's face.

INFERIAE

Spring, and the light and sound of things on earth
Requickening, all within our green sea's girth;
A time of passage or a time of birth
    Fourscore years since as this year, first and last.

The sun is all about the world we see,
The breath and strength of very spring; and we
Live, love, and feed on our own hearts; but he
    Whose heart fed mine has passed into the past.

Past, all things born with sense and blood and breath;
The flesh hears nought that now the spirit saith.   10
If death be like as birth and birth as death,
    The first was fair—more fair should be the last.

Fourscore years since, and come but one month more
The count were perfect of his mortal score
Whose sail went seaward yesterday from shore
    To cross the last of many an unsailed sea.

Light, love and labour up to life's last height,
These three were stars unsettling in his sight;
Even as the sun is life and heat and light
    And sets not nor is dark when dark are we.   20

The life, the spirit, and the work were one
That here--ah, who shall say, that here are done?
Not I, that know not; father, not thy son,
    For all the darkness of the night and sea.

                              March 5, 1877

CYRIL TOURNEUR

A sea that heaves with horror of the night,
    As maddened by the moon that hangs aghast
    With strain and torment of the ravening blast,
Haggard as hell, a bleak blind bloody light;
No shore but one red reef of rock in sight,
    Whereon the waifs of many a wreck were cast
    And shattered in the fierce nights overpast
Wherein more souls toward hell than heaven took flight;
And 'twixt the shark-toothed rocks and swallowing shoals
A cry as out of hell from all these souls
    Sent through the sheer gorge of the slaughtering sea,
Whose thousand throats, full-fed with life by death,
Fill the black air with foam and furious breath;
    And over all these one star—Chastity.

TRANSLATIONS FROM THE FRENCH OF VILLON

THE COMPLAINT OF THE FAIR ARMOURESS

1

Meseemeth I heard cry and groan
    That sweet who was the armourer's maid;
For her young years she made sore moan,
    And right upon this wise she said;
    'Ah fierce old age with foul bald head,

To spoil fair things thou art over fain;
   Who holdeth me? who? would God I were dead!
Would God I were well dead and slain!

2

   'Lo, thou hast broken the sweet yoke
   That my high beauty held above   10
All priests and clerks and merchant-folk;
   There was not one but for my love
   Would give me gold and gold enough,
Though sorrow his very heart had riven,
   To win from me such wage thereof
As now no thief would take if given.

3

   'I was right chary of the same,
   God wot it was my great folly,
For love of one sly knave of them,
   Good store of that same sweet had he;   20
   For all my subtle wiles, perdie,
God wot I loved him well enow;
   Right evilly he handled me,
But he loved well my gold, I trow.

4

   'Though I gat bruises green and black,
   I loved him never the less a jot;
Though he bound burdens on my back,
   If he said 'Kiss me and heed it not'
   Right little pain I felt, God wot,
When that foul thief's mouth, found so sweet,   30
   Kissed me—Much good thereof I got!
I keep the sin and the shame of it.

5

   'And he died thirty year agone.
   I am old now, no sweet thing to see;
By God, though, when I think thereon,
   And of that good glad time, woe's me,
   And stare upon my changed body

Stark naked, that has been so sweet,
    Lean, wizen, like a small dry tree,
I am nigh mad with the pain of it.   40

6

'Where is my faultless forehead's white,
    The lifted eyebrows, soft gold hair,
Eyes wide apart and keen of sight,
    With subtle skill in the amorous air;
    The straight nose, great nor small, but fair,
The small carved ears of shapeliest growth,
    Chin dimpling, colour good to wear,
And sweet red splendid kissing mouth?

7

'The shapely slender shoulders small,
    Long arms, hands wrought in glorious wise,   50
Round little breasts, the hips withal
    High, full of flesh, not scant of size,
    Fit for all amorous masteries;
The large loins, and the flower that was
    Planted above my strong, round thighs
In a small garden of soft grass?

8

'A writhled forehead, hair gone grey,
    Fallen eyebrows, eyes gone blind and red,
Their laughs and looks all fled away,
    Yea, all that smote men's hearts are fled;   60
    The bowed nose, fallen from goodlihead;
Foul flapping ears like water-flags;
    Peaked chin, and cheeks all waste and dead,
And lips that are two skinny rags:

9

'Thus endeth all the beauty of us.
    The arms made short, the hands made lean,
The shoulders bowed and ruinous,
    The breasts, alack! all fallen in;
    The flanks too, like the breasts grown thin;

As for the sweet place, out on it!   70
    For the lank thighs, no thighs but skin,
They are specked with spots like sausage-meat.

    10
    'So we make moan for the old sweet days,
    Poor old light women, two or three
Squatting above the straw-fire's blaze,
    The bosom crushed against the knee,
    Like faggots on a heap we be,
Round fires soon lit, soon quenched and done;
    And we were once so sweet, even we!
Thus fareth many and many an one.'   80

THE EPITAPH IN FORM OF A BALLAD
Which Villon Made for Himself and His Comrades,
Expecting to be Hanged along with Them

Men, brother men, that after us yet live,
    Let not your hearts too hard against us be;
For if some pity of us poor men ye give,
    The sooner God shall take of you pity.
    Here are we five or six strung up, you see,
And here the flesh that all too well we fed
Bit by bit eaten and rotten, rent and shred,
    And we the bones grow dust and ash withal;
Let no man laugh at us discomforted,
    But pray to God that he forgive us all.   10

If we call on you, brothers, to forgive,
    Ye should not hold our prayer in scorn, though we
Were slain by law; ye know that all alive
    Have not wit alway to walk righteously;
    Make therefore intercession heartily
With him that of a virgin's womb was bred,
That his grace be not as a dry well-head
    For us, nor let hell's thunder on us fall;
We are dead, let no man harry or vex us dead,
    But pray to God that he forgive us all.   20

The rain has washed and laundered us all five,
   And the sun dried and blackened; yea, perdie,
Ravens and pies with beaks that rend and rive
   Have dug our eyes out, and plucked off for fee
   Our beards and eyebrows; never are we free,

Not once, to rest; but here and there still sped,
Drive at its wild will by the wind's change led,
   More pecked of birds than fruits on garden-wall;
Men, for God's love, let no gibe here be said,
   But pray to God that he forgive us all. 30

Prince Jesus, that of all art lord and head,
Keep us, that hell be not our bitter bed;
   We have nought to do in such a master's hall.
Be not ye therefore of our fellowhead,
   But pray to God that he forgive us all.

THEOPHILE GAUTIER

Pour mettre une couronne au front d'une chanson,
Il semblait qu'en passant son pied semât des roses,
Et que sa main cueillît comme des fleurs écloses
Les étoiles au fond du ciel en floraison.

Sa parole de marbre et d'or avait le son
Des clairons de l'été chassant les jours moroses;
Comme en Thrace Apollon banni des grands cieux roses,
Il regardait du cœur l'Olympe, sa maison.

Le soleil fut pour lui le soleil du vieux monde,
Et son œil recherchait dans les flots embrasés
Le sillon immortel d'où s'élança sur l'onde
Vénus, que la mer molle enivrait de baisers:
Enfin, dieu ressaisi de sa splendeur première,
Il trône, et son sépulcre est bâti de lumière.

from SONGS OF THE SPRINGTIDES

THALASSIUS

Upon the flowery forefront of the year,
One wandering by the grey-green April sea
Found on a reach of shingle and shallower sand
Inlaid with starrier glimmering jewellery
Left for the sun's love and the light wind's cheer
Along the foam-flowered strand
Breeze-brightened, something nearer sea than land
Though the last shoreward blossom-fringe was near,
A babe asleep with flower-soft face that gleamed
To sun and seaward as it laughed and dreamed,   10
Too sure of either love for either's fear,
Albeit so birdlike slight and light, it seemed
Nor man nor mortal child of man, but fair
As even its twin-born tenderer spray-flowers were,
That the wind scatters like an Oread's hair.

  For when July strewed fire on earth and sea
The last time ere that year,
Out of the flame of morn Cymothoe
Beheld one brighter than the sunbright sphere
Move toward her from its fieriest heart, whence trod   20
The live sun's very God,
Across the foam-bright water-ways that are
As heavenlier heavens with star for answering star,
And on her eyes and hair and maiden mouth
Felt a kiss falling fierier than the South
And heard above afar
A noise of songs and wind-enamoured wings
And lutes and lyres of milder and mightier strings,
And round the resonant radiance of his car
Where depth is one with height,   30
Light heard as music, music seen as light.
And with that second moondawn of the spring's
That fosters the first rose,
A sun-child whiter than the sunlit snows

Was born out of the world of sunless things
That round the round earth flows and ebbs and flows.

   But he that found the sea-flower by the sea
And took to foster like a graft of earth
Was born of man's most highest and heavenliest birth,
Free-born as winds and stars and waves are free;   40
A warrior grey with glories more than years,
Though more of years than change the quick to dead
Had rained their light and darkness on his head;
A singer that in time's and memory's ears
Should leave such words to sing as all his peers
Might praise with hallowing heat of rapturous tears
Till all the days of human flight were fled.
And at his knees his fosterling was fed
Not with man's wine and bread
Nor mortal mother-milk of hopes and fears,   50
But food of deep memorial days long sped;
For bread with wisdom and with song for wine
Clear as the full calm's emerald hyaline.
And from his grave glad lips the boy would gather
Fine honey of song-notes goldener than gold,
More sweet than bees make of the breathing heather,
That he, as glad and bold,
Might drink as they, and keep his spirit from cold.
And the boy loved his laurel-laden hair
As his own father's risen on the eastern air,   60
And that less white brow-binding bayleaf bloom
More than all flowers his father's eyes relume;
And those high songs he heard,
More than all notes of any landward bird,
More than all sounds less free
Than the wind's quiring to the choral sea.

   High things the high song taught him; how the breath
Too frail for life may be more strong than death;
And this poor flash of sense in life, that gleams
As a ghost's glory in dreams,   70
More stabile than the world's own heart's root seems,
By that strong faith of lordliest love which gives

To death's own sightless-seeming eyes a light
Clearer, to death's bare bones a verier might,
Than shines or strikes from any man that lives.
How he that loves life overmuch shall die
The dog's death, utterly:
And he that much less loves it than he hates
All wrong-doing that is done
Anywhere always underneath the sun   80
Shall live a mightier life than time's or fate's.
One fairer thing he shewed him, and in might
More strong than day and night
Whose strengths build up time's towering period:
Yea, one thing stronger and more high than God,
Which if man had not, then should God not be:
And that was Liberty.
And gladly should man die to gain, he said,
Freedom; and gladlier, having lost, lie dead.
For man's earth was not, nor the sweet sea-waves   90
His, nor his own land, nor its very graves,
Except they bred not, bore not, hid not slaves:
But all of all that is,
Were one man free in body and soul, were his.

    And the song softened, even as heaven by night
Softens, from sunnier down to starrier light,
And with its moonbright breath
Blessed life for death's sake, and for life's sake death.
Till as the moon's own beam and breath confuse
In one clear hueless haze of glimmering hues   100
The sea's line and the land's line and the sky's,
And light for love of darkness almost dies,
As darkness only lives for light's dear love,
Whose hands the web of night is woven of,
So in that heaven of wondrous words were life
And death brought out of strife;
Yea, by that strong spell of serene increase
Brought out of strife to peace.

    And the song lightened, as the wind at morn
Flashes, and even with lightning of the wind   110

Night's thick-spun web is thinned
And all its weft unwoven and overworn
Shrinks, as might love from scorn.
And as when wind and light on water and land
Leap as twin gods from heavenward hand in hand,
And with the sound and splendour of their leap
Strike darkness dead, and daunt the spirit of sleep,
And burn it up with fire;
So with the light that lightened from the lyre
Was all the bright heat in the child's heart stirred   120
And blown with blasts of music into flame
Till even his sense became
Fire, as the sense that fires the singing bird
Whose song calls night by name.
And in the soul within the sense began
The manlike passion of a godlike man,
And in the sense within the soul again
Thoughts that make men of gods and gods of men.

    For love the high song taught him: love that turns
God's heart toward man as man's to Godward; love   130
That life and death and life are fashioned of,
From the first breath that burns
Half kindled on the flowerlike yeanling's lip,
So light and faint that life seems like to slip,
To that yet weaklier drawn
When sunset dies of night's devouring dawn.
But the man dying not wholly as all men dies
If aught be left of his in live men's eyes
Out of the dawnless dark of death to rise;
If aught of deed or word   140
Be seen for all time or of all time heard.
Love, that though body and soul were overthrown
Should live for love's sake of itself alone,
Though spirit and flesh were one thing doomed and dead,
Not wholly annihilated.
Seeing even the hoariest ash-flake that the pyre
Drops, and forgets the thing was once afire
And gave its heart to feed the pile's full flame
Till its own heart its own heat overcame,

Outlives its own life, though by scarce a span,   150
As such men dying outlive themselves in man,
Outlive themselves for ever; if the heat
Outburn the heart that kindled it, the sweet
Outlast the flower whose soul it was, and flit
Forth of the body of it
Into some new shape of a strange perfume
More potent than its light live spirit of bloom,
How shall not something of that soul relive,
That only soul that had such gifts to give
As lighten something even of all men's doom   160
Even from the labouring womb
Even to the seal set on the unopening tomb?
And these the loving light of song and love
Shall wrap and lap round and impend above,
Imperishable; and all springs born illume
Their sleep with brighter thoughts than wake the dove
To music, when the hillside winds resume
The marriage-song of heather-flower and broom
And all the joy thereof.

    And hate the song too taught him: hate of all   170
That brings or holds in thrall
Of spirit or flesh, free-born ere God began,
The holy body and sacred soul of man.
And wheresoever a curse was or a chain,
A throne for torment or a crown for bane
Rose, moulded out of poor men's molten pain,
There, said he, should man's heaviest hate be set
Inexorably, to faint not or forget
Till the last warmth bled forth of the last vein
In flesh that none should call a king's again,   180
Seeing wolves and dogs and birds that plague-strike air
Leave the last bone of all the carrion bare.

    And hope the high song taught him: hope whose eyes
Can sound the seas unsoundable, the skies
Inaccessible of eyesight: that can see
What earth beholds not, hear what wind and sea
Hear not, and speak what all these crying in one

Can speak not to the sun.
For in her sovereign eyelight all things are
Clear as the closest seen and kindlier star   190
That marries morn and even and winter and spring
With one love's golden ring.
For she can see the days of man, the birth
Of good and death of evil things on earth
Inevitable and infinite, and sure
As present pain is, or herself is pure.
Yea, she can hear and see, beyond all things
That lighten from before Time's thunderous wings
Through the awful circle of wheel-winged periods,
The tempest of the twilight of all Gods: 20
And higher than all the circling course they ran
The sundawn of the spirit that was man.

    And fear the song too taught him; fear to be
Worthless the dear love of the wind and sea
That bred him fearless, like a sea-mew reared
In rocks of man's foot feared,
Where nought of wingless life may sing or shine.
Fear to wax worthless of that heaven he had
When all the life in all his limbs was glad
And all the drops in all his veins were wine   210
And all the pulses music; when his heart,
Singing, bade heaven and wind and sea bear part
In one live song's reiterance, and they bore:
Fear to go crownless of the flower he wore
When the winds loved him and the waters knew,
The blithest life that clove their blithe life through
With living limbs exultant, or held strife
More amorous than all dalliance aye anew
With the bright breath and strength of their large life,
With all strong wrath of all sheer winds that blew,   220
All glories of all storms of the air that fell
Prone, ineluctable,
With roar from heaven of revel, and with hue
As of a heaven turned hell.
For when the red blast of their breath had made
All heaven aflush with light more dire than shade,

He felt it in his blood and eyes and hair
Burn as if all the fires of the earth and air
Had laid strong hold upon his flesh, and stung
The soul behind it as with serpent's tongue,   230
Forked like the loveliest lightnings: nor could bear
But hardly, half distraught with strong delight,
The joy that like a garment wrapped him round
And lapped him over and under
With raiment of great light
And rapture of great sound
At every loud leap earthward of the thunder
From heaven's most furthest bound:
So seemed all heaven in hearing and in sight,
Alive and mad with glory and angry joy,   240
That something of its marvellous mirth and might
Moved even to madness, fledged as even for flight,
The blood and spirit of one but mortal boy.

    So, clothed with love and fear that love makes great,
And armed with hope and hate,
He set first foot upon the spring-flowered ways
That all feet pass and praise.
And one dim dawn between the winter and spring,
In the sharp harsh wind harrying heaven and earth
To put back April that had borne his birth   250
From sunward on her sunniest shower-struck wing,
With tears and laughter for the dew-dropt thing,
Slight as indeed a dew-drop, by the sea
One met him lovelier than all men may be,
God-featured, with god's eyes; and in their might
Somewhat that drew men's own to mar their sight,
Even of all eyes drawn toward him: and his mouth
Was as the very rose of all men's youth,
One rose of all the rose-beds in the world:
But round his brows the curls were snakes that curled,   260
And like his tongue a serpent's; and his voice
Speaks death, and bids rejoice.
Yet then he spake no word, seeming as dumb,
A dumb thing mild and hurtless; nor at first
From his bowed eyes seemed any light to come,

Nor his meek lips for blood or tears to thirst:
But as one blind and mute in mild sweet wise
Pleading for pity of piteous lips and eyes,
He strayed with faint bare lily-lovely feet
Helpless, and flowerlike sweet: 270
Nor might man see, not having word hereof,
That this of all gods was the great god Love.

   And seeing him lovely and like a little child
That wellnigh wept for wonder that it smiled
And was so feeble and fearful, with soft speech
The youth bespake him softly; but there fell
From the sweet lips no sweet word audible
That ear or thought might reach:
No sound to make the dim cold silence glad,
No breath to thaw the hard harsh air with heat;
Only the saddest smile of all things sweet,
Only the sweetest smile of all things sad.

   And so they went together one green way
Till April dying made free the world for May;
And on his guide suddenly Love's face turned,
And in his blind eyes burned
Hard light and heat of laughter; and like flame
That opens in a mountain's ravening mouth
To blear and sear the sunlight from the south,
His mute mouth opened, and his first word came: 290
'Knowest thou me now by name?'
And all his stature waxed immeasurable,
As of one shadowing heaven and lightening hell;
And statelier stood he than a tower that stands
And darkens with its darkness far-off sands
Whereon the sky leans red;
And with a voice that stilled the winds he said:
'I am he that was thy lord before thy birth,
I am he that is thy lord till thou turn earth:
I make the night more dark, and all the morrow   300
Dark as the night whose darkness was my breath:
O fool, my name is sorrow;
Thou fool, my name is death.'

And he that heard spake not, and looked right on
Again, and Love was gone.

Through many a night toward many a wearier day
His spirit bore his body down its way.
Through many a day toward many a wearier night
His soul sustained his sorrows in her sight.
And earth was bitter, and heaven, and even the sea   310
Sorrowful even as he.
And the wind helped not, and the sun was dumb;
And with too long strong stress of grief to be
His heart grew sere and numb.

And one bright eve ere summer in autumn sank
At stardawn standing on a grey sea-bank
He felt the wind fitfully shift and heave
As toward a stormier eve;
And all the wan wide sea shuddered; and earth
Shook underfoot as toward some timeless birth,   320
Intolerable and inevitable; and all
Heaven, darkling, trembled like a stricken thrall.
And far out of the quivering east, and far
From past the moonrise and its guiding star,
Began a noise of tempest and a light
That was not of the lightning; and a sound
Rang with it round and round
That was not of the thunder; and a flight
As of blown clouds by night,
That was not of them; and with songs and cries   330
That sang and shrieked their soul out at the skies
A shapeless earthly storm of shapes began
From all ways round to move in on the man,
Clamorous against him silent; and their feet
Were as the wind's are fleet,
And their shrill songs were as wild birds' are sweet.

And as when all the world of earth was wronged
And all the host of all men driven afoam
By the red hand of Rome,
Round some fierce amphitheatre overthronged   340

With fair clear faces full of bloodier lust
Than swells and stings the tiger when his mood
Is fieriest after blood
And drunk with trampling of the murderous must
That soaks and stains the tortuous close-coiled wood
Made monstrous with its myriad-mustering brood,
Face by fair face panted and gleamed and pressed,
And breast by passionate breast
Heaved hot with ravenous rapture, as they quaffed
The red ripe full fume of the deep live draught,   350
The sharp quick reek of keen fresh bloodshed, blown
Through the dense deep drift up to the emperor's throne
From the under steaming sands
With clamour of all-applausive throats and hands,
Mingling in mirthful time
With shrill blithe mockeries of the lithe-limbed mime:
So from somewhence far forth of the unbeholden,
Dreadfully driven from over and after and under,
Fierce, blown through fifes of brazen blast and golden,
With sound of chiming waves that drown the thunder   360
Or thunder that strikes dumb the sea's own chimes,
Began the bellowing of the bull-voiced mimes,
Terrible; firs bowed down as briars or palms
Even at the breathless blast as of a breeze
Fulfilled with clamour and clangour and storms of psalms;
Red hands rent up the roots of old-world trees,
Thick flames of torches tossed as tumbling seas
Made mad the moonless and infuriate air
That, ravening, revelled in the riotous hair
And raiment of the furred Bassarides.   370

   So came all those in on him; and his heart,
As out of sleep suddenly struck astart,
Danced, and his flesh took fire of theirs, and grief
Was as a last year's leaf
Blown dead far down the wind's way; and he set
His pale mouth to the brightest mouth it met
That laughed for love against his lips, and bade
Follow: and in following all his blood grew glad
And as again a sea-bird's; for the wind

Took him to bathe him deep round breast and brow   380
Not as it takes a dead leaf drained and thinned,
But as the brightest bay-flower blown on bough,
Set springing toward it singing: and they rode
By many a vine-leafed, many a rose-hung road,
Exalt with exultation; many a night
Set all its stars upon them as for spies
On many a moon-bewildering mountain-height
Where he rode only by the fierier light
Of his dread lady's hot sweet hungering eyes.
For the moon wandered witless of her way,   390
Spell-stricken by strong magic in such wise
As wizards use to set the stars astray.
And in his ears the music that makes mad
Beat always; and what way the music bade,
That alway rode he; nor was any sleep
His, nor from height nor deep.
But heaven was as red iron, slumberless,
And had no heart to bless;
And earth lay sere and darkling as distraught,
And help in her was nought.   400

    Then many a midnight, many a morn and even,
His mother, passing forth of her fair heaven,
With goodlier gifts than all save gods can give
From earth or from the heaven where sea-things live,
With shine of sea-flowers through the bay-leaf braid
Woven for a crown her foam-white hands had made
To crown him with land's laurel and sea-dew,
Sought the sea-bird that was her boy: but he
Sat panther-throned beside Erigone,
Riding the red ways of the revel through   410
Midmost of pale-mouthed passion's crownless crew.
Till on some winter's dawn of some dim year
He let the vine-bit on the panther's lip
Slide, and the green rein slip,
And set his eyes to seaward, nor gave ear
If sound from landward hailed him, dire or dear;
And passing forth of all those fair fierce ranks
Back to the grey sea-banks,

Against a sea-rock lying, aslant the steep,
Fell after many sleepless dreams on sleep.   420

   And in his sleep the dun green light was shed
Heavily round his head
That through the veil of sea falls fathom-deep,
Blurred like a lamp's that when the night drops dead
Dies; and his eyes gat grace of sleep to see
The deep divine dark dayshine of the sea,
Dense water-walls and clear dusk water-ways,
Broad-based, or branching as a sea-flower sprays
That side or this dividing; and anew
The glory of all her glories that he knew.   430
And in sharp rapture of recovering tears
He woke on fire with yearnings of old years,
Pure as one purged of pain that passion bore,
Ill child of bitter mother; for his own
Looked laughing toward him from her midsea throne,
Up toward him there ashore.

   Thence in his heart the great same joy began,
Of child that made him man:
And turned again from all hearts else on quest,
He communed with his own heart, and had rest.   440
And like sea-winds upon loud waters ran
His days and dreams together, till the joy
Burned in him of the boy.
Till the earth's great comfort and the sweet sea's breath
Breathed and blew life in where was heartless death,
Death spirit-stricken of soul-sick days, where strife
Of thought and flesh made mock of death and life.
And grace returned upon him of his birth
Where heaven was mixed with heavenlike sea and earth;
And song shot forth strong wings that took the sun   450
From inward, fledged with might of sorrow and mirth
And father's fire made mortal in his son.
Nor was not spirit of strength in blast and breeze
To exalt again the sun's child and the sea's;
For as wild mares in Thessaly grow great
With child of ravishing winds, that violate

Their leaping length of limb with manes like fire
And eyes outburning heaven's
With fires more violent than the lightning levin's
And breath drained out and desperate of desire,   460
Even so the spirit in him, when winds grew strong,
Grew great with child of song.
Nor less than when his veins first leapt for joy
To draw delight in such as burns a boy,
Now too the soul of all his senses felt
The passionate pride of deep sea-pulses dealt
Through nerve and jubilant vein
As from the love and largess of old time,
And with his heart again
The tidal throb of all the tides keep rhyme   470
And charm him from his own soul's separate sense
With infinite and invasive influence
That made strength sweet in him and sweetness strong,
Being now no more a singer, but a song.

Till one clear day when brighter sea-wind blew
And louder sea-shine lightened, for the waves
Were full of godhead and the light that saves,
His father's, and their spirit had pierced him through,
He felt strange breath and light all round him shed
That bowed him down with rapture; and he knew   480
His father's hand, hallowing his humbled head,
And the old great voice of the old good time, that said:

'Child of my sunlight and the sea, from birth
A fosterling and fugitive on earth;
Sleepless of soul as wind or wave or fire,
A manchild with an ungrown God's desire;
Because thou hast loved nought mortal more than me,
Thy father, and thy mother-hearted sea;
Because thou hast set thine heart to sing, and sold
Life and life's love for song, God's living gold;   490
Because thou hast given thy flower and fire of youth
To feed men's hearts with visions, truer than truth;
Because thou hast kept in those world-wandering eyes
The light that makes me music of the skies;

Because thou hast heard with world-unwearied ears
The music that puts light into the spheres;
Have therefore in thine heart and in thy mouth
The sound of song that mingles north and south,
The song of all the winds that sing of me,
And in thy soul the sense of all the sea.'   500

ON THE CLIFFS

ἱμερόφωνος ἀηδὼν. *Sappho.*

Between the moondawn and the sundown here
The twilight hangs half starless; half the sea
Still quivers as for love or pain or fear
Or pleasure mightier than these all may be
A man's live heart might beat
Wherein a God's with mortal blood should meet
And fill its pulse too full to bear the strain
With fear or love or pleasure's twin-born, pain.
Fiercely the gaunt woods to the grim soil cling
That bears for all fair fruits   10
Wan wild sparse flowers of windy and wintry spring
Between the tortive serpent-shapen roots
Wherethrough their dim growth hardly strikes and shoots
And shews one gracious thing
Hardly, to speak for summer one sweet word
Of summer's self scarce heard.
But higher the steep green sterile fields, thick-set
With flowerless hawthorn even to the upward verge
Whence the woods gathering watch new cliffs emerge
Higher than their highest of crowns that sea-winds fret,   20
Hold fast, for all that night or wind can say,
Some pale pure colour yet,
Too dim for green and luminous for grey.
Between the climbing inland cliffs above
And these beneath that breast and break the bay,
A barren peace too soft for hate or love
Broods on an hour too dim for night or day.

O wind, O wingless wind that walk'st the sea,
Weak wind, wing-broken, wearier wind than we,
Who are yet not spirit-broken, maimed like thee,   30
Who wail not in our inward night as thou
In the outer darkness now,
What word has the old sea given thee for mine ear
From thy faint lips to hear?
For some word would she send me, knowing not how.

Nay, what far other word
Than ever of her was spoken, or of me
Or all my winged white kinsfolk of the sea
Between fresh wave and wave was ever heard,
Cleaves the clear dark enwinding tree with tree   40
Too close for stars to separate and to see
Enmeshed in multitudinous unity?
What voice of what strong God hath stormed and stirred
The fortressed rock of silence, rent apart
Even to the core Night's all-maternal heart?
What voice of God grown heavenlier in a bird,
Made keener of edge to smite
Than lightning—yea, thou knowest, O mother Night,
Keen as that cry from thy strange children sent
Wherewith the Athenian judgement-shrine was rent,   50
For wrath that all their wrath was vainly spent,
Their wrath for wrong made right
By justice in her own divine despite
That bade pass forth unblamed
The sinless matricide and unashamed?
Yea, what new cry is this, what note more bright
Than their song's wing of words was dark of flight,
What word is this thou hast heard,
Thine and not thine or theirs, O Night, what word
More keen than lightning and more sweet than light?   60
As all men's hearts grew godlike in one bird
And all those hearts cried on thee, crying with might,
Hear us, O mother Night.

Dumb is the mouth of darkness as of death:
Light, sound and life are one

In the eyes and lips of dawn that draw the sun
To hear what first child's word with glimmering breath
Their weak wan weanling child the twilight saith;
But night makes answer none.
God, if thou be God,—bird, if bird thou be,—   70
Do thou then answer me.
For but one word, what wind soever blow,
Is blown up usward ever from the sea.
In fruitless years of youth dead long ago
And deep beneath their own dead leaves and snow
Buried, I heard with bitter heart and sere
The same sea's word unchangeable, nor knew
But that mine own life-days were changeless too
And sharp and salt with unshed tear on tear
And cold and fierce and barren; and my soul,   80
Sickening, swam weakly with bated breath
In a deep sea like death,
And felt the wind buffet her face with brine
Hard, and harsh thought on thought in long bleak roll
Blown by keen gusts of memory sad as thine
Heap the weight up of pain, and break, and leave
Strength scarce enough to grieve
In the sick heavy spirit, unmanned with strife
Of waves that beat at the tired lips of life.

Nay, sad may be man's memory, sad may be   90
The dream he weaves him as for shadow of thee,
But scarce one breathing-space, one heartbeat long,
Wilt thou take shadow of sadness on thy song.
Not thou, being more than man or man's desire,
Being bird and God in one,
With throat of gold and spirit of the sun;
The sun whom all our souls and songs call sire,
Whose godhead gave thee, chosen of all our quire,
Thee only of all that serve, of all that sing
Before our sire and king,   100
Borne up some space on time's world-wandering wing,
This gift, this doom, to bear till time's wing tire—
Life everlasting of eternal fire.

Thee only of all; yet can no memory say
How many a night and day
My heart has been as thy heart, and my life
As thy life is, a sleepless hidden thing,
Full of the thirst and hunger of winter and spring,
That seeks its food not in such love or strife
As fill men's hearts with passionate hours and rest.   110
From no loved lips and on no loving breast
Have I sought ever for such gifts as bring
Comfort, to stay the secret soul with sleep.
The joys, the loves, the labours, whence men reap
Rathe fruit of hopes and fears,
I have made not mine; the best of all my days
Have been as those fair fruitless summer strays,
Those water-waifs that but the sea-wind steers,
Flakes of glad foam or flowers on footless ways
That take the wind in season and the sun,   120
And when the wind wills is their season done.

For all my days as all thy days from birth
My heart as thy heart was in me as thee,
Fire: and not all the fountains of the sea
Have waves enough to quench it, nor on earth
Is fuel enough to feed,
While day sows night and night sows day for seed.

We were not marked for sorrow, thou nor I,
For joy nor sorrow, sister, were we made,
To take delight and grief to live and die,   130
Assuaged by pleasures or by pains affrayed
That melt men's hearts and alter; we retain
A memory mastering pleasure and all pain,
A spirit within the sense of ear and eye,
A soul behind the soul, that seeks and sings
And makes our life move only with its wings
And feed but from its lips, that in return
Feed of our hearts wherein the old fires that burn
Have strength not to consume
Nor glory enough to exalt us past our doom.   140

Ah, ah, the doom (thou knowest whence rang that wail)
Of the shrill nightingale!
(From whose wild lips, thou knowest, that wail was thrown)
For round about her have the great gods cast
A wing-borne body, and clothed her close and fast
With a sweet life that hath no part in moan.
But me, for me (how hadst thou heart to hear?)
Remains a sundering with the two-edged spear.

Ah, for her doom! so cried in presage then
The bodeful bondslave of the king of men,   150
And might not win her will.
Too close the entangling dragnet woven of crime,
The snare of ill new-born of elder ill,
The curse of new time for an elder time,
Had caught, and held her yet,
Enmeshed intolerably in the intolerant net,
Who thought with craft to mock the God most high,
And win by wiles his crown of prophecy
From the Sun's hand sublime,
As God were man, to spare or to forget.   160

But thou,—the gods have given thee and forgiven thee
More than our master gave
That strange-eyed spirit-wounded strange-tongued slave
There questing houndlike where the roofs red-wet
Reeked as a wet red grave.
Life everlasting has their strange grace given thee,
Even hers whom thou wast wont to sing and serve
With eyes, but not with song, too swift to swerve;
Yet might not even thine eyes estranged estrange her,
Who seeing thee too, but inly, burn and bleed   170
Like that pale princess-priest of Priam's seed,
For stranger service gave thee guerdon stranger;
If this indeed be guerdon, this indeed
Her mercy, this thy meed—
That thou, being more than all we born, being higher
Than all heads crowned of him that only gives
The light whereby man lives,

The bay that bids man moved of God's desire
Lay hand on lute and lyre,
Set lip to trumpet or deflowered green reed—
If this were given thee for a grace indeed,
That thou, being first of all these, thou alone
Shouldst have the grace to die not, but to live
And lose nor change one pulse of song, one tone
Of all that were thy lady's and thine own,
Thy lady's whom thou criedst on to forgive,
Thou, priest and sacrifice on the altar-stone
Where none may worship not of all that live,
Love's priestess, errant on dark ways diverse;
If this were grace indeed for Love to give,
If this indeed were blessing and no curse.

Love's priestess, mad with pain and joy of song,
Song's priestess, mad with joy and pain of love,
Name above all names that are lights above,
We have loved, praised, pitied, crowned and done thee wrong,
O thou past praise and pity; thou the sole
Utterly deathless, perfect only and whole
Immortal, body and soul.
For over all whom time hath overpast
The shadow of sleep inexorable is cast,
The implacable sweet shadow of perfect sleep
That gives not back what life gives death to keep;
Yea, all that lived and loved and sang and sinned
Are all borne down death's cold sweet soundless wind
That blows all night and knows not whom its breath,
Darkling, may touch to death:
But one that wind hath touched and changed not,—one
Whose body and soul are parcel of the sun;
One that earth's fire could burn not, nor the sea
Quench; nor might human doom take hold on thee;
All praise, all pity, all dreams have done thee wrong,
All love, with eyes love-blinded from above;
Song's priestess, mad with joy and pain of love,
Love's priestess, mad with pain and joy of song.

180

190

200

210

Hast thou none other answer then for me
Than the air may have of thee,
Or the earth's warm woodlands girdling with green girth
Thy secret sleepless burning life on earth,
Or even the sea that once, being woman crowned
And girt with fire and glory of anguish round,   220
Thou wert so fain to seek to, fain to crave
If she would hear thee and save
And give thee comfort of thy great green grave?
Because I have known thee always who thou art,
Thou knowest, have known thee to thy heart's own heart,
Nor ever have given light ear to storied song
That did thy sweet name sweet unwitting wrong,
Nor ever have called thee nor would call for shame,
Thou knowest, but inly by thine only name,
Sappho—because I have known thee and loved, hast thou 230
None other answer now?
As brother and sister were we, child and bird,
Since thy first Lesbian word
Flamed on me, and I knew not whence I knew
This was the song that struck my whole soul through,
Pierced my keen spirit of sense with edge more keen,
Even when I knew not,—even ere sooth was seen,—
When thou wast but the tawny sweet winged thing
Whose cry was but of spring.

And yet even so thine ear should hear me—yea,   240
Hear me this nightfall by this northland bay,
Even for their sake whose loud good word I had,
Singing of thee in the all-beloved clime
Once, where the windy wine of spring makes mad
Our sisters of Majano, who kept time
Clear to my choral rhyme.
Yet was the song acclaimed of these aloud
Whose praise had made mute humbleness misproud,
The song with answering song applauded thus,
But of that Daulian dream of Itylus.   250
So but for love's love haply was it—nay,
How else?—that even their song took my song's part,

For love of love and sweetness of sweet heart,
Or god-given glorious madness of mid May
And heat of heart and hunger and thirst to sing,
Full of the new wine of the wind of spring.

Or if this were not, and it be not sin
To hold myself in spirit of thy sweet kin,
In heart and spirit of song;
If this my great love do thy grace no wrong,   260
Thy grace that gave me grace to dwell therein;
If thy gods thus be my gods, and their will
Made my song part of thy song—even such part
As man's hath of God's heart—
And my life like as thy life to fulfil;
What have our gods then given us? Ah, to thee,
Sister, much more, much happier than to me,
Much happier things they have given, and more of grace
Than falls to man's light race;
For lighter are we, all our love and pain   270
Lighter than thine, who knowest of time or place
Thus much, that place nor time
Can heal or hurt or lull or change again
The singing soul that makes his soul sublime
Who hears the far fall of its fire-fledged rhyme
Fill darkness as with bright and burning rain
Till all the live gloom inly glows, and light
Seems with the sound to cleave the core of night.

The singing soul that moves thee, and that moved
When thou wast woman, and their songs divine   280
Who mixed for Grecian mouths heaven's lyric wine
Fell dumb, fell down reproved
Before one sovereign Lesbian song of thine.
That soul, though love and life had fain held fast,
Wind-winged with fiery music, rose and past
Through the indrawn hollow of earth and heaven and hell,
As through some strait sea-shell
The wide sea's immemorial song,—the sea
That sings and breathes in strange men's ears of thee
How in her barren bride-bed, void and vast,   290
Even thy soul sang itself to sleep at last.

To sleep? Ah, then, what song is this, that here
Makes all the night one ear,
One ear fulfilled and mad with music, one
Heart kindling as the heart of heaven, to hear
A song more fiery than the awakening sun
Sings, when his song sets fire
To the air and clouds that build the dead night's pyre?
O thou of divers-coloured mind, O thou
Deathless, God's daughter subtle-souled—lo, now,⁣ 300
Now too the song above all songs, in flight
Higher than the day-star's height,
And sweet as sound the moving wings of night!
Thou of the divers-coloured seat—behold,
Her very song of old!—
O deathless, O God's daughter subtle-souled!
That same cry through this boskage overhead
Rings round reiterated,
Palpitates as the last palpitated,
The last that panted through her lips and died⁣ 310
Not down this grey north sea's half sapped cliff-side
That crumbles toward the coastline, year by year
More near the sands and near;
The last loud lyric fiery cry she cried,
Heard once on heights Leucadian,—heard not here.

Not here; for this that fires our northland night,
This is the song that made
Love fearful, even the heart of love afraid,
With the great anguish of its great delight.
No swan-song, no far-fluttering half-drawn breath,⁣ 320
No word that love of love's sweet nature saith,
No dirge that lulls the narrowing lids of death,
No healing hymn of peace-prevented strife,—
This is her song of life.

I loved thee,—hark, one tenderer note than all—
Atthis, of old time, once—one low long fall,
Sighing—one long low lovely loveless call,
Dying—one pause in song so flamelike fast—
Atthis, long since in old time overpast—

One soft first pause and last.   330
One,—then the old rage of rapture's fieriest rain
Storms all the music-maddened night again.

Child of God, close craftswoman, I beseech thee,
Bid not ache nor agony break nor master,
Lady, my spirit—
O thou her mistress, might her cry not reach thee?
Our Lady of all men's loves, could Love go past her,
Pass, and not hear it?

She hears not as she heard not; hears not me,
O treble-natured mystery,—how should she   340
Hear, or give ear?—who heard and heard not thee;
Heard, and went past, and heard not; but all time
Hears all that all the ravin of his years
Hath cast not wholly out of all men's ears
And dulled to death with deep dense funeral chime
Of their reiterate rhyme.
And now of all songs uttering all her praise,
All hers who had thy praise and did thee wrong,
Abides one song yet ot her lyric days,
Thine only, this thy song.   350

O soul triune, woman and god and bird,
Man, man at least has heard.
All ages call thee conqueror, and thy cry
The mightiest as the least beneath the sky
Whose heart was ever set to song, or stirred
With wind of mounting music blown more high
Than wildest wing may fly,
Hath heard or hears,—even Æschylus as I.
But when thy name was woman, and thy word
Human,—then haply, surely then meseems   360
This thy bird's note was heard on earth of none,
Of none save only in dreams.
In all the world then surely was but one
Song; as in heaven at highest one sceptred sun
Regent, on earth here surely without fail
One only, one imperious nightingale.

Dumb was the field, the woodland mute, the lawn
Silent; the hill was tongueless as the vale
Even when the last fair waif of cloud that felt
Its heart beneath the colouring moonrays melt, 370
At high midnoon of midnight half withdrawn,
Bared all the sudden deep divine moondawn.
Then, unsaluted by her twin-born tune,
That latter timeless morning of the moon
Rose past its hour of moonrise; clouds gave way
To the old reconquering ray,
But no song answering made it more than day;
No cry of song by night
Shot fire into the cloud-constraining light.
One only, one Æolian island heard 380
Thrill, but through no bird's throat,
In one strange manlike maiden's godlike note,
The song of all these as a single bird.
Till the sea's portal was as funeral gate
For that sole singer in all time's ageless date
Singled and signed for so triumphal fate,
All nightingales but one in all the world
All her sweet life were silent; only then,
When her life's wing of womanhood was furled,
Their cry, this cry of thine was heard again, 390
As of me now, of any born of men,
Through sleepless clear spring nights filled full of thee,
Rekindled here, thy ruling song has thrilled
The deep dark air and subtle tender sea
And breathless hearts with one bright sound fulfilled.
Or at midnoon to me
Swimming, and birds about my happier head
Skimming, one smooth soft way by water and air,
To these my bright born brethren and to me
Hath not the clear wind borne or seemed to bear 400
A song wherein all earth and heaven and sea
Were molten in one music made of thee
To enforce us, O our sister of the shore,
Look once in heart back landward and adore?
For songless were we sea-mews, yet had we

More joy than all things joyful of thee—more,
Haply, than all things happiest; nay, save thee,
In thy strong rapture of imperious joy
Too high for heart of sea-borne bird or boy,
What living things were happiest if not we?   410
But knowing not love nor change nor wrath nor wrong,
No more we knew of song.

Song, and the secrets of it, and their might,
What blessings curse it and what curses bless,
I know them since my spirit had first in sight,
Clear as thy song's words or the live sun's light,
The small dark body's Lesbian loveliness
That held the fire eternal; eye and ear
Were as a god's to see, a god's to hear,
Through all his hours of daily and nightly chime,   420
The sundering of the two-edged spear of time:
The spear that pierces even the sevenfold shields
Of mightiest Memory, mother of all songs made,
And wastes all songs as roseleaves kissed and frayed
As here the harvest of the foam-flowered fields;
But thine the spear may waste not that he wields
Since first the God whose soul is man's live breath,
The sun whose face hath our sun's face for shade,
Put all the light of life and love and death
Too strong for life, but not for love too strong,   430
Where pain makes peace with pleasure in thy song,
And in thine heart, where love and song make strife,
Fire everlasting of eternal life.

from STUDIES IN SONG

GRAND CHORUS OF BIRDS FROM ARISTOPHANES
(685-723)

Come on then, ye dwellers by nature in darkness, and like to the leaves'
generations,
That are little of might, that are moulded of mire, unenduring and
shadowlike nations,

Poor plumeless ephemerals, comfortless mortals, as visions of creatures
  fast fleeing,
Lift up your mind unto us that are deathless, and dateless the date of
  our being:
Us, children of heaven, us, ageless for aye, us, all of whose thoughts are
  eternal;
That ye may from henceforth, having heard of us all things aright as to
  matters supernal,
Of the being of birds and beginning of gods, and of streams, and the
  dark beyond reaching,
Truthfully knowing aright, in my name bid Prodicus pack with his
  preaching.

  It was Chaos and Night at the first, and the blackness of darkness, and
    hell's broad border,
Earth was not, nor air, neither heaven; when in depths of the womb of
  the dark without order   10
First thing first-born of the black-plumed Night was a wind-egg hatched
  in her bosom,
Whence timely with seasons revolving again sweet Love burst out as a
  blossom,
Gold wings glittering forth of his back, like whirlwinds gustily
  turning.
He, after his wedlock with Chaos, whose wings are of darkness, in hell
  broad-burning,
For his nestlings begat him the race of us first, and upraised us to light
  new-lighted.
And before this was not the race of the gods, until all things by Love
  were united;
And of kind united with kind in communion of nature the sky and the
  sea are
Brought forth, and the earth, and the race of the gods everlasting and
  blest. So that we are
Far away the most ancient of all things blest. And that we are of Love's
  generation
There are manifest manifold signs. We have wings, and with us have the
  Loves habitation;   20
And manifold fair young folk that forswore love once, ere the bloom
  of them ended,

Have the men that pursued and desired them subdued, by the help of us
only befriended,

With such baits as a quail, a flamingo, a goose, or a cock's comb staring
and splendid.

All best good things that befall men come from us birds, as is plain
to all reason:

For first we proclaim and make known to them spring, and the winter
and autumn in season;

Bid sow, when the crane starts clanging for Afric, in shrill-voiced
emigrant number,

And calls to the pilot to hang up his rudder again for the season, and
slumber;

And then weave cloak for Orestes the thief, lest he strip men of theirs
if it freezes.

And again thereafter the kite reappearing announces a change in the
breezes,

And that here is the season for shearing your sheep of their spring
wool. Then does the swallow   30

Give you notice to sell your greatcoat, and provide something light
for the heat that's to follow.

Thus are we as Ammon or Delphi unto you, Dodona, nay, Phœbus
Apollo.

For, as first ye come all to get auguries of birds, even such is in all
things your carriage,

Be the matter a matter of trade, or of earning your bread, or of any
one's marriage.

And all things ye lay to the charge of a bird that belong to discerning
prediction:

Winged fame is a bird, as you reckon: you sneeze, and the sign's as a
bird for conviction:

All tokens are 'birds' with you—sounds too, and lackeys, and donkeys.
Then must it not follow

That we ARE to you all as the manifest godhead that speaks in
prophetic Apollo?

October 19, 1880.

BY THE NORTH SEA

I

1

A land that is lonelier than ruin;
  A sea that is stranger than death:
Far fields that a rose never blew in,
  Wan waste where the winds lack breath;
Waste endless and boundless and flowerless
  But of marsh-blossoms fruitless as free:
Where earth lies exhausted, as powerless
    To strive with the sea.

2

Far flickers the flight of the swallows,
  Far flutters the weft of the grass   10
Spun dense over desolate hollows
  More pale than the clouds as they pass:
Thick woven as the weft of a witch is
  Round the heart of a thrall that hath sinned,
Whose youth and the wrecks of its riches
    Are waifs on the wind.

3

The pastures are herdless and sheepless,
  No pasture or shelter for herds:
The wind is relentless and sleepless,
  And restless and songless the birds;   20
Their cries from afar fall breathless,
  Their wings are as lightnings that flee;
For the land has two lords that are deathless:
    Death's self, and the sea.

4

These twain, as a king with his fellow,
  Hold converse of desolate speech:
And her waters are haggard and yellow
  And crass with the scurf of the beach:
And his garments are grey as the hoary
  Wan sky where the day lies dim;   30
And his power is to her, and his glory,
    As hers unto him.

5

In the pride of his power she rejoices,
   In her glory he glows and is glad:
In her darkness the sound of his voice is,
   With his breath she dilates and is mad:
'If thou slay me, O death, and outlive me,
   Yet thy love hath fulfilled me of thee.'
'Shall I give thee not back if thou give me,
      O sister, O sea?'   40

6

And year upon year dawns living,
   And age upon age drops dead:
And his hand is not weary of giving,
   And the thirst of her heart is not fed:
And the hunger that moans in her passion,
   And the rage in her hunger that roars,
As a wolf's that the winter lays lash on,
     Still calls and implores.

7

Her walls have no granite for girder,
   No fortalice fronting her stands: 50
But reefs the bloodguiltiest of murder
   Are less than the banks of her sands:
These number their slain by the thousand;
   For the ship hath no surety to be,
When the bank is abreast of her bows and
     Aflush with the sea.

8

No surety to stand, and no shelter
   To dawn out of darkness but one,
Out of waters that hurtle and welter
   No succour to dawn with the sun,   60
But a rest from the wind as it passes,
   Where, hardly redeemed from the waves,
Lie thick as the blades of the grasses
     The dead in their graves.

9

A multitude noteless of numbers,
    As wild weeds cast on an heap:
And sounder than sleep are their slumbers,
    And softer than song is their sleep;
And sweeter than all things and stranger
    The sense, if perchance it may be,   70
That the wind is divested of danger
        And scatheless the sea.

10

That the roar of the banks they breasted
    Is hurtless as bellowing of herds,
And the strength of his wings that invested
    The wind, as the strength of a bird's;
As the sea-mew's might or the swallow's
    That cry to him back if he cries,
As over the graves and their hollows
        Days darken and rise.   80

11

As the souls of the dead men disburdened
    And clean of the sins that they sinned,
With a lovelier than man's life guerdoned
    And delight as a wave's in the wind,
And delight as the wind's in the billow,
    Birds pass, and deride with their glee
The flesh that has dust for its pillow
        As wrecks have the sea.

12

When the ways of the sun wax dimmer,
    Wings flash though the dusk like beams;   90
As the clouds in the lit sky glimmer,
    The bird in the graveyard gleams;
As the cloud at its wing's edge whitens
    When the clarions of sunrise are heard,
The graves that the bird's note brightens
        Grow bright for the bird.

13

As the waves of the numberless waters
    That the wind cannot number who guides
Are the sons of the shore and the daughters
    Here lulled by the chime of the tides: 100
And here in the press of them standing
    We know not if these or if we
Live truliest, or anchored to landing
        Or drifted to sea.

14

In the valley he named of decision
    No denser were multitudes met
When the soul of the seer in her vision
    Saw nations for doom of them set;
Saw darkness in dawn, and the splendour
    Of judgment, the sword and the rod;   110
But the doom here of death is more tender
        And gentler the god.

15

And gentler the wind from the dreary
    Sea-banks by the waves overlapped,
Being weary, speaks peace to the weary
    From slopes that the tide-stream hath sapped;
And sweeter than all that we call so
    The seal of their slumber shall be
Till the graves that embosom them also
        Be sapped of the sea.   120

II

1

For the heart of the waters is cruel,
    And the kisses are dire of their lips,
And their waves are as fire is to fuel
    To the strength of the sea-faring ships,
Though the sea's eye gleam as a jewel
    To the sun's eye back as he dips.

2

Though the sun's eye flash to the sea's
  Live light of delight and of laughter,
And her lips breathe back to the breeze
  The kiss that the wind's lips waft her   130
From the sun that subsides, and sees
  No gleam of the storm's dawn after.

3

And the wastes of the wild sea-marches
  Where the borderers are matched in their might—
Bleak fens that the sun's weight parches,
  Dense waves that reject his light—
Change under the change-coloured arches
  Of changeless morning and night.

4

The waves are as ranks enrolled
  Too close for the storm to sever: 140
The fens lie naked and cold,
  But their heart fails utterly never:
The lists are set from of old,
  And the warfare endureth for ever.

III

1

Miles, and miles, and miles of desolation!
  Leagues on leagues on leagues without a change!
Sign or token of some eldest nation
  Here would make the strange land not so strange.
Time-forgotten, yea since time's creation,
  Seem these borders where the sea-birds range.   150

2

Slowly, gladly, full of peace and wonder
  Grows his heart who journeys here alone.
Earth and all its thoughts of earth sink under
  Deep as deep in water sinks a stone.
Hardly knows it if the rollers thunder,
  Hardly whence the lonely wind is blown.

3

Tall the plumage of the rush-flower tosses,
    Sharp and soft in many a curve and line
Gleam and glow the sea-coloured marsh-mosses
    Salt and splendid from the circling brine.   160
Streak on streak of glimmering seashine crosses
    All the land sea-saturate as with wine.

4

Far, and far between, in divers orders,
    Clear grey steeples cleave the low grey sky;
Fast and firm as time-unshaken warders,
    Hearts made sure by faith, by hope made high.
These alone in all the wild sea-borders
    Fear no blast of days and nights that die.

5

All the land is like as one man's face is,
    Pale and troubled still with change of cares.   170
Doubt and death pervade her clouded spaces:
    Strength and length of life and peace are theirs;
Theirs alone amid these weary places,
    Seeing not how the wild world frets and fares.

6

Firm and fast where all is cloud that changes
    Cloud-clogged sunlight, cloud by sunlight thinned,
Stern and sweet, above the sand-hill ranges
    Watch the towers and tombs of men that sinned
Once, now calm as earth whose only change is
    Wind, and light, and wind, and cloud, and wind.   180

7

Out and in and out the sharp straits wander,
    In and out and in the wild way strives,
Starred and paved and lined with flowers that squander
    Gold as golden as the gold of hives,
Salt and moist and multiform: but yonder
    See, what sign of life or death survives?

8

Seen then only when the songs of olden
  Harps were young whose echoes yet endure,
Hymned of Homer when his years were golden,
  Known of only when the world was pure,   190
Here is Hades, manifest, beholden,
  Surely, surely here, if aught be sure!

9

Where the border-line was crossed, that, sundering
  Death from life, keeps weariness from rest,
None can tell, who fares here forward wondering;
  None may doubt but here might end his quest.
Here life's lightning joys and woes once thundering
  Sea-like round him cease like storm suppressed.

10

Here the wise wave-wandering steadfast-hearted
  Guest of many a lord of many a land   200
Saw the shape or shade of years departed,
  Saw the semblance risen and hard at hand,
Saw the mother long from love's reach parted,
  Anticleia, like a statue stand.

11

Statue? nay, nor tissued image woven
  Fair on hangings in his father's hall;
Nay, too fast her faith of heart was proven,
  Far too firm her loveliest love of all;
Love wherethrough the loving heart was cloven,
  Love that hears not when the loud Fates call.   210

12

Love that lives and stands up re-created
  Then when life has ebbed and anguish fled;
Love more strong than death or all things fated,
  Child's and mother's, lit by love and led;
Love that found what life so long awaited
  Here, when life came down among the dead.

13

Here, where never came alive another,
    Came her son across the sundering tide
Crossed before by many a warrior brother
    Once that warred on Ilion at his side;   220
Here spread forth vain hands to clasp the mother
    Dead, that sorrowing for his love's sake died.

14

Parted, though by narrowest of divisions,
    Clasp he might not, only might implore,
Sundered yet by bitterest of derisions,
    Son, and mother from the son she bore—
Here? But all dispeopled here of visions
    Lies, forlorn of shadows even, the shore.

15

All too sweet such men's Hellenic speech is,
    All too fain they lived of light to see,   230
Once to see the darkness of these beaches,
    Once to sing this Hades found of me
Ghostless, all its gulfs and creeks and reaches,
    Sky, and shore, and cloud, and waste, and sea.

IV

1

But aloft and afront of me faring
    Far forward as folk in a dream
That strive, between doubting and daring,
    Right on till the goal for them gleam,
Full forth till their goal on them lighten,
    The harbour where fain they would be,   240
What headlands there darken and brighten?
        What change in the sea?

2

What houses and woodlands that nestle
    Safe inland to lee of the hill
As it slopes from the headlands that wrestle

And succumb to the strong sea's will?
Truce is not, nor respite, nor pity,
   For the battle is waged not of hands
Where over the grave of a city
     The ghost of it stands.   250

3

Where the wings of the sea-wind slacken,
   Green lawns to the landward thrive,
Fields brighten and pine-woods blacken,
   And the heat in their heart is alive;
They blossom and warble and murmur,
   For the sense of their spirit is free:
But harder to shoreward and firmer
     The grasp of the sea.

4

Like ashes the low cliffs crumble,
   The banks drop down into dust,   260
The heights of the hills are made humble,
   As a reed's is the strength of their trust:
As a city's that armies environ,
   The strength of their stay is of sand:
But the grasp of the sea is as iron,
     Laid hard on the land.

5

A land that is thirstier than ruin;
   A sea that is hungrier than death;
Heaped hills that a tree never grew in;
   Wide sands where the wave draws breath;   270
All solace is here for the spirit
   That ever for ever may be
For the soul of thy son to inherit,
     My mother, my sea.

6

O delight of the headlands and beaches!
   O desire of the wind on the wold,
More glad than a man's when it reaches

That end which it sought from of old
And the palm of possession is dreary
   To the sense that in search of it sinned;   280
But nor satisfied ever nor weary
     Is ever the wind.

7

The delight that he takes but in living
   Is more than of all things that live:
For the world that has all things for giving
   Has nothing so goodly to give:
But more than delight his desire is,
   For the goal where his pinions would be
Is immortal as air or as fire is,
     Immense as the sea.   290

8

Though hence come the moan that he borrows
   From darkness and depth of the night,
Though hence be the spring of his sorrows,
   Hence too is the joy of his might;
The delight that his doom is for ever
   To seek and desire and rejoice,
And the sense that eternity never
     Shall silence his voice.

9

That satiety never may stifle
   Nor weariness ever estrange   300
Nor time be so strong as to rifle
   Nor change be so great as to change
His gift that renews in the giving,
   The joy that exalts him to be
Alone of all elements living
     The lord of the sea.

10

What is fire, that its flame should consume her?
   More fierce than all fires are her waves:
What is earth, that its gulfs should entomb her?

More deep are her own than their graves. 310
Life shrinks from his pinions that cover
   The darkness by thunders bedinned:
But she knows him, her lord and her lover
     The godhead of wind.

11

For a season his wings are about her,
   His breath on her lips for a space;
Such rapture he wins not without her
   In the width of his worldwide race.
Though the forests bow down, and the mountains
   Wax dark, and the tribes of them flee, 32
His delight is more deep in the fountains
     And springs of the sea.

12

There are those too of mortals that love him,
   There are souls that desire and require,
Be the glories of midnight above him
   Or beneath him the daysprings of fire:
And their hearts are as harps that approve him
   And praise him as chords of a lyre
That were fain with their music to move him
     To meet their desire 330

13

To descend through the darkness to grace them,
   Till darkness were lovelier than light:
To encompass and grasp and embrace them,
   Till their weakness were one with his might:
With the strength of his wings to caress them,
   With the blast of his breath to set free;
With the mouths of his thunders to bless them
     For sons of the sea.

14

For these have the toil and the guerdon
   That the wind has eternally: these 340
Have part in the boon and the burden

Of the sleepless unsatisfied breeze,
That finds not, but seeking rejoices
 That possession can work him no wrong:
And the voice at the heart of their voice is
  The sense of his song.

15

For the wind's is their doom and their blessing;
 To desire, and have always above
A possession beyond their possessing,
 A love beyond reach of their love.   350
Green earth has her sons and her daughters,
 And these have their guerdons; but we
Are the wind's and the sun's and the water's,
  Elect of the sea.

V

1

For the sea too seeks and rejoices,
 Gains and loses and gains,
And the joy of her heart's own choice is
 As ours, and as ours are her pains:
As the thoughts of our hearts are her voices,
 And as hers is the pulse of our veins.   360

2

Her fields that know not of dearth
 Nor lie for their fruit's sake fallow
Laugh large in the depth of their mirth:
 But inshore here in the shallow,
Embroiled with encumbrance of earth,
 Their skirts are turbid and yellow.

3

The grime of her greed is upon her,
 The sign of her deed is her soil;
As the earth's is her own dishonour,
 And corruption the crown of her toil: 370

She hath spoiled and devoured, and her honour
    Is this, to be shamed by her spoil.

4

But afar where pollution is none,
    Nor ensign of strife nor endeavour,
Where her heart and the sun's are one,
    And the soil of her sin comes never,
She is pure as the wind and the sun,
    And her sweetness endureth for ever.

            VI

1

Death, and change, and darkness everlasting
    Deaf, that hears not what the daystar saith,   380
Blind, past all remembrance and forecasting,
    Dead, past memory that it once drew breath;
These, above the washing tides and wasting,
    Reign, and rule this land of utter death.

2

Change of change, darkness of darkness, hidden,
    Very death of very death, begun
When none knows,—the knowledge is forbidden—
    Self-begotten, self-proceeding, one,
Born, not made—abhorred, unchained, unchidden,
    Night stands here defiant of the sun.   390

3

Change of change, and death of death begotten,
    Darkness born of darkness, one and three,
Ghostly godhead of a world forgotten,
    Crowned with heaven, enthroned on land and sea,
Here, where earth with dead men's bones is rotten,
    God of Time, thy likeness worships thee.

4

Lo, thy likeness of thy desolation,
    Shape and figure of thy might, O Lord,

Formless form, incarnate miscreation,
    Served of all things living and abhorred;   400
Earth herself is here thine incarnation,
    Time, of all things born on earth adored.

5

All that worship thee are fearful of thee;
    No man may not worship thee for fear:
Prayers nor curses prove not nor disprove thee,
    Move nor change thee with our change of cheer:
All at last, though all abhorred thee, love thee,
    God, the sceptre of whose throne is here.

6

Here thy throne and sceptre of thy station,
    Here the palace paven for thy feet;   410
Here thy sign from nation unto nation
    Passed as watchword for thy guards to greet,
Guards that go before thine exaltation,
    Ages, clothed with bitter years and sweet.

7

Here, where sharp the sea-bird shrills his ditty,
    Flickering flame-wise through the clear live calm,
Rose triumphal, crowning all a city,
    Roofs exalted once with prayer and psalm,
Built of holy hands for holy pity,
    Frank and fruitful as a sheltering palm.   420

8

Church and hospice wrought in faultless fashion,
    Hall and chancel bounteous and sublime,
Wide and sweet and glorious as compassion,
    Filled and thrilled with force of choral chime,
Filled with spirit of prayer and thrilled with passion,
    Hailed a God more merciful than Time.

9

Ah, less mighty, less than Time prevailing,
    Shrunk, expelled, made nothing at his nod,

Less than clouds across the sea-line sailing,
    Lies he, stricken by his master's rod.   430
'Where is man?' the cloister murmurs wailing;
    Back the mute shrine thunders—'Where is God?'

10

Here is all the end of all his glory—
    Dust, and grass, and barren silent stones.
Dead, like him, one hollow tower and hoary
    Naked in the sea-wind stands and moans,
Filled and thrilled with its perpetual story:
    Here, where earth is dense with dead men's bones.

11

Low and loud and long, a voice for ever,
    Sounds the wind's clear story like a song.   440
Tomb from tomb the waves devouring sever,
    Dust from dust as years relapse along;
Graves where men made sure to rest, and never
    Lie dismantled by the seasons' wrong.

12

Now displaced, devoured and desecrated,
    Now by Time's hands darkly disinterred,
These poor dead that sleeping here awaited
    Long the archangel's re-creating word,
Closed about with roofs and walls high-gated
    Till the blast of judgment should be heard,   450

13

Naked, shamed, cast out of consecration,
    Corpse and coffin, yea the very graves,
Scoffed at, scattered, shaken from their station,
    Spurned and scourged of wind and sea like slaves,
Desolate beyond man's desolation,
    Shrink and sink into the waste of waves.

14

Tombs, with bare white piteous bones protruded,
    Shroudless, down the loose collapsing banks,

Crumble, from their constant place detruded,
    That the sea devours and gives not thanks.   460
Graves where hope and prayer and sorrow brooded
    Gape and slide and perish, ranks on ranks.

15

Rows on rows and line by line they crumble,
    They that thought for all time through to be.
Scarce a stone whereon a child might stumble
    Breaks the grim field paced alone of me.
Earth, and man, and all their gods wax humble
    Here, where Time brings pasture to the sea.

VII

1

But afar on the headland exalted,
    But beyond in the curl of the bay,   470
From the depth of his dome deep-vaulted
    Our father is lord of the day.
Our father and lord that we follow,
    For deathless and ageless is he;
And his robe is the whole sky's hollow,
        His sandal the sea.

2

Where the horn of the headland is sharper,
    And her green floor glitters with fire,
The sea has the sun for a harper,
    The sun has the sea for a lyre.   480
The waves are a pavement of amber,
    By the feet of the sea-winds trod
To receive in a god's presence-chamber
        Our father, the God.

3

Time, haggard and changeful and hoary,
   Is master and God of the land:
But the air is fulfilled of the glory
   That is shed from our lord's right hand.
O father of all of us ever,
   All glory be only to thee   490
From heaven, that is void of thee never,
     And earth, and the sea.

4

O Sun, whereof all is beholden,
   Behold now the shadow of this death,
This place of the sepulchres, olden
   And emptied and vain as a breath.
The bloom of the bountiful heather
   Laughs broadly beyond in thy light
As dawn, with her glories to gather,
     At darkness and night.   500

5

Though the Gods of the night lie rotten
   And their honour be taken away
And the noise of their names forgotten,
   Thou, Lord, art God of the day.
Thou art father and saviour and spirit,
   O Sun, of the soul that is free
And hath grace of thy grace to inherit
     Thine earth and thy sea.

6

The hills and the sands and the beaches,
   The waters adrift and afar,   510
The banks and the creeks and the reaches,
   How glad of thee all these are!
The flowers, overflowing, overcrowded,
   Are drunk with the mad wind's mirth:
The delight of thy coming unclouded
     Makes music of earth.

7

I, last least voice of her voices,
   Give thanks that were mute in me long
To the soul in my soul that rejoices
   For the song that is over my song.   520
Time gives what he gains for the giving
. Or takes for his tribute of me;
My dreams to the wind everliving,
     My song to the sea.

from THE HEPTALOGIA

THE HIGHER PANTHEISM IN A NUTSHELL

One, who is not, we see: but one, whom we see not, is:
Surely this is not that: but that is assuredly this.

What, and wherefore, and whence? for under is over and under:
If thunder could be without lightning, lightning could be without thunder.

Doubt is faith in the main: but faith, on the whole, is doubt:
We cannot believe by proof: but could we believe without?

Why, and whither, and how? for barley and rye are not clover:
Neither are straight lines curves: yet over is under and over.

Two and two may be four: but four and four are not eight:
Fate and God may be twain: but God is the same thing as fate.   10

Ask a man what he thinks, and get from a man what he feels:
God, once caught in the fact, shows you a fair pair of heels.

Body and spirit are twins: God only knows which is which:
The soul squats down in the flesh, like a tinker drunk in a ditch.

More is the whole than a part: but half is more than the whole:
Clearly, the soul is the body: but is not the body the soul?

One and two are not one: but one and nothing is two:
Truth can hardly be false, if falsehood cannot be true.

Once the mastodon was: pterodactyls were common as cocks:
Then the mammoth was God: now is He a prize ox.   20

Parallels all things are: yet many of these are askew:
You are certainly I: but certainly I am not you.

Springs the rock from the plain, shoots the stream from the rock:
Cocks exist for the hen: but hens exist for the cock.

God, whom we see not, is: and God, who is not, we see:
Fiddle, we know, is diddle: and diddle, we take it, is dee.

THE POET AND THE WOODLOUSE

Said a poet to a woodlouse—'Thou art certainly my brother;
    I discern in thee the markings of the fingers of the Whole;
And I recognize, in spite of all the terrene smut and smother,
    In the colours shaded off thee, the suggestions of a soul.

'Yea,' the poet said, 'I smell thee by some passive divination,
    I am satisfied with insight of the measure of thine house;
What had happened I conjecture, in a blank and rhythmic passion,
    Had the æons thought of making thee a man, and me a louse.

'The broad lives of upper planets, their absorption and digestion,
    Food and famine, health and sickness, I can scrutinize and test;   10
Through a shiver of the senses comes a resonance of question,
    And by proof of balanced answer I decide that I am best.

'Man, the fleshly marvel, alway feels a certain kind of awe stick
    To the skirts of contemplation, cramped with nympholeptic weight:
Feels his faint sense charred and branded by the touch of solar caustic,
    On the forehead of his spirit feels the footprint of a Fate.'

'Notwithstanding which, O poet,' spake the woodlouse, very blandly,
    'I am likewise the created,—I the equipoise of thee;

I the particle, the atom, I behold on either hand lie
 The inane of measured ages that were embryos of me.   20

'I am fed with intimations, I am clothed with consequences,
 And the air I breathe is coloured with apocalyptic blush:
Ripest-budded odours blossom out of dim chaotic stenches,
 And the Soul plants spirit-lilies in sick leagues of human slush.

'I am thrilled half cosmically through by cryptophantic surgings,
 Till the rhythmic hills roar silent through a spongious kind of blee:
And earth's soul yawns disembowelled of her pancreatic organs,
 Like a madrepore if mesmerized, in rapt catalepsy.

'And I sacrifice, a Levite—and I palpitate, a poet;—
 Can I close dead ears against the rush and resonance of things? 30
Symbols in me breathe and flicker up the heights of the heroic;
 Earth's worst spawn, you said, and cursed me? look! approve me! I
  have wings.

'Ah, men's poets! men's conventions crust you round and swathe you
  mist-like,
 And the world's wheels grind your spirits down the dust ye overtrod:
We stand sinlessly stark-naked in effulgence of the Christlight,
 And our polecat chokes not cherubs; and our skunk smells sweet
  to God.

'For He grasps the pale Created by some thousand vital handles,
 Till a Godshine, bluely winnowed through the sieve of thunderstorms,
Shimmers up the non-existent round the churning feet of angels;
 And the atoms of that glory may be seraphs, being worms. 40

'Friends, your nature underlies us and your pulses overplay us;
 Ye, with social sores unbandaged, can ye sing right and steer wrong?
For the transient cosmic, rooted in imperishable chaos,
 Must be kneaded into drastics as material for a song.

'Eyes once purged from homebred vapours through humanitarian passion
 See that monochrome a despot through a democratic prism;
Hands that rip the soul up, reeking from divine evisceration,
 Not with priestlike oil anoint him, but a stronger-smelling chrism.

'Pass, O poet, retransfigured! God, the psychometric rhapsode,
    Fills with fiery rhythms the silence, stings the dark with stars that
        blink;   50
All eternities hang round him like an old man's clothes collapsèd,
    While he makes his mundane music—AND HE WILL NOT STOP,
        I THINK'

SONNET FOR A PICTURE

That nose is out of drawing. With a gasp,
    She pants upon the passionate lips that ache
    With the red drain of her own mouth, and make
A monochord of colour. Like an asp,
One lithe lock wriggles in his rutilant grasp.
    Her bosom is an oven of myrrh, to bake
    Love's white warm shewbread to a browner cake.
The lock his fingers clench has burst its hasp.
The legs are absolutely abominable.
    Ah! what keen overgust of wild-eyed woes
    Flags in that bosom, flushes in that nose?
Nay! Death sets riddles for desire to spell,
    Responsive. What red hem earth's passion sews,
But may be ravenously unripped in hell?

NEPHELIDIA

From the depth of the dreamy decline of the dawn through a notable
    nimbus of nebulous moonshine,
    Pallid and pink as the palm of the flag-flower that flickers with fear
      of the flies as they float,
Are they looks of our lovers that lustrously lean from a marvel of mystic
    miraculous moonshine,
    These that we feel in the blood of our blushes that thicken and
      threaten with throbs through the throat?
Thicken and thrill as a theatre thronged at appeal of an actor's appalled
    agitation,
    Fainter with fear of the fires of the future than pale with the promise
      of pride in the past;

Flushed with the famishing fullness of fever that reddens with radiance
 of rathe recreation,
  Gaunt as the ghastliest of glimpses that gleam through the gloom of
   the gloaming when ghosts go aghast?
Nay, for the nick of the tick of the time is a tremulous touch on the
 temples of terror,
  Strained as the sinews yet strenuous with strife of the dead who is
   dumb as the dust-heaps of death: 10
Surely no soul is it, sweet as the spasm of erotic emotional exquisite
 error,
  Bathed in the balms of beatified bliss, beatific itself by beatitude's
   breath.

Surely no spirit or sense of a soul that was soft to the spirit and soul of
 our senses
  Sweetens the stress of suspiring suspicion that sobs in the semblance
   and sound of a sigh;
Only this oracle opens Olympian, in mystical moods and triangular
 tenses—
  'Life is the lust of a lamp for the light that is dark till the dawn of the
   day when we die.'
Mild is the mirk and monotonous music of memory, melodiously mute as
 it may be,
  While the hope in the heart of a hero is bruised by the breach of men's
   rapiers, resigned to the rod;
Made meek as a mother whose bosom-beats bound with the bliss-bringing
 bulk of a balm-breathing baby,
  As they grope through the grave-yard of creeds, under skies growing
   green at a groan for the grimness of God.   20
Blank is the book of his bounty beholden of old, and its binding is
 blacker than bluer:
  Out of blue into black is the scheme of the skies, and their dews are
   the wine of the bloodshed of things;
Till the darkling desire of delight shall be free as a fawn that is freed from
 the fangs that pursue her,
  Till the heart-beats of hell shall be hushed by a hymn from the hunt
   that has harried the kennel of kings.

from TRISTRAM OF LYONESSE

PRELUDE

TRISTRAM AND ISEULT

Love, that is first and last of all things made,
The light that has the living world for shade,
The spirit that for temporal veil has on
The souls of all men woven in unison,
One fiery raiment with all lives inwrought
And lights of sunny and starry deed and thought,
And alway through new act and passion new
Shines the divine same body and beauty through,
The body spiritual of fire and light
That is to worldly noon as noon to night;   10
Love, that is flesh upon the spirit of man
And spirit within the flesh whence breath began;
Love, that keeps all the choir of lives in chime;
Love, that is blood within the veins of time;
That wrought the whole world without stroke of hand,
Shaping the breadth of sea, the length of land,
And with the pulse and motion of his breath
Through the great heart of the earth strikes life and death,
The sweet twain chords that make the sweet tune live
Through day and night of things alternative,   20
Through silence and through sound of stress and strife,
And ebb and flow of dying death and life;
Love that sounds loud or light in all men's ears,
Whence all men's eyes take fire from sparks of tears,
That binds on all men's feet or chains or wings;
Love, that is root and fruit of terrene things;
Love, that the whole world's waters shall not drown,
The whole world's fiery forces not burn down;
Love, that what time his own hands guard his head
The whole world's wrath and strength shall not strike dead;   30
Love, that if once his own hands make his grave
The whole world's pity and sorrow shall not save;
Love, that for very life shall not be sold,
Nor brought nor bound with iron nor with gold;

So strong that heaven, could love bid heaven farewell,
Would turn to fruitless and unflowering hell;
So sweet that hell, to hell could love be given,
Would turn to splendid and sonorous heaven;
Love that is fire within thee and light above,
And lives by grace of nothing but of love;   40
Through many and lovely thoughts and much desire
Led these twain to the life of tears and fire;
Through many and lovely days and much delight
Led these twain to the lifeless life of night.

　　So shine above dead chance and conquered change
The spherèd signs, and leave without their range
Doubt and desire, and hope with fear for wife,
Pale pains, and pleasures long worn out of life.
Yea, even the shadows of them spiritless,
Through the dim door of sleep that seem to press,   50
Forms without form, a piteous people and blind,
Men and no men, whose lamentable kind
The shadow of death and shadow of life compel
Through semblances of heaven and false-faced hell,
Through dreams of light and dreams of darkness tost
On waves innavigable, are these so lost?
Shapes that wax pale and shift in swift strange wise,
Void faces with unspeculative eyes,
Dim things that gaze and glare, dead mouths that move,
Featureless heads discrowned of hate and love,   60
Mockeries and masks of motion and mute breath,
Leavings of life, the superflux of death—
If these things and no more than these things be
Left when man ends or changes, who can see?
Or who can say with what more subtle sense
Their subtler natures taste in air less dense
A life less thick and palpable than ours,
Warmed with faint fires and sweetened with dead flowers
And measured by low music? how time fares
In that wan time-forgotten world of theirs,   70
Their pale poor world too deep for sun or star
To live in, where the eyes of Helen are,
And hers who made as God's own eyes to shine

The eyes that met them of the Florentine,
Wherein the godhead thence transfigured lit
All time for all men with the shadow of it?
Ah, and these too felt on them as God's grace
The pity and glory of this man's breathing face;
For these too, these my lovers, these my twain,
Saw Dante, saw God visible by pain,   80
With lips that thundered and with feet that trod
Before men's eyes incognisable God;
Saw love and wrath and light and night and fire
Live with one life and at one mouth respire,
And in one golden sound their whole soul heard
Sounding, one sweet immitigable word.
　　They have the night, who had like us the day;
We, whom day binds, shall have the night as they.
We, from the fetters of the light unbound,
Healed of our wound of living, shall sleep sound.   90
All gifts but one the jealous God may keep
From our soul's longing, one he cannot—sleep.
This, though he grudge all other grace to prayer,
This grace his closed hand cannot choose but spare.
This, though his ear be sealed to all that live,
Be it lightly given or lothly, God must give.
We, as the men whose name on earth is none,
We too shall surely pass out of the sun;
Out of the sound and eyeless light of things,
Wide as the stretch of life's time-wandering wings,   100
Wide as the naked world and shadowless,
And long-lived as the world's own weariness.
Us too, when all the fires of time are cold,
The heights shall hide us and the depths shall hold.
Us too, when all the tears of time are dry,
The night shall lighten from her tearless eye.
Blind is the day and eyeless all its light,
But the large unbewildered eye of night
Hath sense and speculation; and the sheer
Limitless length of lifeless life and clear,   110
The timeless space wherein the brief worlds move
Clothed with light life and fruitful with light love,
With hopes that threaten, and with fears that cease,

Past fear and hope, hath in it only peace.
　　Yet of these lives inlaid with hopes and fears,
Spun fine as fire and jewelled thick with tears,
These lives made out of loves that long since were,
Lives wrought as ours of earth and burning air,
Fugitive flame, and water of secret springs,
And clothed with joys and sorrows as with wings,　　　　　　120
Some yet are good, if aught be good, to save
Some while from washing wreck and wrecking wave.
Was such not theirs, the twain I take and give
Out of my life to make their dead life live
Some days of mine, and blow my living breath
Between dead lips forgotten even of death?
So many and many of old have given my twain
Love and live song and honey-hearted pain,
Whose root is sweetness and whose fruit is sweet,
So many and with such joy have tracked their feet,　　　　　130
What should I do to follow? yet I too,
I have the heart to follow, many or few
Be the feet gone before me; for the way,
Rose-red with remnant roses of the day
Westward, and eastward white with stars that break,
Between the green and foam is fair to take
For any sail the sea-wind steers for me
From morning into morning, sea to sea.

from A CENTURY OF ROUNDELS

'HAD I WIST'

Had I wist, when life was like a warm wind playing
Light and loud through sundawn and the dew's bright mist,
How the time should come for hearts to sigh in saying
　　　'Had I wist'—

Surely not the roses, laughing as they kissed,
Not the lovelier laugh of seas in sunshine swaying,
Should have lured my soul to look thereon and list.

Now the wind is like a soul cast out and praying
Vainly, prayers that pierce not ears when hearts resist:
Now mine own soul sighs, adrift as wind and straying,
    'Had I wist.'

PLUS INTRA

Soul within sense, immeasurable, obscure,
Insepulchred and deathless, through the dense
Deep elements may scarce be felt as pure
    Soul within sense.

From depth and height by measures left immense,
Through sound and shape and colour, comes the unsure
Vague utterance, fitful with supreme suspense.

All that may pass, and all that must endure,
Song speaks not, painting shows not: more intense
And keen than these, art wakes with music's lure
    Soul within sense.

THE ROUNDEL

A roundel is wrought as a ring or a starbright sphere,
With craft of delight and with cunning of sound unsought,
That the heart of the hearer may smile if to pleasure his ear
    A roundel is wrought.

Its jewel of music is carven of all or of aught—
Love, laughter, or mourning—remembrance of rapture or fear—
That fancy may fashion to hang in the ear of thought.

As a bird's quick song runs round, and the hearts in us hear
Pause answer to pause, and again the same strain caught,
So moves the device whence, round as a pearl or tear,
    A roundel is wrought.

A SINGING LESSON

Far-fetched and dear-bought, as the proverb rehearses,
Is good, or was held so, for ladies: but nought
In a song can be good if the turn of the verse is
    Far-fetched and dear-bought.

As the turn of a wave should it sound, and the thought
Ring smooth, and as light as the spray that disperses
Be the gleam of the words for the garb thereof wrought.

Let the soul in it shine through the sound as it pierces
Men's heart with possession of music unsought;
For the bounties of song are no jealous god's mercies,
    Far-fetched and dear-bought.

THREE FACES

1

VENTIMIGLIA

The sky and sea glared hard and bright and blank:
Down the one steep street, with slow steps firm and free,
A tall girl paced, with eyes too proud to thank
    The sky and sea.

One dead flat sapphire, void of wrath or glee,
Through bay on bay shone blind from bank to bank
The weary Mediterranean, drear to see.

More deep, more living, shone her eyes that drank
The breathless light and shed again on me,
Till pale before their splendour waned and shrank
    The sky and sea.

EROS

I

Eros, from rest in isles far-famed,
With rising Anthesterion rose,
And all Hellenic heights acclaimed
      Eros.

The sea one pearl, the shore one rose,
All round him all the flower-month flamed
And lightened, laughing off repose.

Earth's heart, sublime and unashamed,
Knew, even perchance as man's heart knows,
The thirst of all men's nature named
      Eros.

II

Eros, a fire of heart untamed,
A light of spirit in sense that glows,
Flamed heavenward still ere earth defamed
      Eros.

Nor fear nor shame durst curb or close
His golden godhead, marred and maimed,
Fast round with bonds that burnt and froze.

Ere evil faith struck blind and lamed
Love, pure as fire or flowers or snows,
Earth hailed as blameless and unblamed
      Eros.

III

Erose, with shafts by thousands aimed
At laughing lovers round in rows,
Fades from their sight whose tongues proclaimed
      Eros.

But higher than transient shapes or shows
The light of love in life inflamed
Springs, toward no goal that these disclose.

Above those heavens which passion claimed
Shines, veiled by change that ebbs and flows,
The soul in all things born or framed,
    Eros.

ON THE RUSSIAN PERSECUTION OF THE JEWS

O SON of man, by lying tongues adored,
  By slaughterous hands of slaves with feet red-shod
  In carnage deep as ever Christian trod
Profaned with prayer and sacrifice abhorred
And incense from the trembling tyrant's horde,
  Brute worshippers or wielders of the rod,
  Most murderous even of all that call thee God,
Most treacherous even that ever called thee Lord;
Face loved of little children long ago,
  Head hated of the priests and rulers then,
    If thou see this, or hear these hounds of thine
    Run ravening as the Gadarean swine,
Say, was not this thy Passion, to foreknow
  In death's worst hour the works of Christian men?

January 23, 1882.

JOHN FORD

Hew hard the marble from the mountain's heart
  Where hardest night holds fast in iron gloom
  Gems brighter than an April dawn in bloom,
That his Memnonian likeness thence may start
Revealed, whose hand with high funereal art
  Carved night, and chiselled shadow: be the tomb
  That speaks him famous graven with signs of doom
Intrenched inevitably in lines athwart,
As on some thunder-blasted Titan's brow
  His record of rebellion. Not the day
    Shall strike forth music from so stern a chord,
Touching this marble: darkness, none knows how,
  And stars impenetrable of midnight, may.
    So looms the likeness of thy soul, John Ford.

from A MIDSUMMER HOLIDAY

A SEA-MARK

Rains have left the sea-banks ill to climb:
Waveward sinks the loosening seaboard's floor:
Half the sliding cliffs are mire and slime.
Earth, a fruit rain-rotted to the core,
Drops dissolving down in flakes, that pour
Dense as gouts from eaves grown foul with grime.
One soul rock which years that scathe not score
Stands a sea-mark in the tides of time.

Time were even as even the rainiest clime,
Life were even as even this lapsing shore,
Might not aught outlive their trustless prime:
Vainly fear would wail or hope implore,
Vainly grief revile or love adore
Seasons clothed in sunshine, rain, or rime.
Now for me one comfort held in store
Stands a sea-mark in the tides of time.

Once, by fate's default or chance's crime,
Each apart, our burdens each we bore;
Heard, in monotones like bells that chime,
Chime the sounds of sorrows, float and soar
Joy's full carols, near or far before;
Heard not yet across the alternate rhyme
Time's tongue tell what sign set fast of yore
Stands a sea-mark in the tides of time.

Friend, the sign we knew not heretofore
Towers in sight here present and sublime.
Faith in faith established evermore
Stands a sea-mark in the tides of time.

IN SEPULCRETIS

Vidistis ipso rapere de rogo cœnam.—Catullus, LIX. 3.

To publish even one line of an author which he himself has not intended for the
public at large—especially letters which are addressed to private persons—is to
commit a despicable act of felony.—*Heine.*

I

It is not then enough that men who give
    The best gifts given of man to man should feel,
    Alive, a snake's head ever at their heel:
Small hurt the worms may do them while they live—
Such hurt as scorn for scorn's sake may forgive.
    But now, when death and fame have set one seal
    On tombs whereat Love, Grief, and Glory kneel,
Men sift all secrets, in their critic sieve,
Of graves wherein the dust of death might shrink
    To know what tongues defile the dead man's name
    With loathsome love, and praise that stings like shame.
Rest once was theirs, who had crossed the mortal brink:
    No rest, no reverence now: dull fools undress
    Death's holiest shrine, life's veriest nakedness.

II

A man was born, sang, suffered, loved, and died.
    Men scorned him living: let us praise him dead.
    His life was brief and bitter, gently led
And proudly, but with pure and blameless pride.
He wrought no wrong toward any; satisfied
    With love and labour, whence our souls are fed
    With largesse yet of living wine and bread.
Come, let us praise him: here is nought to hide.
Make bare the poor dead secrets of his heart,
    Strip the stark-naked soul, that all may peer,
    Spy, smirk, sniff, snap, snort, snivel, snarl, and sneer:
Let none so sad, let none so sacred part
    Lie still for pity, rest unstirred for shame,
    But all be scanned of all men. This is fame.

A SOLITUDE

Sea beyond sea, sand after sweep of sand,
    Here ivory smooth, here cloven and ridged with flow
    Of channelled waters soft as rain or snow,
Stretch their lone length at ease beneath the bland
Grey gleam of skies whose smile on wave and strand
    Shines weary like a man's who smiles to know
    That now no dream can mock his faith with show,
Nor cloud for him seem living sea or land.

Is there an end at all of all this waste,
These crumbling cliffs defeatured and defaced,
These ruinous heights of sea-sapped walls that slide
    Seaward with all their banks of bleak blown flowers
Glad yet of life, ere yet their hope subside
    Beneath the coil of dull dense waves and hours?

from POEMS AND BALLADS, THIRD SERIES

A REIVER'S NECK-VERSE

Some die singing, and some die swinging,
    And weel mot a' they be:
Some die playing, and some die praying,
    And I wot sae winna we, my dear,
    And I wot sae winna we.

Some die sailing, and some die wailing,
    And some die fair and free:
Some die flyting, and some die fighting,
    But I for a fause love's fee, my dear,
    But I for a fause love's fee.   10

Some die laughing, and some die quaffing,
    And some die high on tree:
Some die spinning, and some die sinning,
    But faggot and fire for ye, my dear,
    Faggot and fire for ye.

Some die weeping, and some die sleeping,
    And some die under sea:
Some die ganging, and some die hanging,
    And a twine of a tow for me, my dear,
    A twine of a tow for me.   20

THE WITCH-MOTHER

'O where will ye gang to and where will ye sleep.
    Against the night begins?'
'My bed is made wi' cauld sorrows,
    My sheets are lined wi' sins.

'And a sair grief sitting at my foot,
    And a sair grief at my head;
And dule to lay me my laigh pillows,
    And teen till I be dead.

'And the rain is sair upon my face,
    And sair upon my hair;   10
And the wind upon my weary mouth,
    That never may man kiss mair.

'And the snow upon my heavy lips,
    That never shall drink nor eat;
And shame to cledding, and woe to wedding,
    And pain to drink and meat.

'But woe be to my bairns' father,
    And ever ill fare he:
He has tane a braw bride hame to him,
    Cast out my bairns and me.'   20

from ASTROPHEL AND OTHER POEMS

A NYMPHOLEPT

Summer, and noon, and a splendour of silence, felt,
    Seen, and heard of the spirit within the sense.
Soft through the frondage the shades of the sunbeams melt,

Sharp through the foliage the shafts of them, keen and dense,
   Cleave, as discharged from the string of the God's bow, tense
As a war-steed's girth, and bright as a warrior's belt.
   Ah, why should an hour that is heaven for an hour pass hence?

I dare not sleep for delight of the perfect hour,
   Lest God be wroth that his gift should be scorned of man.
The face of the warm bright world is the face of a flower,   10
     The word of the wind and the leaves that the light winds fan
     As the word that quickened at first into flame, and ran,
Creative and subtle and fierce with invasive power,
     Through darkness and cloud, from the breath of the one God, Pan.

The perfume of earth possessed by the sun pervades
     The chaster air that he soothes but with sense of sleep.
Soft, imminent, strong as desire that prevails and fades,
     The passing noon that beholds not a cloudlet weep
     Imbues and impregnates life with delight more deep
Than dawn or sunset or moonrise on lawns or glades   20
     Can shed from the skies that receive it and may not keep.

The skies may hold not the splendour of sundown fast;
     It wanes into twilight as dawn dies down into day.
And the moon, triumphant when twilight is overpast,
     Takes pride but awhile in the hours of her stately sway.
     But the might of the moon, though the light of it pass away.
Leaves earth fulfilled of desires and of dreams that last;
     But if any there be that hath sense of them none can say.

For if any there be that hath sight of them, sense, or trust
     Made strong by the might of a vision, the strength of a dream,   30
His lips shall straiten and close as a dead man's must,
     His heart shall be sealed as the voice of a frost-bound stream.
     For the deep mid mystery of light and of heat that seem
To clasp and pierce dark earth, and enkindle dust,
     Shall a man's faith say what it is? or a man's guess deem?

Sleep lies not heavier on eyes that have watched all night
     Than hangs the heat of the noon on the hills and trees.
Why now should the haze not open, and yield to sight

A fairer secret than hope or than slumber sees?
I seek not heaven with submission of lips and knees,   40
With worship and prayer for a sign till it leap to light:
I gaze on the gods about me, and call on these.

I call on the gods hard by, the divine dim powers
    Whose likeness is here at hand, in the breathless air,
In the pulseless peace of the fervid and silent flowers,
    In the faint sweet speech of the waters that whisper there.
    Ah, what should darkness do in a world so fair?
The bent-grass heaves not, the couch-grass quails not or cowers;
    The wind's kiss frets not the rowan's or aspen's hair.

But the silence trembles with passion of sound suppressed,   50
    And the twilight quivers and yearns to the sunward, wrung
With love as with pain; and the wide wood's motionless breast
    Is thrilled with a dumb desire that would fain find tongue
    And palpitates, tongueless as she whom a mansnake stung,
Whose heart now heaves in the nightingale, never at rest
    Nor satiated ever with song till her last be sung.

Is it rapture or terror that circles me round, and invades
    Each vein of my life with hope—if it be not fear?
Each pulse that awakens my blood into rapture fades,
    Each pulse that subsides into dread of a strange thing near   60
    Requickens with sense of a terror less dread than dear.
Is peace not one with light in the deep green glades
    Where summer at noonday slumbers? Is peace not here?

The tall thin stems of the firs, and the roof sublime
    That screens from the sun the floor of the steep still wood,
Deep, silent, splendid, and perfect and calm as time,
    Stand fast as ever in sight of the night they stood,
    When night gave all that moonlight and dewfall could.
The dense ferns deepen, the moss glows warm as the thyme:
    The wild heath quivers about me: the world is good.   70

Is it Pan's breath, fierce in the tremulous maidenhair,
    That bids fear creep as a snake through the woodlands, felt
In the leaves that it stirs not yet, in the mute bright air,

In the stress of the sun? For here has the great God dwelt:
For hence were the shafts of his love or his anger dealt.
For here has his wrath been fierce as his love was fair,
    When each was as fire to the darkness its breath bade melt.

Is it love, is it dread, that enkindles the trembling noon,
.   That yearns, reluctant in rapture that fear has fed,
As man for woman, as woman for man? Full soon,   80
    If I live, and the life that may look on him drop not dead,
    Shall the ear that hears not a leaf quake hear his tread,
The sense that knows not the sound of the deep day's tune
    Receive the God, be it love that he brings or dread.

The naked noon is upon me: the fierce dumb spell,
    The fearful charm of the strong sun's imminent might,
Unmerciful, steadfast, deeper than seas that swell,
    Pervades, invades, appals me with loveless light,
    With harsher awe than breathes in the breath of night.
Have mercy, God who art all! For I know thee well,   90
    How sharp is thine eye to lighten, thine hand to smite.

The whole wood feels thee, the whole air fears thee: but fear
    So deep, so dim, so sacred, is wellnigh sweet.
For the light that hangs and broods on the woodlands here,
    Intense, invasive, intolerant, imperious, and meet
    To lighten the works of thine hands and the ways of thy feet,
Is hot with the fire of the breath of thy life, and dear
    As hope that shrivels or shrinks not for frost or heat.

Thee, thee the supreme dim godhead, approved afar,
    Perceived of the soul and conceived of the sense of man,   100
We scarce dare love, and we dare not fear: the star
    We call the sun, that lit us when life began
    To brood on the world that is thine by his grace for a span,
Conceals and reveals in the semblance of things that are
    Thine immanent presence, the pulse of thy heart's life, Pan.

The fierce mid noon that wakens and warms the snake
    Conceals thy mercy, reveals thy wrath: and again
The dew-bright hour that assuages the twilight brake

Conceals thy wrath and reveals thy mercy: then
  Thou art fearful only for evil souls of men   110
That feel with nightfall the serpent within them wake,
  And hate the holy darkness on glade and glen.

Yea, then we know not and dream not if ill things be,
. Or if aught of the work of the wrong of the world be thine.
We hear not the footfall of terror that treads the sea,
  We hear not the moan of winds that assail the pine:
   We see not if shipwreck reign in the storm's dim shrine;
If death do service and doom bear witness to thee
  We see not,—know not 'if blood for thy lips be wine.

But in all things evil and fearful that fear may scan,   120
  As in all things good, as in all things fair that fall,
We know thee present and latent, the lord of man;
  In the murmuring of doves, in the clamouring of winds that call
  And wolves that howl for their prey; in the midnight's pall,
In the naked and nymph-like feet of the dawn, O Pan,
  And in each life living, O thou the God who art all.

Smiling and singing, wailing and wringing of hands,
  Laughing and weeping, watching and sleeping, still
Proclaim but and prove but thee, as the shifted sands
  Speak forth and show but the strength of the sea's wild will   130
  That sifts and grinds them as grain in the storm-wind's mill.
In thee is the doom that falls and the doom that stands:
  The tempests utter thy word, and the stars fulfil.

Where Etna shudders with passion and pain volcanic
  That rend her heart as with anguish that rends a man's,
Where Typho labours, and finds not his thews Titanic,
  In breathless torment that ever the flame's breath fans,
  Men felt and feared thee of old, whose pastoral clans
Were given to the charge of thy keeping; and soundless panic
  Held fast the woodland whose depths and whose heights were Pan's.
                         [140

And here, though fear be less than delight, and awe
  Be one with desire and with worship of earth and thee,
So mild seems now thy secret and speechless law,

So fair and fearless and faithful and godlike she,
   So soft the spell of thy whisper on stream and sea,
Yet man should fear lest he see what of old men saw
   And withered: yet shall I quail if thy breath smite me.

Lord God of life and of light and of all things fair,
   Lord God of ravin and ruin and all things dim,
Death seals up life, and darkness the sunbright air,   150
   And the stars that watch blind earth in the deep night swim
   Laugh, saying, 'What God is your God, that ye call on him?
What is man, that the God who is guide of our way should care
   If day for a man be golden, or night be grim?'

But thou, dost thou hear? Stars too but abide for a span,
   Gods too but endure for a season; but thou, if thou be
God, more than shadows conceived and adored of man,
   Kind Gods and fierce, that bound him or made him free,
   The skies that scorn us are less in thy sight than we,
Whose souls have strength to conceive and perceive thee, Pan,   160
   With sense more subtle than senses that hear and see.

Yet may not it say, though it seek thee and think to find
   One soul of sense in the fire and the frost-bound clod,
What heart is this, what spirit alive or blind,
   That moves thee: only we know that the ways we trod
   We tread, with hands unguided, with feet unshod,
With eyes unlightened; and yet, if with steadfast mind,
   Perchance may we find thee and know thee at last for God.

Yet then should God be dark as the dawn is bright,
   And bright as the night is dark on the world—no more.   170
Light slays not darkness, and darkness absorbs not light;
   And the labour of evil and good from the years of yore
   Is even as the labour of waves on a sunless shore.
And he who is first and last, who is depth and height,
   Keeps silence now, as the sun when the woods wax hoar.

The dark dumb godhead innate in the fair world's life
   Imbues the rapture of dawn and of noon with dread,
Infects the peace of the star-shod night with strife,

Informs with terror the sorrow that guards the dead.
No service of bended knee or of humbled head   180
May soothe or subdue the God who has change to wife:
And life with death is as morning with evening wed.

And yet, if the light and the life in the light that here
Seem soft and splendid and fervid as sleep may seem
Be more than the shine of a smile or the flash of a tear,
Sleep, change, and death are less than a spell-struck dream,
And fear than the fall of a leaf on a starlit stream.
And yet, if the hope that hath said it absorb not fear,
What helps it man that the stars and the waters gleam?

What helps it man, that the noon be indeed intense,   190
The night be indeed worth worship? Fear and pain
Were lords and masters yet of the secret sense,
Which now dares deem not that light is as darkness, fain
Though dark dreams be to declare it, crying in vain.
For whence, thou God of the light and the darkness, whence
Dawns now this vision that bids not the sunbeams wane?

What light, what shadow, diviner than dawn or night,
Draws near, makes pause, and again—or I dream—draws near?
More soft than shadow, more strong than the strong sun's light,
More pure than moonbeams—yea, but the rays run sheer   200
As fire from the sun through the dusk of the pinewood, clear
And constant; yea, but the shadow itself is bright
That the light clothes round with love that is one with fear.

Above and behind it the noon and the woodland lie,
Terrible, radiant with mystery, superb and subdued,
Triumphant in silence; and hardly the sacred sky
Seems free from the tyrannous weight of the dumb fierce mood
Which rules as with fire and invasion of beams that brood
The breathless rapture of earth till its hour pass by
And leave her spirit released and her peace renewed.   210

I sleep not: never in sleep has a man beholden
This. From the shadow that trembles and yearns with light
Suppressed and elate and reluctant—obscure and golden

As water kindled with presage of dawn or night—
    A form, a face, a wonder to sense and sight,
Grows great as the moon through the month; and her eyes embolden
    Fear, till it change to desire, and desire to delight.

I sleep not: sleep would die of a dream so strange;
    A dream so sweet would die as a rainbow dies,
As a sunbow laughs and is lost on the waves that range   220
    And reck not of light that flickers or spray that flies.
    But the sun withdraws not, the woodland shrinks not or sighs,
No sweet thing sickens with sense or with fear of change;
    Light wounds not, darkness blinds not, my steadfast eyes.

Only the soul in my sense that receives the soul
    Whence now my spirit is kindled with breathless bliss
Knows well if the light that wounds it with love makes whole,
    If hopes that carol be louder than fears that hiss,
    If truth be spoken of flowers and of waves that kiss,
Of clouds and stars that contend for a sunbright goal.   230
    And yet may I dream that I dream not indeed of this?

An earth-born dreamer, constrained by the bonds of birth,
    Held fast by the flesh, compelled by his veins that beat
And kindle to rapture or wrath, to desire or to mirth,
    May hear not surely the fall of immortal feet,
    May feel not surely if heaven upon earth be sweet;
And here is my sense fulfilled of the joys of earth,
    Light, silence, bloom, shade, murmur of leaves that meet.

Bloom, fervour, and perfume of grasses and flowers aglow,
    Breathe and brighten about me: the darkness gleams,   240
The sweet light shivers and laughs on the slopes below,
    Made soft by leaves that lighten and change like dreams;
    The silence thrills with the whisper of secret streams
That well from the heart of the woodland: these I know:
    Earth bore them, heaven sustained them with showers and beams.

I lean my face to the heather, and drink the sun
    Whose flame-lit odour satiates the flowers: mine eyes
Close, and the goal of delight and of life is one:

No more I crave of earth or her kindred skies.
    No more? But the joy that springs from them smiles and flies: 250
The sweet work wrought of them surely, the good work done,
    If the mind and the face of the season be loveless, dies.

Thee, therefore, thee would I come to, cleave to, cling,
    If haply thy heart be kind and thy gifts be good,
Unknown sweet spirit, whose vesture is soft in spring,
    In summer splendid, in autumn pale as the wood
    That shudders and wanes and shrinks as a shamed thing should,
In winter bright as the mail of a war-worn king
    Who stands where foes fled far from the face of him stood.

My spirit or thine is it, breath of thy life or of mine,   260
    Which fills my sense with a rapture that casts out fear?
Pan's dim frown wanes, and his wild eyes brighten as thine,
    Transformed as night or as day by the kindling year.
    Earth-born, or mine eye were withered that sees, mine ear
That hears were stricken to death by the sense divine,
    Earth-born I know thee: but heaven is about me here.

The terror that whispers in darkness and flames in light,
    The doubt that speaks in the silence of earth and sea,
The sense, more fearful at noon than in midmost night,
    Of wrath scarce hushed and of imminent ill to be,   270
    Where are they? Heaven is as earth, and as heaven to me
Earth: for the shadows that sundered them here take flight;
    And nought is all, as am I, but a dream of thee.

A SWIMMER'S DREAM
November 4, 1889

Somno mollior unda

I

Dawn is dim on the dark soft water,
    Soft and passionate, dark and sweet.
Love's own self was the deep sea's daughter,
    Fair and flawless from face to feet,

Hailed of all when the world was golden,
Loved of lovers whose names beholden
Thrill men's eyes as with light of olden
　　Days more glad than their flight was fleet.

So they sang: but for men that love her,
　　Souls that hear not her word in vain,
Earth beside her and heaven above her
　　Seem but shadows that wax and wane.
Softer than sleep's are the sea's caresses,
Kinder than love's that betrays and blesses,
Blither than spring's when her flowerful tresses
　　Shake forth sunlight and shine with rain.

All the strength of the waves that perish
　　Swells beneath me and laughs and sighs,
Sighs for love of the life they cherish,
　　Laughs to know that it lives and dies,
Dies for joy of its life, and lives
Thrilled with joy that its brief death gives—
Death whose laugh or whose breath forgives
　　Change that bids it subside and rise.

II
Hard and heavy, remote but nearing,
　　Sunless hangs the severe sky's weight,
Cloud on cloud, though the wind be veering
　　Heaped on high to the sundawn's gate.
Dawn and even and noon are one,
Veiled with vapour and void of sun;
Nought in sight or in fancied hearing
　　Now less mighty than time or fate.

The grey sky gleams and the grey seas glimmer,
　　Pale and sweet as a dream's delight,
As a dream's where darkness and light seem dimmer,
　　Touched by dawn or subdued by night.
The dark wind, stern and sublime and sad,
Swings the rollers to westward, clad
With lustrous shadow that lures the swimmer,
　　Lures and lulls him with dreams of light.

10

20

30

40

Light, and sleep, and delight, and wonder,
   Change, and rest, and a charm of cloud,
Fill the world of the skies whereunder
   Heaves and quivers and pants aloud
All the world of the waters, hoary
Now, but clothed with its own live glory,
That mates the lightning and mocks the thunder
   With light more living and word more proud.

   III

Far off westward, whither sets the sounding strife,
   Strife more sweet than peace, of shoreless waves whose glee   50
   Scorns the shore and loves the wind that leaves them free,
Strange as sleep and pale as death and fair as life,
   Shifts the moonlight-coloured sunshine on the sea.

Toward the sunset's goal the sunless waters crowd,
   Fast as autumn's days toward winter: yet it seems
   Here that autumn wanes not, here that woods and streams
Lose not heart and change not likeness, chilled and bowed,
   Warped and wrinkled: here the days are fair as dreams.

   IV

O russet-robed November,
   What ails thee so to smile?   60
Chill August, pale September,
   Endured a woful while,
And fell as falls an ember
   From forth a flameless pile:
But golden-girt November
   Bids all she looks on smile.

The lustrous foliage, waning
   As wanes the morning moon,
Here falling, here refraining,
   Outbraves the pride of June   70
With statelier semblance, feigning
   No fear lest death be soon:
As though the woods thus waning
   Should wax to meet the moon.

As though, when fields lie stricken
   By grey December's breath,
These lordlier growths that sicken
   And die for fear of death
Should feel the sense requicken
   That hears what springtide saith
And thrills for love, spring-stricken
   And pierced with April's breath.

                                               80

The keen white-winged north-easter
   That stings and spurs thy sea
Doth yet but feed and feast her
   With glowing sense of glee:
Calm chained her, storm released her,
   And storm's glad voice was he:
South-wester or north-easter,
   Thy winds rejoice the sea.

                                               90

     V
A dream, a dream is it all—the season,
   The sky, the water, the wind, the shore?
A day-born dream of divine unreason,
   A marvel moulded of sleep—no more?
For the cloudlike wave that my limbs while cleaving
Feel as in slumber beneath them heaving
Soothes the sense as to slumber, leaving
   Sense of nought that was known of yore.

A purer passion, a lordlier leisure,
   A peace more happy than lives on land,
Fulfils with pulse of diviner pleasure
   The dreaming head and the steering hand.
I lean my cheek to the cold grey pillow,
The deep soft swell of the full broad billow,
And close mine eyes for delight past measure,
   And wish the wheel of the world would stand.

                                           100

The wild-winged hour that we fain would capture
   Falls as from heaven that its light feet clomb,
So brief, so soft, and so full the rapture

Was felt that soothed me with sense of home.   120
To sleep, to swim, and to dream, for ever—
Such joy the vision of man saw never;
For here too soon will a dark day sever
    The sea-bird's wing from the sea-wave's foam.

A dream, and more than a dream, and dimmer
    At once and brighter than dreams that flee,
The moment's joy of the seaward swimmer
    Abides, remembered as truth may be.
Not all the joy and not all the glory
Must fade as leaves when the woods wax hoary;   130
For there the downs and the sea-banks glimmer,
    And here to south of them swells the sea.

THE PALACE OF PAN

Inscribed To My Mother

September, all glorious with gold, as a king
    In the radiance of triumph attired,
Outlightening the summer, outsweetening the spring,
Broods wide on the woodlands with limitless wing,
    A presence of all men desired.

Far eastward and westward the sun-coloured lands
    Smile warm as the light on them smiles;
And statelier than temples upbuilded with hands,
Tall column by column, the sanctuary stands
    Of the pine-forest's infinite aisles.   10

Mute worship, too fervent for praise or for prayer,
    Possesses the spirit with peace,
Fulfilled with the breath of the luminous air,
The fragrance, the silence, the shadows as fair
    As the rays that recede or increase.

Ridged pillars that redden aloft and aloof,
    With never a branch for a nest,
Sustain the sublime indivisible roof,

To the storm and the sun in his majesty proof,
    And awful as waters at rest.   20

Man's hand hath not measured the height of them; thought
    May measure not, awe may not know;
In its shadow the woofs of the woodland are wrought;
As a bird is the sun in the toils of them caught,
    And the flakes of it scattered as snow.

As the shreds of a plumage of gold on the ground
    The sun-flakes by multitudes lie,
Shed loose as the petals of roses discrowned
On the floors of the forest engilt and embrowned
    And reddened afar and anigh.   30

Dim centuries with darkling inscrutable hands
    Have reared and secluded the shrine
For gods that we know not, and kindled as brands
On the altar the years that are dust, and their sands
    Time's glass has forgotten for sign.

A temple whose transepts are measured by miles,
    Whose chancel has morning for priest,
Whose floor-work the foot of no spoiler defiles,
Whose musical silence no music beguiles,
    No festivals limit its feast.   40

The noon's ministration, the night's and the dawn's,
    Conceals not, reveals not for man,
On the slopes of the herbless and blossomless lawns,
Some track of a nymph's or some trail of a faun's
    To the place of the slumber of Pan.

Thought, kindled and quickened by worship and wonder
    To rapture too sacred for fear
On the ways that unite or divide them in sunder,
Alone may discern if about them or under
    Be token or trace of him here.   50

With passionate awe that is deeper than panic
   The spirit subdued and unshaken
Takes heed of the godhead terrene and Titanic
Whose footfall is felt on the breach of volcanic
   Sharp steeps that their fire has forsaken.

By a spell more serene than the dim necromantic
   Dead charms of the past and the night,
Or the terror that lurked in the noon to make frantic
Where Etna takes shape from the limbs of gigantic
   Dead gods disanointed of might,   60

The spirit made one with the spirit whose breath
   Makes noon in the woodland sublime
Abides as entranced in a presence that saith
Things loftier than life and serener than death,
   Triumphant and silent as time.

Pine Ridge: September 1893.

from A CHANNEL PASSAGE

THE LAKE OF GAUBE

The sun is lord and god, sublime, serene,
   And sovereign on the mountains: earth and air
Lie prone in passion, blind with bliss unseen
   By force of sight and might of rapture, fair
   As dreams that die and know not what they were.
The lawns, the gorges, and the peaks, are one
Glad glory, thrilled with sense of unison
In strong compulsive silence of the sun.

Flowers dense and keen as midnight stars aflame
   And living things of light like flames in flower   10
That glance and flash as though no hand might tame
   Lightnings whose life outshone their stormlit hour
   And played and laughed on earth, with all their power
Gone, and with all their joy of life made long
And harmless as the lightning life of song,
Shine sweet like stars when darkness feels them strong.

The deep mild purple flaked with moonbright gold
   That makes the scales seem flowers of hardened light,
The flamelike tongue, the feet that noon leaves cold,
   The kindly trust in man, when once the sight   20
   Grew less than strange, and faith bade fear take flight,
Outlive the little harmless life that shone
And gladdened eyes that loved it, and was gone
Ere love might fear that fear had looked thereon.

Fear held the bright thing hateful, even as fear,
   Whose name is one with hate and horror, saith
That heaven, the dark deep heaven of water near,
   Is deadly deep as hell and dark as death.
   The rapturous plunge that quickens blood and breath
With pause more sweet than passion, ere they strive   30
To raise again the limbs that yet would dive
Deeper, should there have slain the soul alive.

As the bright salamander in fire of the noonshine exults and is glad of
     his day,
The spirit that quickens my body rejoices to pass from the sunlight
     away,
To pass from the glow of the mountainous flowerage, the high
     multitudinous bloom,
Far down through the fathomless night of the water, the gladness of
     silence and gloom.
Death-dark and delicious as death in the dream of a lover and dreamer
     may be,
It clasps and encompasses body and soul with delight to be living and
     free:
Free utterly now, though the freedom endure but the space of a perilous
     breath,
And living, though girdled about with the darkness and coldness and
     strangeness of death: 40
Each limb and each pulse of the body rejoicing, each nerve of the spirit
     at rest,
All sense of the soul's life rapture, a passionate peace in its blindness
     blest.
So plunges the downward swimmer, embraced of the water unfathomed
     of man,

The darkness unplummeted, icier than seas in midwinter, for blessing
    or ban;
And swiftly and sweetly, when strength and breath fall short, and the
    dive is done,
Shoots up as a shaft from the dark depth shot, sped straight into sight
    of the sun;
And sheer through the snow-soft water, more dark than the roof of the
    pines above,
Strikes forth, and is glad as a bird whose flight is impelled and sustained
    of love.
As a sea-mew's love of the sea-wind breasted and ridden for rapture's
    sake
Is the love of his body and soul for the darkling delight of the soundless
    lake: 50
As the silent speed of a dream too living to live for a thought's space
    more
Is the flight of his limbs through the still strong chill of the darkness
    from shore to shore.
Might life be as this is and death be as life that casts off time as a robe,
The likeness of infinite heaven were a symbol revealed of the lake of
    Gaube.

Whose thought has fathomed and measured
    The darkness of life and of death,
The secret within them treasured,
    The spirit that is not breath?
Whose vision has yet beholden
    The splendour of death and of life?   60
Though sunset as dawn be golden,
    Is the word of them peace, not strife?
Deep silence answers: the glory
    We dream of may be but a dream,
And the sun of the soul wax hoary
    As ashes that show not a gleam.
But well shall it be with us ever
    Who drive through the darkness here,
If the soul that we live by never,
    For aught that a lie saith, fear.   70

from **POSTHUMOUS POEMS**

DISGUST

A Dramatic Monologue

A woman and her husband, having been converted from free thought to Calvinism, and being utterly miserable in consequence, resolve to end themselves by poison. The man dies, but the woman is rescued by application of the stomach-pump.

A.C.S.

I

Pills? talk to me of your pills? Well, that, I must say, is cool.
Can't bring my old man round? he was always a stubborn old fool.
If I hadn't taken precautions—a warning to all that wive—
He might not have been dead, and I might not have been alive.

II

You would like to know, if I please, how it was that our troubles began?
You see, we were brought up Agnostics, I and my poor old man.
And we got some idea of selection and evolution, you know—
Professor Huxley's doing—where does he expect to go!

III

Well, then came trouble on trouble on trouble—I may say, a peck—
And his cousin was wanted one day on the charge of forging a
     cheque—   10
And his puppy died of the mange—my parrot choked on its perch.
This was the consequence was it, of not going weekly to church?

IV

So we felt that the best if not only thing that remained to be done
On an earth everlastingly moving about a perpetual sun,
Where worms breed worms to be eaten of worms that have eaten their
     betters—
And reviewers are barely civil—and people get spiteful letters—
And a famous man is forgot ere the minute hand can tick nine—
Was to send in our P.P.C., and purchase a packet of strychnine.

V

Nay—but first we thought it was rational—only fair—
To give both parties a hearing—and went to the meeting-house
     there,   20
At the curve of the street that runs from the Stag to the old Blue Lion.
'Little Zion' they call it—a deal more 'little' than 'Zion'.

VI

And the preacher preached from the text, 'Come out of her.' Hadn't
    we come?
And we thought of the shepherd in Pickwick—and fancied a flavour
    of rum
Balmily borne on the wind of his words—and my man said, 'Well,
Let's get out of this, my dear—for his text has a brimstone smell.'

VII

So we went, O God, out of chapel—and gazed, ah God, at the sea.
And I said nothing to him. And he said nothing to me.

VIII

And there, you see was an end of it all. It was obvious, in fact,
That, whether or not you believe in the doctrine taught in a tract,   30
Life was not in the least worth living. Because, don't you see?
Nothing that can't be, can, and what must be must. Q.E.D.
And the infinitesimal sources of Infinite Unideality
Curve in to the central abyss of a sort of a queer Personality
Whose refraction is felt in the nebulæ strewn in the pathway of Mars
Like the parings of nails Æonian—clippings and snippings of stars—
Shavings of suns that revolve and evolve and involve and at times
Give a sweet astronomical twang to remarkably hobbling rhymes.

IX

And the sea curved in with a moan—and we thought how once—before
We fell out with those atheist lecturers—once, ah, once and no more,   40
We read together, while midnight blazed like the Yankee flag,
A reverend gentleman's work—the Conversion of Colonel Quagg.
And out of its pages we gathered this lesson of doctrine pure—
Zephaniah Stockdolloger's gospel—a word that deserves to endure
Infinite millions on millions of infinite Æons to come—
'Vocation,' says he, 'is vocation, and duty duty. Some.'

X

And duty, said I, distinctly points out—and vocation, said he,
Demands as distinctly—that I should kill you, and that you should
    kill me.
The reason is obvious—we cannot exist without creeds—who can?
So we went to the chemist's—a highly respectable church-going man— 50

And bought two packets of poison. You wouldn't have done so?—Wait.
It's evident, Providence is not with you, ma'am, the same thing as Fate.
Unconscious cerebration educes God from a fog,
But spell God backwards, what then? Give it up? the answer is, dog.
(I don't exactly see how this last verse is to scan,
But that's a consideration I leave to the secular man.)

XI

I meant of course to go with him—as far as I pleased—but first
To see how my old man liked it—I thought perhaps he might burst.
I didn't wish it—but still it's a blessed release for a wife—
And he saw that I thought so—and grinned in derision—and threatened
    my life   60
If I made wry faces—and so I took just a sip—and he—
Well—you know how it ended—he didn't get over me.

XII

Terrible, isn't it? Still, on reflection, it might have been worse.
He might have been the unhappy survivor, and followed my hearse.
'Never do it again?' Why certainly not. You don't
Suppose I should think of it, surely? But anyhow—there—I won't.

NOTES

from ROSAMOND. The opening scene in the maze at Woodstock. Rosamond Clifford, mistress of Henry II and hated by Queen Eleanor, describes the dangers of her position to her companion Constance.

from ATALANTA. S. prefaces the work with the following argument.

The argument

Althaea, daughter of Thestius and Eurythemis, queen of Calydon, being with child of Meleager her first-born son, dreamed that she brought forth a brand burning; and upon his birth came the three Fates and prophesied of him three things, namely these; that he should have great strength of his hands, and good fortune in this life, and that he should live no longer when the brand then in the fire were consumed: wherefore his mother plucked it forth and kept it by her. And the child being a man grown sailed with Jason after the fleece of gold, and won himself great praise of all men living; and when the tribes of the north and west made war upon Aetolia, he fought against their army and scattered it. But Artemis, having at the first stirred up these tribes to war against Oeneus king of Calydon, because he had offered sacrifice to all the gods saving her alone, but her he had forgotten to honour, was yet more wroth because of the destruction of this army, and sent upon the land of Calydon a wild boar which slew many and wasted all their increase, but him could none slay, and many went against him and perished. Then were all the chief men of Greece gathered together, and among them Atalanta daughter of Iasius the Arcadian, a virgin; for whose sake Artemis let slay the boar, seeing she favoured the maiden greatly; and Meleager having despatched it gave the spoil thereof to Atalanta, as one beyond measure enamoured of her; but the brethren of Althaea his mother, Toxeus and Plexippus, with such others as misliked that she only should bear off the praise whereas many had borne the labour, laid wait for her to take away her spoil; but Meleager fought against them and slew them: whom when Althaea their sister beheld and knew to be slain of her son, she waxed for wrath and sorrow like as one mad, and taking the brand whereby the measure of her son's life was meted to him, she cast it upon a fire; and with wasting thereof his life likewise wasted away, that being brought back to his father's house he died in a brief space; and his mother also endured not long after for very sorrow; and this was his end, and the end of that hunting.

2. *mother of months*: Artemis, invoked at the poem's opening as mistress also of chastity and hunting, and of the dead.

6. *Itylus*: killed by his mother Procne and fed to her husband Tereus, king of Thrace, to avenge his rape of Philomela, sister to Procne. Philomela

lived in exile with her tongue cut out,but recorded Tereus' treachery in a tapestry sent to her sister. Philomela was metamorphosed into a nightingale, Procne into a swallow, and Terreus into a hoopoe. The legend is one of Swinburne's favourites.

41.   *Pan . . . Bacchus:* respectively the goat-god and the god of religious ecstasy (Dionysus), presented here as diurnal and nocturnal expressions of the life-force.

44.   *Maenad . . . Bassarid:* female followers of Dionysus. Their names betoken frenzy and being clad in fox-skin, a condition and symbol of union with nature.

49.   *Bacchanal:* also maenadic, wreathed in ivy sacred to Bacchus.

57.   Althaea has just reviewed the circumstances of Meleager's birth and resolved to ready him for the hunt.

105.   Meleager describes his experience with Jason and the Argonauts in their quest for the Golden Fleece.

115.   *Nereids:*   sea-nymphs, daughters of Nereus, king of the Mediterranean.

121.   *Symplegades:*   clashing rocks through which the Argonauts pass into the Hellespont after the rocks have claimed the dove released by Jason.

135.   *Euxine:* the Black Sea.

138.   *Medea:*   'the cunning one', the Colchian princess who betrays her family for love of Jason.

140.   *this one:* Atalanta.

144.   the chorus comments on the quarrelling that precedes the commencement of the hunt.

183.   *the weeping Seven:*   the Pleiades, daughters of Atlas, form a constellation that rises in May and sets in November, and is associated with showers and autumn storms.

209.   *the draught that quickeneth:* conferring mortality, unlike nectar, the elixir of the gods.

215.   *the fates that spun:* strictly speaking, of the three Fates (*Moirai*), Klotho spins the thread of life, apportioned by Lachesis, that will eventually be severed by Atropos.

216.   *The lips that made us:* S. seems to be thinking of gods breathing life into man. For the breath of life, see e.g. Aeschylus, *Persae* 507.

261ff. the description of the mysterious genesis of Fate is true to the earliest Greek sources, while the catalogue of relationships and attributes suggests the movement from unitary moira to the three moirai responsible for birth, life, and death. Fate remains distinct from Death itself (*thanatos*), as in Hesiod et al.

from CHASTELARD. Act one, scene two. Mary Queen of Scots has just given the besotted Chastelard 'stuff for riddles'. He will be discovered in her chamber and executed.

17. *Corrichie:* In Act Two, scene one, the Queen tells Chastelard of the battle near Aberdeen in 1562 where her forces, led by Moray, quashed an abortive Catholic uprising led by George Gordon, 4th Earl of Huntly.

from POEMS AND BALLADS, FIRST SERIES.

A BALLAD OF LIFE: in 1876 S. requested that an epigraph be added, 'In Honorem D. Lucretiae Estensis Borgiae,' one of his favourite femmes fatales.

LAUS VENERIS: 'In Praise of Venus': S. wrote a bogus Renaissance French account of the Tannhaüser legend to precede the poem:

Lors dit en plourant; Hélas trop malheureux homme et mauldict pescheur, oncques ne verrai-je clémence et miséricorde de Dieu. Ores m'en irai-je d'icy et me cacherai dedans le mont Horsel, en requérant de faveur et d'amoureuse merci ma doulce dame Vénus, car pour son amour serai-je bien à tout jamais damné en enfer. Voicy la fin de tous mes faicts d'armes et de toutes mes belles chansons. Hélas, trop belle estoyt la face de ma dame et ses yeulx, et en mauvais jour je vis ces chouses-là. Lors s'en alla tout en gémissant et se retourna chez elle, et là vescut tristement en grand amour près de sa dame. Puis après advint que le pape vit un jour esclater sur son baston force belles fleurs rouges et blanches et maints boutons de feuilles, et ainsi vit-il reverdir toute l'escorce. Ce dont il eut grande crainte et moult s'en esmut, et grande pitié lui prit de ce chevalier qui s'en estoyt départi sans espoir comme un homme misérable et damné. Doncques envoya force messaigers devers luy pour le ramener, disant qu'il aurait de Dieu grace et bonne absolution de son grand pesché d'amour. Mais oncques plus ne le virent; car toujours demeura ce pauvre chevalier auprès de Vénus la haulte et forte déesse ès fiancs de la montagne amoureuse.

Livre des grandes merveilles d'amour, escript en latin et en françoys par Maistre Antoine Gaget. 1530.

193. *the marvellous mouth:* Helen of Troy. Cf. Aeschylus, *Agamemnon* 689ff.

198. *the Queen:* Cleopatra. Cf. Shakespeare, *Antony and Cleopatra* I.i. 33ff.

200. *Semiramis:* mythical Assyrian Queen, builder of Babylon.

267. *slotwise:* from the trail or spoor left by an animal. S. commits the common error of applying the term to smell.

278. *vair:* squirrel fur used for trimming hoods, expecially in the 13th and 14th centuries.

283. *tears . . . of Magdalen:* typically, contrition of a reformed whore.

284. *Dove:* the Holy Spirit.

439. *his knees:* the Pope's.

355. *the spot:* Cf. Jeremiah 13:23.

390. *As when she came out of the naked sea:* transferred epithet. Aphrodite Anadyomene (Venus) sprang from ocean's foam, as her name may suggest in Greek. Cf. Hesiod, *Theognis* 192ff.

THE TRIUMPH OF TIME: probably addressed to S.'s cousin, Mary Gordon, after the announcement of her engagement to Colonel Disney Leith.

56. *The strong sea-daisies feast on the sun:* an ironic adjustment of the troubadour sun-flower convention to the tenacious habits of *armeria maritima*. For similar *floraisons grasses* cf. Baudelaire, 'Une Charogne' and 'Duellum'.

62.ff. *The sweet sea* etc.: S. is eclectic and eccentric here, choosing from the catalogue of qualities associated with Aphrodite, her links with the sea (*pontias*), with the seasons (*Horae*) and with the conditions of fair voyage (*euploia*), and affirming her barrenness and chastity in paradoxical terms that echo the Hermaphroditus legend while severing connections with the fertility of Aphrodite Genetrix.

83. *the great third wave: trikumia* (Latin *fluctus decumanus*), the third or largest wave. Cf. Aeschylus, *Prometheus* 1015 for a similar metaphoric application.

168. *the gate is strait:* Cf. Luke 13:24.

237. *'What should such fellows as I do': Hamlet* III. i. 132-3 continues, 'crawling between earth and heaven?' S. saw Hamlet as the victim of 'a strong conflux of contending forces.'

253. *Though the swords in my heart for one were seven:* S. ironically appropriates to his own virgin anguish the Seven Sorrows of the Virgin Mary.

301. *thou art older than earth:* S.'s marine version of the Great Mother is unconventional. But the cosmogonical priority of water is supported by Homer's claims for Okeanos at *Iliad* XIV. 200, 301 and by the theories of Thales. Cf. Aristotle, *De Caelo* B 13, 294 a 28.

321ff. *There lived a singer in France of old:* Jaufré Rudel, a 12th century Provençal poet, fell in love with Queen Melisande of Tripoli and composed six lyrics for her before his fateful journey.

365. *an armed archangel:* traditionally Michael, champion over Satan and enforcer of the Last Judgement. S.'s tribute to the power of music is typical of his Religion of Beauty in its exploitation of Christian materials—including the sacrament here—to aesthetic ends.

LES NOYADES: those executed by drowning, including so-called *mariages républicains*, by Carrier in 1793. Cf. Carlyle, *The French Revolution* IV, iii.

ANACTORIA: one of the young women beloved by Sappho of Lesbos, the 7th Century B.C. Greek poetess and teacher greatly admired by S. for her lyric gifts. S. does not attempt to translate Sappho's 'Ode to Anactoria'.

That had been tried by others, and only Catullus came close to pleasing S. who tries 'instead to reproduce in a diluted and dilated form the spirit of a poem which could not be reproduced in the body.'

Epigraph: a corrupt version of lines 18-19 of the 'Prayer to Aphrodite': S. wrongly has Sappho ask herself 'Of whom by persuasion hast thou in vain caught love.'

15. *lesser loves:* in Fr.86 Sappho suggests Anactoria married and settled in Sardis in Lydia.

22. *Erotion or Erinna:* a male lover (literally a little cupid) or one of Sappho's female companions.

64. *Paphos:* city on Cyprus near where Aphrodite was thought to have risen from the sea. Her Paphian shrine was one of the most famous.

161-62. *wind-blown hair / Of comets:* the Greek epithet for bearded (*kometes*) was applied to the luminous tail of the comet. Cf. Aristotle, *Meteorology* I. 6, 8.

195-200. *high Pierian flower . . . lordlier leaf:* S. seems to borrow the terms of Sappho's rebuke to a woman who neglected the Muses (Fr.71). Pieria, the birthplace of Orpheus and home of the Muses, furnished symbols of immortal song in its rose-garlands and laurel that bound the brows of victorious poets.

220-21. *the one star . . . sleepless moon:* S. seems to add Orion, love-lorn pursuer of the Pleiades, to Sappho's picture of her nocturnal loneliness after the setting of Moon and Pleiades in Fr. III.

259-60. S. invokes the tradition of the New Comedy and Ovid whereby Sappho threw herself off the Leucadian cliff to die in the sea for the love of Phaon.

286. *Atthis:* Sappho addressed several poems to this Athenian woman.

HYMN TO PROSERPINE: S. intended this to be a hymn of the 'Last Pagan' of the Roman Empire. Proserpine, daughter of Zeus and Demeter who shares her time between earth and Hades, is celebrated in the Eleusinian Mysteries described sketchily in the Homeric Hymn to Demeter. The Mysteries were very popular until the final victory of Christianity, partly no doubt because no fixed doctrine attached to them.

Vicisti, Galilaee: 'Thou hast conquered, Galilaean [Christ],' said by his zealous Christian opponents to be the dying words of Julian the Apostate (331-63), Emperor of Rome. Julian wrote only in Greek including two prose hymns, 'To King Helios' and 'To the Mother of the Gods.' Chapters 22 to 24 of Gibbon's *History of the Decline and Fall of the Roman Empire* give a superb, sympathetic account of this 'extraordinary man.'

1. *I have lived long enough:* Macbeth's words in face of the imminent dissolution of his world (V. iii. 22).

43-44. True to the allegations of persecution hurled at each other by Christians and Pagans. Cf. Gibbon, Ch.24.

52ff. This passage seems to recall details from Turner's *Slave Ship*, and

Ruskin's impassioned commentary on this painting in 'Of Truth of Water, As Painted by Turner', *Modern Painters* I (1843).

73ff. *Cytherean:* Aphrodite, who will be flatteringly compared with the Virgin Mary.

80. *Mother of Rome;* as mother of Aeneas Aphrodite came to be celebrated as such. S. resorts once again to the argument from antiquity.

108. Slightly less direct than the Greek S. quotes and was at some pains to have printed correctly. This finely phrased rebuke to human vanity is recorded by Marcus Aurelius, *Meditations* IV. 41. Epictetus (c. A.D.55 to c.135), a Phrygian slave who became a great stoic teacher and intimate of emperors, remained one of S.'s favourite authors throughout his life.

DOLORES: Our Lady of the Seven Sorrows is an anti-Madonna in the manner of Baudelaire's 'A une Madone'.

10. Cf. Matthew 19: 21-22: 'Then came Peter to him and said, Lord, how oft shall my brother sin against me, and I forgive him? till seven times? Jesus saith unto him. I say unto thee, Until seven times: but, Until seventy times seven.'

11. *Seven ages:* Cf. *As You Like It*, II. viii, 139ff.

19. Cf. Song of Solomon 7: 4: 'Thy neck is as a tower of ivory.' This phrase was later applied to the Virgin.

51. *Libitina:* was a goddess of the dead in whose temples funeral supplies were sold. S. follows Plutarch in confusing her with Lubentia, subject of a Venus cult. Priapus was a Greek fertility god symbolised by the phallus.

175-76. S. transposes associations once again. The Cypress was associated with mourning, the myrtle with Venus. Cf. respectively Ovid, *Metamorphoses* X; Aristophanes, *Lysistrata* 1004.

230ff. *A sand never moist from the main:* S. alludes to Christian persecution at the *Circus Gaii et Neronis*. Cf., e.g., Pliny, *Natural History*, XXVI, 74.

281. *Vestal:* Vesta was the Roman hearth-goddess whose shrines contained a perpetual flame tended by the Vestal Virgins.

299. *Alciphron . . . Arisbe:* S. shared Landor's liking for Alciphron, a contemporary of Lucian. In the fourth book of Alciphron's *Epistulae* —letters ostensibly written by courtesans—there is a good deal of priapic detail. A modern translator of the letters, F.A.Wright, reverts to Latin at IV. 12 and 13 when the situation becomes especially sportive. The Arisbe referred to seems to be the daughter of Macar, legendary king of Lesbos, S. deviously insinuating a lesbian alternative for Dolores.

303. *the garden-god:* Priapus.

307. S. is more tactful than Catullus who attributes Priapic activities at Lampsacus to the availability of aphrodisiac oysters. Cf. lines 340-41.

326. *Ipsithilla:* addressee of some of Catullus' most carnal verses. Cf. *Carmina*, xxxii.

330ff. *the Phrygian is priest:* the Galli, priests of the Anatolian earth mother Cybele, were self-castrated eunuchs. S. bewails the spread of the cult of Cybele who was worshipped on mountain-tops, including Ida and Dindymus. Her cult was officially brought to Rome in 205-4. S. alludes to further traditional features of her legend and rituals in the chariot drawn by two lions, fasting and purgation, the Day of Blood when Attis' castration and death was commemorated, and the concluding 'baptism' (*lavatio*) of her image in the Almo.

371ff. Cf. Exodus 7. Aaron's rod changes to a serpent and back again in a similar contest of religious powers. S. suggests that the Phrygian and other enfeeblements of the true pagan way will be assimilated and outlived by Dolores and her followers.

379-80. If one follows Milton, as S. seems to intend (rather than St. James or Gower) then the prophet, preacher and poet is an inversion of the 'Yelling Monsters' that dwell in Sin's nether parts, just as Dolores is an inversion of the Virgin Mary. Cf. *Paradise Lost* II, 727ff.

406. *Aphaca:* village near the source of the River Adonis, site of a celebrated shrine to Aphrodite destroyed by Constantine.

409-10. *Cotytto . . . Astarte or Ashtaroth:* Cotys, a Thracian derivative from Cybele, was worshipped orgiastically. Astarte is the Phoenician equivalent of Ishtar or Ashtaroth, an Assyro-Babylonian goddess of love.

438. Cf. the parable of tares and wheat, Matthew 13: 25-40.

THE SUNDEW: S. associated this carnivorous marsh-plant with the Borders and his cousin Mary. It is also found on the Isle of Wight where they spent so many vacations.

FELISE.

Mais où sont les neiges d'antan: 'But where are the snows of yesteryear,' refrain in 'Ballade Des Dames Du Temps Jadis' by François Villon (1431-63), a poet greatly admired in Pre-Raphaelite circles for his poetry and scandalous life.

197. *Who are most sad, being cruel:* S. seems to be punning covertly on the name of the Marquis de Sade, laureate of cruelty.

229ff. Cf. Matthew 23: 17, 19: '*Ye* fools and blind: for whether is greater, the gold or the temple that sanctifieth the gold?'

245. *Stones to bread:* one of Satan's challenges to Christ in the desert. Cf. Matthew 4: 3.

HENDECASYLLABICS: Verse in lines of eleven syllables. S. may be offering a serious complement to the third of Tennyson's 'Attempts at Classic Meters in Quantity' in the *Cornhill Magazine* in 1863: 'O you chorus of indolent reviewers, / Irresponsible, indolent reviewers' etc. S. shared Landor's admiration of the Hendecasyllabics of Catullus.

SAPPHICS: S. uses the Saphhic stanza of three lesser Sapphics (logaoedic hendecasyllables with a dactyl in the third place) and an Adonic (five syllables: —ᴗᴗ—ᴗ). The theme and imagery derive largely from Sappho.

30. *the tenth, the Lesbian:* Sappho herself, traditionally characterized
    thus. Cf., e.g., Antipater's tribute, *Palatine Anthology* VII, 14.

DEDICATION 1865

27-28. Heroines in this volume. 'Faustine' presents a gladiatorial tribute
    to the Roman Empress Faustine. 'Fragoletta' (little strawberry) ex-
plores the ambiguities of love, philosophical and physical. Yolande de
Sallières is beloved of the speaker in 'The Leper'. S. ends his list of
heroines with another allusion to de Sade; in particular to *Juliette, ou
les prospérités du vice,* a work less notorious than *Justine, ou les malheurs
de la vertu* and *La Philosophie dans le boudoir.*

53ff. S. addresses the dedicatee of this volume, Edward Burne-Jones
    (1833-98), his friend and contemporary at Oxford, and the most
talented painter among the second generation of Pre-Raphaelites.

THE EVE OF REVOLUTION: for S. 'the centre poem and mainspring
of my volume.'

1. Cf. John Donne, Holy Sonnets vii: 'At the round earth's imagined
    corners, blow / Your trumpets, Angels, and arise, arise' etc.

8ff. *Dead leaves of sleep:* Hypnos, god of sleep, touched men with a
    branch. S. exploits the relationship in Greek mythology between
Hypnos, his mother Night (Nyx), and his son (Morpheus), maker of dreams.

33. Cf. the final defiance of Browning's 'Childe Roland': 'And yet /
    Dauntless the Slughorn to my lips I set, / And blew. *"Childe Roland
to the Dark Tower Came."* '

47-48. S. seems to give a pagan version of Miltonic Right Reason. For
    a similar linking of Athene, Aphrodite and Helios, cf. Julian, 'Hymn
to King Helios', 150 A-C.

78ff. S. adapts Genesis I.

84ff. Evocative topography, primarily Spartan in detail and association.
    Like Shelley in *Hellas,* S. is inspired by Aeschylus' *Persae.* From Mt.
Taygetus flow the Cephisus and Eurotas that mark the boundaries of
Sparta. At Thermopylae in 480 B.C. Leonidas and 300 Spartans died
defending Greece against the hordes of Xerxes. At Salamis the same year
the Greeks inflicted a severe naval defeat on the Persians. The plains of
Marathon witnessed the first Greek victory over the Persians in 490 B.C.
Athene, protectress of heroes, is seen in terms that seem to recall her
wooden talismans (*xoana*).

124ff. S. echoes the polar details of his unsuccessful prize poem of 1860
    on 'The Death of Sir John Frnaklin' who died trying to discover the
north west passage.

145. *Light, light, and light:* Cf. Milton, *Samson Agonistes,* I. 80: 'O
    dark, dark, dark, amid the blaze of noon.'

159-60. S. adapts the 'mind-forged manacles' of Blake's 'London'.

187ff. S. follows the conventions of the 19th century Republican
    muse once again. Byron's perception of parallels is typical: The

Greeks 'have turned out Mavrocordato, who was the only *Washington* or *Kosciusko* kind of man amongst them'. Kosciusko led the Polish insurrection against the Russians.

236-37. *The golden-headed worm / Made headless for a term:* the British monarchy, in the person of Charles the First.

300ff. The French attitude towards Italian unification alternated between treachery and active opposition. The support of the Papal states was crucial. In 1849 S.'s hero, Mazzini, had held Rome for the *Risorgimento*, but the Roman republic fell to the French, and Papal despotism returned, bolstered now by a foreign garrison. In 1867 Garibaldi's forces, once again intent on 'liberating' Rome, were defeated by the French at Mentano. Only with France's defeat in 1870 in the Franco-Prussian War did Italian troops claim Rome for a united Italy.

HERTHA: Teutonic goddess of earth and fertility. For Tacitus (*Germania* XL), Hertha could intercede in the affairs of men. For S. this is the most successful of his 'mystic atheistic democratic anthropologic poem[s]'.

15. S. ironically echoes the words of Christ in the temple, John 8: 58: 'Verily, verily, I say unto you, Before Abraham was, I am.'

41ff. Hertha interrogates man in the manner of God, the Voice out of the Whirlwind: Job 38 and 39.

96. The great tree Yggdrasil of Norse mythology. S. follows the language and sentiments of Carlyle's first lecture in *On Heroes, Hero-worship And the Heroic in History* (1841), where the 'Ash-tree of Existence' is memorably praised.

181. *twilight:* S. applies *ragna rökkr* (Norse twilight of the Gods) to God.

GENESIS.

32. *divine contraries:* A Blakean sentiment. Cf., e.g., *Annotations to Swedenborg's Divine Love*, p.56: 'Good & Evil are here both Good & the contraries Married.'

MATER DOLOROSA: 'Stabat Mater Dolorosa / Iuxta Crucem lacrimosa.' Jacopone da Todi's couplet is translated thus in the *English Hymnal*: 'At the cross her station keeping / Stood the mournful mother weeping.' S.'s epigraph, from Hugo's enormous novel of 1862, is typical of the 'métaphores demi-énigmatiques, mais significatives,' of the republican Enjolras.

26. *Can these bones live?* Ezekiel 37: 3.

TIRESIAS: A legendary blind, hermaphrodite Theban seer. S. glosses his political allegory thus: 'Tiresias at the grave of Antigone—i.e. (understand) Dante at the grave of Italy. I do not say the living heir and successor Dante as patriot, for *he* sees her slowly but hopefully rising, though with pain and shame and labour.'

6. *Antigone:* daughter of Iocasta and Oedipus. Sophocles has her commit suicide after her burial of her brother Polynices incurs the wrath

of her uncle Creon.

18.   *Cadmus . . . Harmonia:* founders of Thebes. In old age, after much grief, they went to Illyria where they were changed into serpents. Cf. Ovid, *Metamorphoses* III and IV.

67.   *Dircean spring:* Dirce and her husband Lycus tortured Antiope, mother of Amphion whose music raised the walls of Thebes. Amphion and his brother Zethos avenged their mother by killing or disthroning Lycus and tying Dirce to the horns of a bull. When she died thereon she was turned into a stream, and her bones were burned and thrown into the stream that bears her name.

69ff. Oedipus blinds himself on discovering the truth of his incest. His sons Eteocles and Polynices rule alternately in his stead. However, they quarrel, and Polynices musters a force in Argos and returns to take Thebes. Champions of the two forces meet at each of the city's seven gates. The brothers die at each other's hands in the ensuing struggle, and the curse of Oedipus is fulfilled. Cf. Aeschylus, *The Seven Against Thebes.*

74ff. Pentheus was king of Thebes when Dionysus returned to Greece. When the king refused to acknowledge the god's divinity, Dionysus drove the Theban women and the Queen Mother mad. Pentheus tried to witness their rituals on Mt. Cithaeron and was torn to pieces by them. Cf. Euripides, *Bacchae.*

86.   *bloody-footed child:* Laius drove a spike through the feet of Oedipus before exposing the child to nature. This action may have been intended to prevent Oedipus' ghost from walking.

310. Thebes was plagued by a Sphinx which Oedipus vanquished before marrying his mother.

351ff. S. alludes to the final vision of the Trinity granted Dante through his love for Beatrice at the end of *Paradiso.*

NON DOLET: 'It does not hurt': Words spoken by Arria to her husband, Caecina Paetus, when she urges him to suicide after stabbing herself. See, e.g., Pliny, *Letters,* III, xvi.

from BOTHWELL: Act Two, Scene nineteen. Henry Stuart, Lord Darnley (?1545-1567), Mary's cousin and her junior by three years, married her in 1565. They became estranged after the murder of David Riccio, the Queen's secretary. Darnley was strangled at Kirk O'Field in 1567 while escaping from an explosion arranged by Bothwell. Darnley's dream occurs shortly before his death.

5.   *Cittern:* like the guitar, but strung with wire and played with a plectrum or quill. This instrument was very popular in the 16th and 17th centuries.

10-11. Darnley shows the same ambivalence to the spectre of David Riccio now as at the time of his murder. Riccio, an accomplished musician, was much valued by his music-loving Queen.

from ERECTHEUS: lines spoken by the Chorus near the end of the drama. Chthonia, daughter of Erectheus, legendary King of Athens, and his Queen, Praxithea, has killed herself at the behest of Athena in order to save Athens from the Thracian forces of Eumolpus, son of Poseidon. Erectheus leads the Athenians in the final battle wherein he will lose his life while securing victory.

1ff. S. draws on the Athenian state-cult devoted to the north wind, Boreas, for his destruction of the Persian fleet.

THE LAST ORACLE: The Greek epigraph is translated in lines 7 to 10. S. describes his subject 'which starts from the message sent back (to the effect that there was none) from Delphi to Julian when he sent to consult the oracle the year of his accession, and passes into an invocation of the healing and destroying God of song and of the sun, taken as the type of the 'light of thought' and spirit of speech which makes and un-makes gods within the soul that it makes vocal and articulate from age to age; not really therefore son of Zeus the son of Chronos, but older than all time we take count of, and father of all possible gods fashioned by the human spirit out of itself for types of worship. This sounds rather metaphysical, but I don't think the verse is obscure or turbid—the form of a hymn or choral chant, and the alternate metre of twelve long trochaic lines and twelve shorter anapaestic, carry the thought on and carry off the symbolic or allegoric amibguity: at least so I flatter myself.'

23. *Paian:* Physician of the gods. After Homer the name and office of healer were transferred to Apollo, whose invocation in these terms gave rose to paean as chant or hymn of thanksgiving.

138. Cf. Judges 2: 10: 'and there arose another generation after them, which knew not the Lord, nor yet the works which he had done for Israel.'

IN THE BAY.

10. *freak:* to fleck or streak with colour.

31ff. Hades was always a person, never a place in classical Greek. One of the sons of Kronos, his domain was the underworld. Elysium, originally Isles of the Blest at the end of the world, was later transferred underground to accommodate the favoured dead. Lethe and Styx are two of the nine rivers of the underworld.

45. *Son of the songs of morning:* Marlowe. S. sees Shelley as Marlowe's true heir.

59. *Sirius:* the dog-star, brightest in the heavens.

90ff. S. refers to the defeat of the Spanish Armada in 1588.

129. our mightiest: Shakespeare. S. echoes Sonnet 87: 'Thus have I had thee, as a dream doth flatter, / In sleep a king, but, waking, no such matter.'

142. Beaumont and Fletcher.

145ff. John Ford (fl. 1639). S. refers to *Tis Pity She's A Whore* which deals with the incestuous passion of Giovanni for his sister Annabella. This passion is consummated and continues after her husband Sorenzo confines her behind 'bride-house bars', but all three lose their lives.

152. *Phosphor:* the morning star (and evening star also), Venus.

157. Both Shelley and Marlowe died aged 29.

RELICS.

2. *laurustine:* an ever-green, winter-flowering shrub.

54ff. On his Italian journey S. visited the small town of San Gimignano near Siena. It is famous for its thirteen towers and the Church of Santa Fina.

AT A MONTH'S END.

81. *read his weird:* construe his fate.

119. *anthers:* pollen-bearing organs in flowers.

AVE ATQUE VALE: HAIL AND FAREWELL. Cf. Catullus, *Carmina* C1. The epigraph is taken from 'Tableaux Parisiens', poem 100 of the 1861 text of *Fleurs du mal*. S. alters the punctuation to suit his own elegiac purposes.

14ff. Cf. Baudelaire's 'Lesbos'.

45. *It is enough:* S. contradicts Baudelaire's poem 'Sed Non Satiata'.

59ff. Cf. Baudelaire's 'La Géante'.

120-21. Orestes laid a lock of his own hair on the tomb of Agamemnon, his murdered father.

129. *Electra:* Sister to Orestes.

157. the Venus of the Tannhäuser legend. S. is less ghoulish than Baudelaire in his 'Voyage A Cythère': 'Dans ton île, ô Vénus je n'ai trouvé debout / Qu'un gibet symbolique où pendait mon image.' S. knew Baudelaire's praise of Wagner's *Tannhäuser* in the *Révue Européenne* in 1861.

160. *Erycine:* Venus was worshipped at a famous temple at Mt. Eryx in Sicily.

192. Niobe, wife of Amphion, had at least twelve children. She boasted that she was at least the equal of Leto who had had only two children, Apollo and Artemis. Leto's children thereupon destroyed all Niobe's brood. The mother's grief is a favourite subject for classical poets.

SONNET (WITH A COPY OF *MADEMOISELLE DE MAUPIN):* This novel by Théophile Gautier (1811-72) was a celebrated contribution to French romanticism, and one that profoundly influenced the young S. who contributed this poem, another in French, two in English, one in Latin, and five short pieces in Greek to the commemorative volume, *Le Tombeau de Théophile Gautier* (1873).

INFERIAE: Rites and offerings to honour and propitiate the dead. S. honours his father, Admiral Charles Henry Swinburne (1797-1877).

CYRIL TOURNEUR: (?1575-1626). S. admired the lurid charms of *The Revenger's Tragedy* and *The Atheist's Tragedy*.

THE COMPLAINT OF THE FAIR ARMOURESS: a rendering of 'Les Regrets de la Belle Heaumière'. In stanzas 7 and 9 the last three lines of each were suppressed in favour of a series of asterisks. They are restored here from the versions given in T.J. Wise's *Bibliography* (1919), i, 292.

THE EPITAPH IN FORM OF A BALLAD: Villon's poem was occasioned by his being sentenced to hang in Paris in 1462, after an affray in which a papal notary was wounded. He appealed the sentence successfully, but was exiled from Paris for ten years for his persistent profligacy.

THEOPHILE GAUTIER: Another of S.'s contributions to the commemorative volume.

THALASSIUS: '[Born] of the sea': S.'s 'symbolical quasi-autobiographical poem after the fashion of Shelley or of Hugo, concerning the generation, birth and rearing of a by-blow of Amphitrite's.' Cf. the discovery of the infant Perdita on the sea-shore, *Winter's Tale* II, iii.

18. *Cymothoe:* literally 'Wave-swift'. A sea-nymph in *Iliad* xviii, 41 and Hesiod. She is mother to S. here, and Apollo is his father.

37. *he:* Walter Savage Landor (1775-1864), S.'s spiritual foster-parent.

53. *hyaline:* resembling glass, transparent.

71. *stabile:* firmly established, enduring. This rare form was used by Landor, and by S. in *Atalanta*.

133. *yeanling:* a young lamb or kid.

409. *panther-throned beside Erigone:* daughter of Icarius, King of Attica, she was loved by Dionysus, who wooed her in the form of a grape-cluster. On discovering her father's murder, she killed herself and was transformed into the constellation Virgo. The panther was sacred to Dionysus. S. refers here to his earlier drunken excesses.

455ff. Boreas became a stallion to woo the mares of Ericthonius. From this union were born 12 mares of wonderful celerity. Cf. *Iliad* xx, 233.

459. *levin's:* flash's.

ON THE CLIFFS: the Greek epigraph, 'lovely-voiced songstress', forms part of Sappho's tribute to the nightingale as harbinger of spring, cited by Scholiast re. Sophocles, *Electra* 149.

49. *thy strange children:* the Erinyes or Furies, daughters of Night. In Aeschylus, *Eumenides* 321ff., they demand of Athena the death of Orestes for killing his mother, Clytemnestra. These demands are not heeded because Orestes had righteously obeyed Apollo in the matricide.

115. *Rathe:* early.

141ff. Aeschylus again, *Agamemnon* 1150ff. Cassandra, brought back from Troy with Agamemnon, foresees the death of both of them at the hands of Clytemnestra.

152. *the entangling dragnet:* literal as well as symbolic. Clytemnestra

threw a net round her husband before stabbing him to death.

157ff.   Cassandra, 'pale princess-priest of Priam's seed', would not submit to the source of her power of prophecy, Apollo. He cursed her by spitting in her mouth in mid-embrace, so that her prophecies would not be believed.

241ff.   S. alludes to his Italian journey of 1864, when he met Landor and read his verses to a new circle of literary acquaintances. Landor celebrates the poetic and bird voices of the small Tuscan town of Maiano in his 'Ode To A Friend' and 'Dante of Maiano'.

299ff.   S. renders the opening of Sappho's 'Ode to Aphrodite'.

326ff.   S. renders a fragment to Atthis, from the poem that probably opened Book Two of Sappho's poems. S. is sensitive to the prosodic beauty of the line: Ἠράμαν μὲν ἔγω σέθεν, Ἄτθι, πάλαι πότα.

333ff.   Another variation on the opening plea of the 'Ode to Aphrodite'.

422-23.   Cf. the seven-fold shield of Ajax, *Iliad* VII, 220 etc.

THE BIRDS: S. provides the following note:

I was allured into the audacity of this experiment by consideration of a fact which hitherto does not seem to have been taken into consideration by any translator of the half divine humourist in whose incomparable genius the highest qualities of Rabelais were fused and harmonized with the supremest gifts of Shelley: namely, that his marvellous metrical invention of the anapaestic heptameter was almost exactly reproducible in a language to which all variations and combinations of anapaestic, iambic, or trochaic metre are as natural and pliable as all dactylic and spondaic forms of verse are unnatural and abhorrent. As it happens, this highest central interlude of a most adorable masterpiece is as easy to detach from its dramatic setting, and even from its lyrical context, as it was easy to give line for line of it in English. In two metrical points only does my version vary from the verbal pattern of the original. I have of course added rhymes, and double rhymes, as necessary makeweights for the imperfection of an otherwise inadequate language; and equally of course I have not attempted the impossible and undesirable task of reproducing the rare exceptional effect of a line overcharged on purpose with a preponderance of heavy-footed spondees: and this for the obvious reason that even if such a line—which I doubt—could be exactly represented, foot by foot and pause for pause, in English, this English line would no more be a verse in any proper sense of the word than is the line I am writing at this moment. And my main intention, or at least my main desire, in the undertaking of this brief adventure, was to renew as far as possible for English ears the music of this resonant and triumphant metre, which goes ringing at full gallop as of horses who

> 'dance as 'twere to the music
> Their own hoofs make.'

I would not seem over curious in search of an apt or inapt quotation: but nothing can be fitter than a verse of Shakespeare's to praise at once and to describe the most typical verse of Aristophanes.

8.   *Prodicus:*   a sophist from Ceos, contemporary with Socrates, esteemed for his fine semantic discriminations.

11.   Aristophanes departs from Hesiod in order to further the primogenitive claims of the Birds. In Orphic tradition Phanes, the precursor of the erotic creator of all things, is born from a mystic egg.

34.   All sites of oracles.

BY THE NORTH SEA: S. enquired of Lord Houghton, 'Do you know the "dead cathedral city" which I have tried to describe . . . Dunwich, in Suffolk? The whole picture is from life—salt marshes, ruins, and bones protruding seawards through the soil of the crumbling sandbanks.'

50.   *fortalice:* a small fort.

105. Cf. Joel 3: 13-14: 'Multitudes, multitudes in the valley of decision,' will suffer God's vengeance.

204. *Anticlea:* the mother of Odysseus who died of grief for her son. He tries vainly to embrace her shade when he visits the underworld in *Odyssey* XI.

THE HIGHER PANTHEISM IN A NUTSHELL: a parody of Tennyson's 'The Higher Pantheism'.

19-20. S. uses pre-historic creatures to ridicule Tennyson's grapplings with Darwin.

THE POET AND THE WOODLOUSE: a parody of Elizabeth Barrett Browning.

14.   *nympholeptic:* ecstatic because of something unattainable. 'Nympholepsy' appears in Mrs. Browning's 'Lady Geraldine's Courtship' viii; but S. was aware that the term had serious uses, his own later poem, 'A Nympholept', demonstrating this.

15.   *solar caustic:* S. adapts lunar caustic, nitrate of silver used medically to burn living tissue, to express his amusement at the searing intellectual difficulties of Mrs. Browning's personae.

25.   *cryptophantic:* this nonsensical neologism yokes pseudo-meaningfully the ideas of concealment and disclosure.

26.   *spongeous kind of blee:* archaic nonsense suggesting a spongy hue, and also the nonsense poems of Edward Lear which S. admired.

28.   *madrepore:* perforate coral.

44.   *drastics:* severe purgatives. S. exploits the therapeutic associations of poetry—as in the *katharmoi* (purgations) of Empedocles—and the echo in *drastics* of *dactylics.*

48.   *chrism:* oil mixed with balm, consecrated for use as an unguent in the administration of certain sacraments in the Eastern and Western Churches.

SONNET FOR A PICTURE: a parody of D. G. Rosetti.

5. *rutilant:* an archaism in the Pre-Raphaelite manner, signifying gleaming or glittering with a red or golden light.

7. *Shewbread:* the twelve loaves that were placed every sabbath 'before the Lord' on a table beside the altar of incense, and at the end of the week were eaten by the priests alone. S. parodies Rossetti's adaptation of religious symbols to carnal purposes.

NEPHELIDIA: Little Clouds. This is a self-parody.

TRISTRAM AND ISEULT: The Prelude was written in response to Tennyson's *Holy Grail and Other Poems* (1870). It was followed by nine cantos.

41ff. Tristram and Iseult unwittingly drink a love-potion while he escorts her to her waiting bridegroom, King Mark of Cornwall. Their love necessitates separation, and Tristram leaves for Brittany where he marries a younger Breton Iseult. Her brother Ganhardine protests the non-consummation of this marriage, but is persuaded of Tristram's rectitude by seeing Queen Iseult in Cornwall. Tristram and the Queen have a final period together at Camelot before she is recalled to Cornwall while he goes off to fight the giant Urgan in Wales. On his way home to Brittany victorious, Tristram is tempted to one more battle where he is seriously wounded. He dies on being misled by his wife about the colour of sail of the vessel bringing Queen Iseult to his side.

73-74. Beatrice and Dante.

79-80. Cf. *Inferno* V. S. assumes that Iseult is with Tristram.

HAD I WIST: Proverbial: Most versions stress either the danger or the futility of regrets after the fact. Cf. Tristram's testament at the end of 'Tristram of Lyonesse': 'Had I wist, / Ye had never sinned nor died thus, nor had I / Borne in this doom that bade you sin and die / So sore a part of sorrow.'

PLUS INTRA: Further within.

THREE FACES: S. wrote to Watts, 'As to women, I saw at Venice one of the three most beautiful I ever saw (the other two were one at Genoa, the other at Ventimiglia in the Riviera.)'

EROS.

2. *Anthesterion:* eighth month of the Attic year, answering to the end of February and the beginning of March, the time of the Feast of Flowers (*Anthesteria*).

ON THE RUSSIAN PERSECUTION OF THE JEWS.

12. *Gadarean swine:* a herd of crazed swine which perished much like lemmings. Cf. Matthew 8: 32.

JOHN FORD: this sonnet draws on the tradition of the colossus of Memnon in Egypt, and its emission of music when struck by first light each morning.

IN SEPULCRETIS: Title and Latin epigraph form a sequence, lines 2 and 3 of *Carmina* LIX, where Catullus presents Rufa from Bologna, wife of Menenius, 'seen at a funeral pyre stealing the food baking there.' The implication of deplorable scavenging is reinforced by the second epigraph. The poem is a protest against H. B. Forman's edition of *Letters of John Keats to Fanny Brawne, Written in the Years MDCCCIX and MDCCCXX* (1878).

A REIVER'S NECK-VERSE: In his novel *Lesbia Brandon*, S. prefaces this poem (minus the second stanza) thus: 'I like much better that song of a border thief whom his wife or some other woman betrayed into the hands of justice.'

8. *Flyting:* quarrelling.

A NYMPHOLEPT.

136. *Typho:* Titan rebel against Zeus, he was vanquished and buried under Etna.

A SWIMMER'S DREAM: I have not been able to trace the Latin epigraph. The idea of the softer, less troubled sleep of waters is commonplace. Perhaps S. is adapting Virgil at *Eclogue* vii. 45: 'Somno mollior herba.'

THE LAKE OF GAUBE: situated in the Pyrenees. S. comments, 'I myself like the Lake of Gaube as well as any. But perhaps the reviewer was right who said that only swimmers could properly appreciate and relish that poem.'

33. *salamander:* a lizard-like creature supposed to live in, or to be able to endure fire.

DISGUST: A DRAMATIC MONOLOGUE: A parody of Tennyson's 'Despair: A Dramatic Monologue'.

8. *Professor Huxley:* T. H. Huxley, F.R.S. (1825-95) became an ardent evolutionist after the appearance of Darwin's *Origin of Species* (1859). Huxley coined the term 'agnostic', and was popularly known as Doubting Thomas.

18. *P.P.C.: Pour Prendre Congé*, an application to take leave.

24. *the shepherd in Pickwick:* The Reverend Mr. Stiggins, when attending Mrs. Weller, 'always brings now, a flat bottle as holds about a pint and a-half, and fills it with the pine-apple rum afore he goes away.'

FURTHER READING

Swinburne studies will be much encouraged by the completion of two major projects, John S. Mayfield's *Bibliography*, and the edition of the *Complete Poems* by Timothy Burnett and Terry Meyers, The following will continue to be especially useful:

Eliot, T. S., *The Sacred Wood* (1920).

Fletcher, I. and M. Bradbury, eds., *Decadence and the 1890s*, Stratford-upon-Avon Studies, 17 (1979).

Henderson, P., *Swinburne: Portrait of a Poet* (1974).

Hyder, C. K., *Swinburne: The Critical Heritage* (1970).

Lafourcade, G., *La Jeunesse de Swinburne 1837-1867* (1928).

Lang, C. Y., ed., *Victorian Poetry*, nos.1-2 (1972). A special Swinburne issue.

McGann, J. J., *Swinburne: An Experiment in Criticism* (1972).

Meyers, T. L., 'Shelley and Swinburne's Aesthetic of Melody', *Papers on Language and Literature* (1978), 284-95.

Murfin, R. C., *Swinburne, Hardy, Lawrence, and the Burden of Belief* (1978).

Peters, R. L., *The Crowns of Apollo* (1965).

Praz, M., *The Romantic Agony* (1933).

Ridenour, G., 'Time and Eternity in Swinburne: Minute Particulars in Five Poems', *English Literary History* (1978), 107-30.

Rosenberg, J.D., 'Swinburne', *Victorian Studies* (1967), 131-52.

Rosenblatt, L., *L'Idée de l'Art pour l'Art Dans La Littérature Anglaise Pendant La Période Victorienne* (1931).

Rutland, W. R., *Swinburne: A Nineteenth-Century Hellene* (1931).

Small, Ian, ed., *The Aesthetes: A Sourcebook* (1979).

Temple, R. Z., *The Critic's Alchemy: A Study of the Introduction of French Symbolism into England* (1953).

INDEX OF FIRST LINES